Microsoft System Center Data Protection Manager 2012 SP1

Learn how to deploy, monitor, and administer System Center Data Protection Manager 2012 SP1

Steve Buchanan

Islam Gomaa

Robert Hedblom

Flemming Riis

[PACKT] enterprise
PUBLISHING   professional expertise distilled

BIRMINGHAM - MUMBAI

Microsoft System Center Data Protection Manager 2012 SP1

First published: June 2013

Production Reference: 2010713

Published by Packt Publishing Ltd
Livery Place
35 Livery Street
Birmingham B3 2PB, UK.

ISBN 978-1-84968-630-3

www.packtpub.com

Cover Image by Tina Negus (tina_manthorpe@sky.com)

Credits

Authors
Steve Buchanan
Islam Gomaa
Robert Hedblom
Flemming Riis

Reviewers
Mike Resseler
Yegor Startsev

Acquisition Editor
Mary Nadar

Lead Technical Editor
Arun Nadar

Technical Editor
Hardik B. Soni

Project Coordinators
Abhishek Kori
Wendell Palmer

Proofreaders
Dan McMahon
Bernie Watkins

Indexer
Rekha Nair

Graphics
Ronak Dhruv
Abhinash Sahu

Production Coordinator
Pooja Chiplunkar

Cover Work
Pooja Chiplunkar

About the Authors

Steve Buchanan is an infrastructure consultant at RBA with a focus on System Center. He has 13 years of experience in information technology around systems management and systems administration. Steve authored System Center Data Protection Manager (SCDPM) 2010 SP1 and was a technical reviewer for the *System Center Service Manager 2012 Cookbook* and *System Center Virtual Machine Manager 2012 Cookbook, Packt Publishing*. Steve is a Microsoft System Center MVP and holds the following certifications: Linux +, MCP, MCTS, MCSA, MCITP: Server Administrator, and MCSE: Private Cloud.

Steve can be found blogging at www.buchatech.com.

I want to first and foremost give thanks to God for making opportunities such as this possible. I would like to thank my wife, Aya, and my three sons for being patient and supportive as I work on time consuming projects like this. I would also like to thank all of my other family and friends. I want to give a big thanks to the other System Center MVPs Robert Hedblom, Islam Gomaa, Flemming Riis, Yegor Startsev, and Mike Resseler for being a part of the team on this book, as it takes a great amount of effort to put something like this together. I also want to thank the Packt Publishing team for supporting all the authors and reviewers during this project. I would also like to say thanks to my employer RBA for being supportive and encouraging these types of community-based efforts. Last but not least, thank you to the System Center community for being supporters of books like this.

Islam Gomaa is a System Architect at Kivuto Solutions Inc, the global leader in complex digital distribution solutions. Islam has over 15 years of expertise in helping organizations align their business goals using Microsoft technology and deploying Microsoft-based solutions, which helped Kivuto become ISO 27001 certified and achieve the Microsoft Gold competency as an ISV.

Islam is an SCDM MVP and member of the Windows Springboard Technical Expert Panel (STEP) for Windows 8 and Server 2012, having delivered STEP presentations as an evangelist across Canada and the USA. He has also authored select advanced webcasts on Microsoft private cloud. Islam presented at both TechEd 2013 North America and Europe, and is welcomed each year to present for TechEd and MMS as a guest speaker.

Islam has a Bachelor's in computer science from Montreal University, holds several Microsoft technical designations, and is an active member of the IT community.

Islam enjoys sharing his adventures and ideas about system administration through his blog at `http://blog.islamgomaa.com` and `http://www.IslamGomaa.com`.

First of all, I would like to thank God for allowing me to participate in a great project like the writing of this book. I would like to thank my wife Marwa and son Yassine for being patient and supportive. I can't thank enough everyone that participated in the making of this book, Robert Hedblom, Steve Buchanan, Flemming Riis, Yegor Startsev, and Mike Resseler. They have invested a lot of their time to this project; a special thanks to Steve Buchanan for taking the lead on this project and guiding each of the authors. I also want to thank the Packt Publishing team for their outstanding work and support rendered to all the authors and reviewers during this project; I know it wasn't easy to coordinate between four authors living in four different countries.

Robert Hedblom is a Microsoft Most Valuable Professional (MVP) for System Center Cloud and Datacenter Management and works as a Solution Architect for System Center for hosters, EPG, and SMB customers globally. He was previously an MVP for DPM. Robert's knowledge is often used by Microsoft as a reviewing partner and consultant via Microsoft Consultant Services (MCS) or Premier Field Engineers (PFE) on a global scale.

He also runs one of the largest DPM blogs (`http://robertanddpm.blogspot.com`) where he blogs frequently about DPM and also other System Center products for the System Center community.

Robert has written several DPM trainings for versions 2010, 2012, and 2012 SP1 that a large number of training centers are using. Robert is often seen as a speaker on MMS, TechEd, and several other seminars that Microsoft runs. He was involved in the previous book for System Center Data Protection Manager as a technical reviewer.

> I would like to dedicate a big thank you to my family, and especially my wife Hanna, who is the reason that I can fulfill my dream.

Flemming Riis is an infrastructure consultant at Kompetera with a focus on System Center.

He has been working there since 1997 in various roles, starting with repairing PCs and then presales support. He is now a consultant who started with management software, then became Operations Manager, and hasn't looked back since.

Flemming is a Microsoft System Center MVP and holds the following certifications: MCP, MCTS, MCSA, and MCITP.

Flemming can be found blogging at www.flemmingriis.com.

I want to first and foremost give thanks to Steve Buchanan and the rest of the team on this book for allowing me to contribute to the great team, and in general to the whole community around Microsoft Solutions, where everyone is very helpful across company relations; this is a true inspiration for others to follow.

I want to give a big thanks to the other System Center MVPs Robert Hedblom, Islam Gomaa, Mike Resseler, and Yegor Startsev.

I also want to thank the Packt Publishing team for supporting all the authors and reviewers during this project.

About the Reviewers

Mike Resseler is a Product Strategy Specialist for Veeam. Mike is focused on technologies around Hyper-V and System Center. With years of experience in the field, he presents regularly at large events such as MMS, TechEd, and TechDays. Mike has been awarded the MVP for System Center Cloud and Datacenter Management since 2010. His major hobby is discussing and developing solid Disaster Recovery scenarios. Additionally, he has enterprise-class experience in Private Cloud architecture, deployment with marked focus on protection from the bottom to the top. He holds certifications in many Microsoft Technologies including MCITP. You can also follow Mike on Twitter @MikeResseler and @Veeam.

Yegor Startsev is a System Center Cloud and Datacenter Management MVP from Samara, Russia. Yegor has worked in the IT industry for over 11 years, starting as a systems administrator and working up to his current role as a Chief Information Officer at VTS. Yegor is focused on managing IT departments and budgets, architecting and developing IT projects in a large group of construction companies. He is a regular speaker at regional Microsoft and IT Pro community events. Yegor also runs the DPM blog, *The recovery point* (http://ystartsev.wordpress.com). Yegor is married and a proud father of triplets (two boys and a girl).

> I'm thankful for the great opportunity to work with Steve, Robert, Islam, and Flemming. I would also like to thank my wife, Olga, for her support and patience throughout this project.

www.PacktPub.com

Support files, eBooks, discount offers and more

You might want to visit www.PacktPub.com for support files and downloads related to your book.

Did you know that Packt offers eBook versions of every book published, with PDF and ePub files available? You can upgrade to the eBook version at www.PacktPub.com and as a print book customer, you are entitled to a discount on the eBook copy. Get in touch with us at service@packtpub.com for more details.

At www.PacktPub.com, you can also read a collection of free technical articles, sign up for a range of free newsletters and receive exclusive discounts and offers on Packt books and eBooks.

PACKTLiB®

http://PacktLib.PacktPub.com

Do you need instant solutions to your IT questions? PacktLib is Packt's online digital book library. Here, you can access, read and search across Packt's entire library of books.

Why Subscribe?

- Fully searchable across every book published by Packt
- Copy and paste, print and bookmark content
- On demand and accessible via web browser

Free Access for Packt account holders

If you have an account with Packt at www.PacktPub.com, you can use this to access PacktLib today and view nine entirely free books. Simply use your login credentials for immediate access.

Instant Updates on New Packt Books

Get notified! Find out when new books are published by following @PacktEnterprise on Twitter, or the *Packt Enterprise* Facebook page.

Table of Contents

Preface

Microsoft Data Protection Manager (DPM) 2012 SP1 is a protection and recovery solution, which provides continuous data protection for Windows application and file servers to seamlessly integrated disk, tape, and cloud.

This book includes deep dive contributions from seven experienced System Center MVPs, with hands-on and real-life experience in deploying, managing, and configuring DPM. This book will show you how to effectively plan and deploy DPM and how to effectively back up your business-critical data using Microsoft DPM 2012 SP1. This book will focus on Microsoft's best practices as well as the authors' own real-world experience.

What this book covers

Chapter 1, What is Data Protection Manager?, will give you an overview on System Center Data Protection Manager (SCDPM), what it is, and how it works using underlying components in the operating system such as VSS and PowerShell.

Chapter 2, Backup Strategies, will help you understand protection planning and show you how to create a backup and custom recovery strategy for your own enterprise.

Chapter 3, DPM Server Management Tasks, will provide guidance on how to manage your DPM server, including the most common DPM management task and DPM third-party add-ons.

Chapter 4, Monitoring and Managing Performance of DPM, will help you in monitoring your DPM server using standard Windows tools as well as operation manager.

Chapter 5, Workload Protection, will cover an introduction on how to protect Microsoft workloads using DPM with a workaround on how to back up non-Microsoft workloads.

Chapter 6, DPM-aware Windows Workload Protection, will cover how DPM is aware of certain workloads and how it protects and recovers these workloads.

Chapter 7, DPM Non-aware Windows Workload Protection, will cover how DPM can protect and recover some non-Microsoft workloads.

Chapter 8, Managing Tapes in DPM, will help you understand how DPM manages tapes and how it will write data to a tape using different recovery goals.

Chapter 9, Client Protection in DPM, will cover how DPM can protect trusted clients, off-site protection, and the challenges that this presents.

Chapter 10, Workgroups and Untrusted Domains, will focus on how DPM can protect untrusted and workgroup clients using various authentication methods.

Chapter 11, Disaster Recovery, will look at the steps we need to take to ensure that we can always recover our organization's data, even if multiple events occurs at the same time.

Chapter 12, DPM PowerShell, Automation, and Private Cloud, will cover DPM and PowerShell along with some new cmdlets, using PowerShell ISE with DPM. It will also help you understand DPM's role in private cloud, automating DPM with System Center Orchestrator, and how to deploy the DPM Remote Administration console via SCCM.

Who this book is for

This book is for IT professionals who are looking to expand their knowledge on how to use and monitor DPM to protect their enterprise and its mission-critical data.

What you need for this book

In order to perform the demo and examples within this book, a functional DPM installation 2012 SP1 is required. DPM SP1 is resource-intensive; in terms of storage, there are some areas in which you will need to have more than one server, especially when you are practicing the Cluster Shared Volume.

The configuration you decide to use will most likely need some type of virtualization software such as Hyper-V or VMware.

The following are the core software components that you will need to perform the demos and examples:

- Windows Server 2008
- Windows Server 2012
- Exchange server 2012/2013
- SQL Server 2008 R2 / 2012 in a cluster or mirroring scenario
- SharePoint 2010/2013
- File Server on Windows 2008 R2 / Windows 2012
- Hyper-V 2012 in cluster or standalone mode
- Reporting services 2008 R2

The book doesn't cover the installation of the workload that needs to be backed up by the DOM servers and nor does it cover troubleshooting the DPM installation. In order to know more about these tasks, refer to `http://technet.com`.

Conventions

In this book, you will find a number of styles of text that distinguish between different kinds of information. Here are some examples of these styles, and an explanation of their meaning.

Code words in text, database table names, folder names, filenames, file extensions, pathnames, dummy URLs, user input, and Twitter handles are shown as follows: "Open the restored files and you will see a catalog with the structure name `DPM_date_time`."

A block of code is set as follows:

```
DECLARE @w int
SET @w = (SELECT [WorkHoursTransmissionRate] from tbl_AM_
InstalledAgent WHERE InstallID = '2083CDAA-2872-4D2D-BAEA-
ADF033021EB9')
DECLARE @n int
SET @n = (SELECT [NonWorkHoursTransmissionRate] from tbl_AM_
InstalledAgent WHERE InstallID = '2083CDAA-2872-4D2D-BAEA-
ADF033021EB9')
DECLARE @t nvarchar(max)
SET @t = (SELECT [ThrottlingSettings] from tbl_AM_InstalledAgent WHERE
InstallID = '2083CDAA-2872-4D2D-BAEA-ADF033021EB9')
UPDATE [DPMDB].[dbo].[tbl_AM_InstalledAgent]
SET
```

```
[IsThrottled] = 1
, [WorkHoursTransmissionRate] = @w
, [NonWorkHoursTransmissionRate] = @n
, [ThrottlingSettings] = @t
GO
```

Any command-line input or output is written as follows:

```
start /wait setup.exe /i /f <path>\DPMsetup.ini /l <path>\dpmlog.txt
```

New terms and **important words** are shown in bold. Words that you see on the screen, in menus or dialog boxes for example, appear in the text like this: "In the **Getting Started** wizard, click on **Chart Wizard**."

 Warnings or important notes appear in a box like this.

 Tips and tricks appear like this.

Reader feedback

Feedback from our readers is always welcome. Let us know what you think about this book—what you liked or may have disliked. Reader feedback is important for us to develop titles that you really get the most out of.

To send us general feedback, simply send an e-mail to feedback@packtpub.com, and mention the book title via the subject of your message.

If there is a topic that you have expertise in and you are interested in either writing or contributing to a book, see our author guide on www.packtpub.com/authors.

Customer support

Now that you are the proud owner of a Packt book, we have a number of things to help you to get the most from your purchase.

Errata

Although we have taken every care to ensure the accuracy of our content, mistakes do happen. If you find a mistake in one of our books—maybe a mistake in the text or the code—we would be grateful if you would report this to us. By doing so, you can save other readers from frustration and help us improve subsequent versions of this book. If you find any errata, please report them by visiting http://www.packtpub.com/submit-errata, selecting your book, clicking on the **errata submission form** link, and entering the details of your errata. Once your errata are verified, your submission will be accepted and the errata will be uploaded on our website, or added to any list of existing errata, under the Errata section of that title. Any existing errata can be viewed by selecting your title from http://www.packtpub.com/support.

Piracy

Piracy of copyright material on the Internet is an ongoing problem across all media. At Packt, we take the protection of our copyright and licenses very seriously. If you come across any illegal copies of our works, in any form, on the Internet, please provide us with the location address or website name immediately so that we can pursue a remedy.

Please contact us at copyright@packtpub.com with a link to the suspected pirated material.

We appreciate your help in protecting our authors, and our ability to bring you valuable content.

Questions

You can contact us at questions@packtpub.com if you are having a problem with any aspect of the book, and we will do our best to address it.

1
What is Data Protection Manager?

This chapter will give you a good understanding of what System Center **Data Protection Manager** (**DPM**) is and how it works, using the underlying components in the operating system.

There are many different backup software vendors that claim the market today. They have all got one thing in common, they perform backups. The big difference between third-party backup software and DPM is that DPM isn't a backup software, it's a restore product. This was the primary idea from Microsoft when introducing DPM to the market. You shouldn't need to be a DBA to restore your SQL databases nor should you need to be a SharePoint administrator to be able to perform fast, optimized, and fully supported restore operations in your Microsoft environment. As a DPM administrator, you will have the ability to perform all restore operations possible in your datacenter or smaller server environments.

DPM uses many different components and functions to be able to give you that great experience when protecting your Microsoft environment. Though DPM relies on different components in the operating system, there are three different key components that you must be aware of:

- PowerShell
- DPMDB
- Volume Shadow Copy Services (VSS)

All the configurations made in DPM regarding deployed agents, throttling, protection groups, and so on, are stored in a local or remote SQL database called DPMDB. It is very important that you backup your DPMDB database when it comes to restoring your DPM server. The DPMDB database can be placed in a local SQL that is also shipped with your DPM media or it can be placed on a remote SQL that is already in place in your Microsoft environment.

VSS is the most important component. VSS gives DPM the ability to make online snapshots of online and live data that are read during the backup process. In this chapter we will cover:

- Planning for your DPM deployment
- The Windows applications
- The DPM disk pool
- Dependent services, local accounts, and groups
- VSS
- How does the DPM agent operate?
- A GUI walkthrough
- Additional functions and roles within DPM
- PSDataSourceConfig.XML
- Troubleshooting backups
- Upgrading scenarios

Planning for your DPM deployment

When it comes to planning your deployment of DPM there are several scenarios you need to consider. The first thing is the number of DPM servers you would like to deploy, whether to use a backup network or not, agent deployment, the total size of the DPM disk pool, and so on. First, let's have a look at the hardware requirements.

Hardware requirements

There is a major difference between minimum requirements and recommended requirements, regarding the performance of the DPM server. In the planning phase, you probably have some expectations regarding what performance DPM will have in your environment.

Remember that DPM stores its configurations in SQL (DPMDB) and if you are using a local SQL installation, you may consider using a slightly higher amount of RAM than the recommended requirements. Since hardware isn't a big cost or investment for companies these days, you may consider buying hardware that will give DPM of the hardware resources it really needs.

Minimum requirements

The minimum hardware requirements are as follows:

Processor	1 GHz dual-core CPU
RAM	4 GB
Page file	0.2 percent of all combined size of all recovery point volumes
Disk space	DPM installation location: 3 GB
	Database files drive: 900 MB
	System drive: 1 GB
DPM disk pool	1.5 times the size of the protected data

Recommended requirements

The recommended hardware requirements are as follows:

Processor	2.33 GHz quad-core CPU
RAM	8 GB
Page file	1.5 times the amount of RAM
Disk space	Always has at least 3 GB of free disk space on the volume that the DPM is installed on.
DPM disk pool	1.5 times the size of the protected data

Limitations of DPM

Depending on the load you put on the DPM server, it will be able to protect different numbers of servers. In your DPM deployment, it is important that you are aware of the limitation based on the minimum requirements of DPM.

There are some guidelines you should be aware of. First off, based on the minimum hardware requirements, a DPM server can protect 75 servers and 150 clients. The DPM disk pool can have a total number of 600 volumes, of which 300 are replica volumes and 300 are recovery points.

In the disk pool you can have 64 recovery points for file data and 512 online snapshots for other workloads.

Based on the minimum requirements, a DPM server can have 80 TB of disk storage in the disk pool and 40 TB of this is the maximum recovery point size.

DPM is a 64-bit software that can protect both 32-bit and 64-bit operating systems. DPM must be installed on a 64-bit operating system.

The Windows applications

DPM was designed to be fully supported and fully optimized for backup, restore, and disaster recovery scenarios of the Windows workloads. Since DPM only follows a predefined definition from the product groups that states the backup and restore operation, this will give you an advance regarding restore scenarios compared with different vendors. DPM protects Windows applications that have a defined VSS writer. If these Windows applications are clustered, DPM will be fully aware of the cluster configuration and also inform you if you haven't installed a DPM agent on all of your cluster members.

The Exchange server

DPM protects the Exchange Windows application with the following Service Pack levels:

- 2003 SP2
- 2007
- 2010
- 2013

The SQL Server

DPM protects the following versions of the SQL Windows applications:

- 2000 SP4
- 2005 SP1
- 2008
- 2008 R2
- 2012

SharePoint

DPM protects the following versions of the SharePoint Windows applications:

- Windows SharePoint Services 3.0
- Windows SharePoint Services 3.0 SP Search
- Microsoft Office SharePoint Server 2007
- SharePoint 2010
- SharePoint 2013

Virtual platforms

DPM protects the following virtual platforms:

- Hyper-V 1.0
- Hyper-V 2.0
- Hyper-V 3.0

The Windows clients

DPM protects the following Windows clients:

- Windows XP SP2
- Vista
- Windows 7
- Windows 8

The system state

DPM can protect the system state as a workload (the Active Directory).

The DPM disk pool

Before you can start protecting a production environment, you must attach a disk or disks to the DPM disk pool to be able to perform fast disk recovery.

The choice of disk type or technology is really made easy with DPM. The only important part is that the storage used for the DPM disk pool must be presented as a local attached storage, which means that SAN, NAS, DAS, and local disks will work.

You cannot use USB or IEEE 1394 FireWire disks since they are presented as removable storage in the operating system.

Since the DPM disk pool is based on the disk management and its underlying technologies, there are some limitations that you must be aware of:

- **Master Boot Record (MBR)** disks have a 2 TB physical disk limit.
- Don't make your GPT disk larger than 17 TB even if Microsoft supports it. This is a recommendation from the DPM development group.
- The NTFS supports up to 16 TB volume size using the default cluster size.
- The **Virtual Disk Service (VDK)** supports up to 32 member spanned volumes, which means that you shouldn't use more than 32 disks in the DPM disk pool.
- Don't exceed 80 TB of storage for production data in the DPM disk pool with a maximum recovery point size of 40 TB.
- You can have up to 600 volumes in your DPM disk pool.

The RAID levels for the disk pool

When it comes to planning the DPM disk pool, selecting the RAID level is a strategic choice since this will be one area that will give you good or poor performance of the DPM disk pool.

There are four categories that you must consider when planning for the DPM disk pool:

- Capacity
- Cost
- Reliability
- Performance and scalability

Many companies will use the RAID 5 for their RAID level since this gives you an ok score in all four categories. One thing that is often forgotten is the actual number of disks that could be included in a RAID 5 before it will impact the reliability and performance. This differs among different vendors and you should verify the maximum limits permitted from each storage vendor.

The following matrix will give you a good understanding of the RAID level you should choose to fit your company performance need and disk cost. The value 1 in the matrix is poor and 4 is very good.

RAID level	Capacity	Cost	Reliability	Performance and scalability
JBOD	4	4	1	4
RAID 0	4	4	1	4
RAID 1	1	1	4	3
RAID 5	3	3	3	3
RAID 10	1	1	4	4
JBOD	5	5	1	2
RAID 0	5	5	1	5
RAID 1	1	2	3	3
RAID 5	4	4	2	3
RAID 6	3	3	5	2
RAID 10	1	1	4	5
RAID 50	3	2	4	4

If your company would like to have good performance in their DPM disk pool you should choose the RAID 10 level. This choice isn't the most cost effective but gives you great performance.

Software controllers versus hardware controllers

Regarding the choice of software versus hardware, Microsoft always recommends that you use a hardware controller. DPM will work with a software controller but if you are looking for stability, performance, and reliability for your DPM disk pool, you should always use a hardware controller.

The sector size

When planning your DPM disk pool for an enterprise deployment, there are two critical issues that you must consider:

- How the data stream is being written
- The size of the data being written to disk

This is important in those scenarios where you need to plan your SAN being used for the DPM disk pool. DPM will write the data in a sequential I/O with the size of 64 KB.

The custom volumes

DPM 2012 has some auto-heal functions; one of these is automatically growing the volumes that were introduced in DPM 2010. In some cases you might like to place your more important or critical protected production data on a storage solution that has a better I/O performance for your restore process. As a DPM administrator, the only way to choose which disk in the DPM disk pool to host the protected data is to use the custom volumes. Consider the scenario where you would like to place your protected Exchange mailbox databases on a performance SAN instead of cheaper storage so you can manage your SLA. A custom volume can also be encrypted.

By using the custom volumes you will be able to manage the creation of the volume for the replica and the volume for the recovery point yourself in disk management. During the creation of a protection group, you can associate the created volumes with the data source you want to protect. The custom volumes will not grow automatically and, as an administrator, you need to be able to increase the size when needed.

Deduplication

DPM doesn't do deduplication for the DPM disk pool. It can be done by using third-party software or by using hardware that performs deduplication on the disks that are presented to the DPM server operating system.

For the software deduplication there is one piece of vendor software that you should use. The software name is BitWackr and the vendor is Exar.

For hardware-based deduplication, there are two options. If your SAN supports deduplication for the disks that will be used for the DPM disk pool then you will be able to have the deduplicated data in your disk pool. The second option is to use a product called CRUNCH from the company BridgeSTOR.

Dependent services, local accounts, and groups

After the installation of DPM, you will have some new services running in your operating system and also two specific accounts that you will have been prompted to enter a password for. We will now explain the purpose of these services and the local accounts.

Services

After the installation is finished, the following DPM processes are present in your DPM server's operating system:

- DPM
- DPM AccessManager
- DPM Agent Coordinator
- DPM CPWrapper
- DPM Writer
- DPMLA
- DPMRA

DPM

The DPM service is used by the DPM server to implement and manage shadow copy creation and synchronization of your production servers.

The DPM AccessManager service

The DPM AccessManager service will manage access to the DPM server.

The DPM Agent Coordinator service

When you are deploying, updating, or uninstalling the agent, the DPM Agent Coordinator service is the service that manages these processes.

The DPM CPWrapper service

The DPM CPWrapper service is used for the DCOM-WCF bridge service in association with the dpmcmd proc. It is used when wrapping the data for the **certificate-based authentication (CBA)** protection.

The DPM Writer service

The DPM Writer service manages the backed up shadow copies of the replicas. The DPM Writer service is also used when you are backing up the local DPMDB or reporting databases.

The DPMLA service

The DPMLA service is used by DPM for managing the libraries attached to the DPM.

The DPMRA service

The DPMRA service is the DPM replication agent and is found on the protected servers and also on the DPM server. The purpose is to back up and restore file and application data to the DPM.

Local accounts and groups

During the installation process of DPM, you will be prompted to type in a password for two accounts that will be placed locally on the DPM server. Both accounts are low-privilege accounts in the operating system. The accounts are as follows:

- `DPMR$YOUR_DPM_SERVER_NAME`
- `MICROSOFT$DPM$Acct`

The `DPMR$YOUR_DPM_SERVER_NAME` account is used by the local SQL Server reporting services with the purpose of generating reports in the DPM console.

The `MICROSOFT$DPM$Acct` account is used by the local SQL Server and SQL agent services.

There are also six groups, as follows:

- **DPMDBReaders$your_dpm_server_name**: This contains the computer account for your DPM server, so it has the privilege to read information in the DPMDB
- **DPMDRTrustedMachines**: This contains the computer account for the secondary DPM server associated with your DPM server
- **DPMRADcomTrustedMachines**: This contains the primary and secondary DPM servers' computer accounts
- **DPMRADmTrustedMachines**: This contains the computer account that has an associated DPM agent with your DPM server
- **MSDPMTrustedMachines**: This contains the computer accounts of those production servers that have an associated DPM agent with the DPM server
- **MSDPMTrustedUsers**: This is used for the centralized management features

Volume Shadow Copy Services (VSS)

The VSS is a key feature of the DPM backup and restore processes for your Microsoft production environment. For a few minutes you will get a deep dive into how VSS works and "what makes it tick".

VSS was first introduced in the Windows Server 2003 release and has been developed since. The VSS enables you to make a backup of your production servers while they are still running their production processes.

The VSS consists of four different blocks:

- **The VSS requester**: The DPM agent is a requester and the purpose of this is to initiate a request for a snapshot to happen.
- **The VSS writer**: SQL, Exchange, SharePoint, and so on all have a defined VSS writer. The VSS writer guarantees that there is a consistent data set for backup.
- **The VSS provider**: The VSS provider is software- or hardware-based. The VSS provider creates and maintains the shadow copies. By default, you are using a software provider that resides within the operating system. The software provider uses a copy-on-write technique that will be explained shortly.
- **The VSS service**: To make the requester, writer, and provider work together, you will need a coordination service. The VSS service is the coordinator that makes the communication between the different components work.

The creation of a shadow copy

Let's have a look at how the different components of the shadow copy services interact with each other to be able to make a consistent shadow copy of your production environment. The following diagram is a graphical explanation of the process:

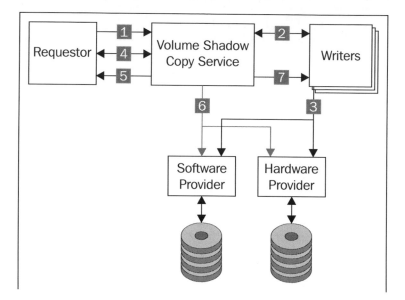

The DPM agent sends a query to the VSS to enumerate the writers and the writer metadata within the protected servers' operating system and prepare for the creation of a shadow copy:

1. The VSS writer creates an XML file that will describe the components and data stores that need to be included in the backup and also a definition of the restore process. The information is transferred to the VSS that will provide the VSS Requestor with the VSS writer's description. The VSS Requestor will select the components for the backup process.

2. The VSS will receive the VSS Requestor's choice for backup and will instruct the VSS writers to prepare their data for creating a shadow copy.

3. The VSS writer will complete all open transactions, rolling transaction logs, and flushing caches. When this process is done, the VSS writer notifies the VSS that the data is ready to be shadow copied.

4. The VSS instructs the VSS writers to freeze their write I/O requests for that specific application. During the freeze state, the shadow copy is created. This takes just a few seconds but there is a time-out limit of 60 seconds. The shadow copy service will flush the file system buffer and freeze the filesystem. This process makes the recording of the system metadata and verifies that it is correct and that the data that will be shadow copied is written in a consistent order.

5. The VSS initiates the provider to create a shadow copy. This takes 10 seconds and, during this time, the write I/O is frozen. However, you are still able to read the data being processed.

6. The VSS releases the file system write I/O.

7. The VSS tells the application to un-freeze the I/O requests.

8. If any error occurs then the requester can retry the process.

9. If the shadow copy creation was successful the VSS returns the location of the files to the VSS Requestor.

A different creation of a shadow copy

When the VSS coordinates a creation of a shadow copy, there are three different techniques to achieve this:

- **Complete copy**: This technique makes a full copy or a clone of a disk
- **Copy-on-write**: This is a technique that only copies data that has changed and is used by the DPM
- **Redirect-on-write**: When the original volume receives a change, the change is made to another volume that stores the shadow copy storage area

How does the DPM agent operate?

The DPM agent is the communication channel between the production server that is protected with DPM and the DPM server. There are several important things to know regarding how DPM agent works and why.

Distributed Component Object Model (DCOM)

Distributed Component Object Model (DCOM) is the technology for the communication between the software components for computers on a network.

DCOM objects that reside within the operating system are located in **Administrative Tools | Component Services**. If you expand **Component Services | Computers | My Computer | DCOM Config** you will see all the DCOM objects.

The DCOM object for the DPMRA service is most significant for the backup and restore operation. Within the security settings for the DPM RA service, you will find the security settings for launching and activation. If you are looking at a production server that is protected with DPM, you will find the computer account for the primary (and secondary) DPM server. These computer accounts must be allowed to have the following permissions:

- Local launch
- Remote launch
- Local activation
- Remote activation

Direction of communication

When you are protecting a production server or a Windows client, the communication is initialized in different ways:

- In a production server scenario, the DPM server initializes the communication
- In a Windows client scenario, the DPM agent initializes the communication

The firewall settings for DPM

The following is a list of the TCP and UDP ports used by the DPM communication. If the firewall is not configured correctly DPM will not work:

Protocol	Port
DNS	53 UDP
Kerberos	88 UDP/TCP
DCOM	135 TCP dynamic allocation 1024-65535
NetBIOS	137 UDP
	138 UDP
	139 UDP
	445 TCP
LDAP	389 UDP/TCP
TCP	5718 TCP
TCP	5719 TCP

Underlying technologies

When DPM is performing its backups and restore operations, there are several underlying technologies that are used to be able to track those block-level changes that are associated with a Windows application or files.

Change Journal

The Change Journal was first introduced in the Windows 2000 server operating system and has been developed over the years. The Change Journal enables you to keep track of the changes made to files on an NTFS formatted volume. The Change Journal exists on the volume itself and is stored as a sparse file of each volume present in the operating system.

The File System filter

The File System Filter is a driver that intercepts requests targeted at a filesystem. By doing the interception, the File Filter driver can extend or replace functionality that is provided by the original target of the request.

The DPM File filter

The DPM File filter is the technology that provides the delta change tracking of a protected volume.

A GUI walkthrough

The first thing you will discover in the new GUI of DPM is that DPM has got the same look as the other System Center family applications. The new GUI of DPM enables you to navigate through the product with ease. You now have the ability to work with ribbons and outlook navigation. The console is still based on **Microsoft Management Console (MMC)** but this doesn't mean that you can attach your DPM server console via MMC on other operating systems. If you wish to administrate your DPM server, you should use the Remote Administration function.

Let's take a look at the different task areas in the GUI:

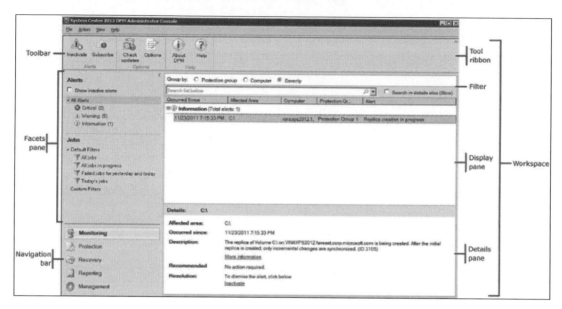

The Navigation bar

The DPM console consists of the following five buttons:

- **Monitoring**
- **Protection**
- **Recovery**
- **Reporting**
- **Management**

The different buttons will provide you with different management tasks or scenarios and we will start off by looking at the **Monitoring** task area.

Monitoring

Regardless of what is going on in your DPM environment or DPM server, the **Monitoring** task pane will give you the information to see the health of your SCDPM server. The **Monitoring** task pane consists of two parts: **Alerts** and **Jobs**. They can both be filtered with the new context bar feature that resides at the top of the display pane.

Alerts

There are three types of **Alerts** that DPM will provide:

- The **Critical** alerts are alerts regarding functions or features that have failed their backup or restore process of the production environment.
- The **Warning** alerts inform you that something needs your attention.
- The **Information** alerts inform you of the result of a restore and so on. This type of alert is just information regarding the result of a successful operation.

As a DPM administrator, you can also deactivate alerts. To do this you will need to right-click on **Alert** and choose **Show inactive alerts**. Inactivating an alert will clear that specific alert from the console. If the error reoccurs, a new alert will be published.

You can also subscribe to alerts via e-mail. If you choose to do this, your DPM server will send your alerts to a specified e-mail address or addresses. To do this you must first define an SMTP server that DPM has the rights to use and then configure your notifications. To do this click on the **Subscribe** icon in your ribbon. If you cannot see the **Subscribe** icon, remember that the ribbon interacts with your navigation in the console, click on an **Alert** type and the **Subscribe** icon should appear. Clicking on the **Subscribe** icon, a new window will appear, click on the **SMTP** tab and fill in the information regarding your SMTP server that should be used for this operation. When you have finished filling in the configuration for your SMTP server, click on the **Notifications** tab. Now choose the different alert types that you want to have forwarded and fill in the recipient list. To separate multiple e-mail addresses use a comma. For example: `john.doe@gmail.com, john.doe@yahoo.com`.

You can now press the **Send Test Notification** button and shortly an e-mail will appear in those specified e-mail inboxes.

Jobs

When you schedule a backup within a protection group, the backup schedule will be presented in the DPM console within the standard filters. There are four **Default Filters**:

- **All jobs**
- **Al jobs in progress**
- **Failed jobs for yesterday and today**
- **Today's jobs**

You can also create custom filters, which will consist of different job types and status. To create a custom filter, click on filters in the DPM console and then click on the **Create** button. Now a window appears, enter you filter name, set the time interval, and choose what job types and statuses should be used in your custom filter. You can also narrow down the output of the filter by choosing explicit computers or protection groups under the **Protection** tab. If your custom filter should include information regarding time elapsed or data transferred for your tape-based backup, this is defined under the **Other** tab.

Protection

In the **Protection** area, you will need to define your protection groups that contain the backup schedules for your Microsoft environment.

Facets pane

Outlook Navigation has two parts: **Data Source Health** and **All Protection groups**. These two parts are filters that help DPM administrators filter the information regarding the DPM server's protection group and health:

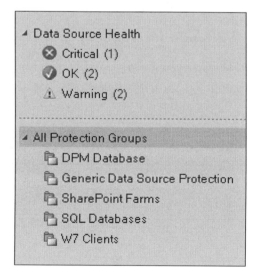

Ribbons

Ribbons enable you to create new protection groups, modify them, and delete them. The ribbon is context sensitive meaning that, depending on your selection, you will get other tasks presented in the ribbon:

On-the-wire

You can also perform an optimization on protection group level by using **Enable on-the-wire compression**. When you are using this function, the DPM agent will compress the data it backs up before sending it to the DPM server. This will not impact the performance of your production environment severely, but it will take some CPU and RAM.

If you are looking for what tapes are associated to a specific protection group, just mark the **Protection group** area and click on the **View tapes** list. A new window will appear and prompt you with that information. If you want to perform a consistency check on your data sources just mark the protection group and click on the **Consistency check** ribbon button:

Resume backups

Resume backups will clear out all the VSS inconsistencies and synchronize the replicas and can be done for disk tapes and Azure:

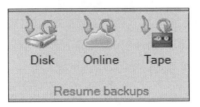

With **Online protection**, you can configure your DPM server to replicate its data to Azure.

With **Self service recovery**, you can configure your DPM server to let the DBAs in your organization restore SQL databases to an alternative location without contacting the DPM administrator.

With **Tape catalog retention**, you specify the tape catalog retention and set an alert limit for the growth of the DPMDB.

In the **Protection** area you can create a recovery point status report by clicking on the **Recovery point status** ribbon button.

To download the latest update available, you click on the **Check updates** ribbon button. To determine your DPM version and applied updates, click on the **About DPM** ribbon button as seen in the following screenshot:

Recovery

In the **Recovery** task area you will see what DPM is all about, restore.

In the **Navigation** pane you will see **Browse**. In the **Filter servers** text field you enter a server name that you want to restore data from and hit *Enter*. DPM will provide you with a list of all the servers and data sources that were found from your search under **Recoverable Data**.

Under **Search** in the facets pane you will be able to make your searches for recoverable data within three different categories:

- Files and folders
- Exchange mailboxes
- SharePoint

Within those three search categories you will be able to perform a more detailed search.

On the right side in the display pane you will see all of your recoverable items that were the output of your searches. In the calendar you will see some dates in bold numbers; this is an indication that DPM has recovery points for those dates. After you have chosen your recovery time, you can then restore a recoverable item by right-clicking on the data source and choosing **Recover**.

Reporting

It is important to know the status of your DPM server and the present recovery point status. By default, DPM is shipped with six standard reports that will provide you with information regarding different areas in the DPM server. The reports are:

- **Disk Utilization**: This report provides you with information regarding disk capacity, disk allocation, and disk usage in the DPM storage pool.
- **Recovery**: The Recovery report provides you with details about recovery items and statistics of recovery jobs.
- **Recovery Point Status**: This report provides you with the information if there is a recovery point present or not within the defined time window.
- **Status**: This report provides the status of all recovery points for a specific time period.
- **Tape Management**: This report provides details for managing tape rotation.
- **Tape Utilization**: This report provides information on the trends for the tape utilization and capacity planning.

To keep a track of changes in your DPM server environment, you are now able to schedule your creations of reports for future comparing. You are also able to subscribe to the reports after you have created them, but this feature needs to have a defined SMTP server. The reports can be sent in three different formats:

- HTML
- Excel
- PDF

Management

In the **Management** task area, you will be able to manage your DPM server. In the facets pane you will find three different parts:

- **Agents**
- **Disks**
- **Libraries**

Before DPM can start to protect the server-side production data, a DPM agent must be installed and attached to the DPM server. In the **Agents** part, you are able to install, update, disable protection, uninstall, throttle, or just refresh your agents by right-clicking the protected server name. You can also install the DPM agents to the production servers from here by clicking on the **Install** button in the toolbar.

All the information about your DPM storage pool can be found under the disks link in the facets pane. Within the GUI, you are able to add or rescan disks in the disk pool.

Under the **Libraries** part, you will find the attached tape library or stand-alone tape drive. DPM is not picky regarding the tape vendor of your tape solution. The only important thing to consider is that the tape drives and library media changer is populated correctly in the device manager. A good thing to do is to verify your drivers for your tape solution. If you have Microsoft signed drivers or the vendor has verified that their drivers work with DPM, you are ready to use your new tape solution.

Additional functions and roles within DPM

In this section we will discuss some additional features and roles within DPM that can ease the administrative burden of the IT staff or helpdesk.

End-user Restore Recovery (EUR)

In the first version of DPM that was released in 2006, **End-user Restore Recovery (EUR)** was introduced. This is a feature that is based on the shadow copy client that is included in the client operating system from Vista and newer. XP can also be protected but you need to install a shadow copy client and also have SP2 installed.

EUR gives the end user the ability to restore previous versions of files on file shares. The EUR function will verify the users restoring files or folders by verifying the **Access Control List** (**ACL**) in the NTFS rights of the file or folder.

To enable the EUR feature you must perform an update of the schema in your Active Directory. Keep in mind that those changes are not reversible. If you need to undo the changes made you will need to restore the Active Directory.

DPM Self-service Recovery Tool (SSRT)

SQL server has been around for sometime and with that, the need to restore databases. Many database administrators would like to be able to perform their own database restores without having to contact the restore admin.

With the **Self-Service Recovery Tool (SSRT)**, DBAs can perform the restore process without contacting any restore administrator.

The DPM admin will need to specify the group or user within the Active Directory that will be able to perform a restore and will need to define where the restored databases should be placed. The DBAs will not be able to restore any databases to their original location; just alternative locations or network folders.

The configuration of SSRT will be covered in *Chapter 6, DPM-aware Windows Workload Protection.*

Single Instance Storage (SIS)

Single Instance Storage (SIS) is a feature included in Window Storage Server 2003 and 2008. SIS is Microsoft's former answer to deduplication of data.

DPM is SIS-aware, which means that DPM can protect SIS-enabled volumes of the Windows Storage Server, which is why the SIS component is installed during the DPM server installation.

DPM cannot leverage SIS by itself to achieve a deduplicated DPM disk pool. If your goal is to have a deduplicated DPM disk pool you can use hardware deduplication of the SAN that stores the DPM disk pool or you can use third-party software such as BitWackr.

PSDataSourceConfig.XML

After you have deployed your DPM agents, attached them, and created a protection group with data sources, a configuration file is created on the production server. The configuration file is PSDatasourceConfig.XML and we will have a closer look at the file and explain how it is structured.

The PSDataSourceConfig.XML file is the configuration file for the DPM agent that holds the definition of which VSS should be used for what purpose. For example, if you are performing a system state backup of a 2008 R2 Windows Server, the PSDataSourceConfig.XML file instructs the DPM agent to use the VSS with the VSS WriterId tag: 8c3d00f9-3ce9-4563-b373-19837bc2835e.

Let's have a closer look at all the lines in the PSDataSourceConfig.XML file that are associated with the system state backup:

```
- <DatasourceConfig>
    <WriterId>8c3d00f9-3ce9-4563-b373-19837bc2835e</WriterId>
    <Version>01.00.0000.00</Version>
    <VssWriterInvolved>false</VssWriterInvolved>
    <LogicalPath>Computer</LogicalPath>
    <ComponentName>System Protection</ComponentName>
    <FilesToProtect>C:\WindowsImageBackup\*</FilesToProtect>
    <Size>51200</Size>
    <UseDRWithCC>true</UseDRWithCC>
  </DatasourceConfig>
```

The following are the attributes of the previous screenshot:

- The WriterId tag identifies the VSS writer that should be used for the VSS process
- The Version tag of the VSS is the VSS version that is used for the VSS writer
- The VssWriterInvolved tag identifies any cooperative VSS writers used for the backup process
- The LogicalPath and ComponentName tags are used by the VSS writer to backup reporting
- The FilesToProtect tag identifies which files should be included in the system state backup
- The Size tag in the PSDataSourceConfig.XML file indicates the size that is allocated in KB for the VSS area
- The UseDRWithCC tag is used for the disaster recovery process

Troubleshooting backups

DPM only uses technologies that are already installed to back up and restore the production servers. It is good to know where the DPM agent and DPM server store the logfiles that are written during this process in case something goes wrong. Understanding the logfiles is critical if you are facing an error, when backing up, that you are unable to resolve.

The local Windows logs

The operating system writes useful troubleshooting information in the local Windows logs regarding what is causing a backup to fail. The **Application** and the **System** log will provide somewhat detailed information that will aid you in the troubleshooting process.

Troubleshooting VSS

Since DPM uses the underlying VSS technology, this is the first place you should look for any errors. Since VSS has certain needs, such as enough free disk space on the volumes that the shadow copy operates on or VSS writers that are in a stable state, it is a simple troubleshooting process.

To verify the VSS state, just open a command prompt and type `vssadmin list writers`. The output will be a list of all the VSS writers present in the operating system and their state. If the state is 1 (stable) or 5 (waiting for completion), everything is normal.

The DPM agent logs

If you don't find anything wrong with the VSS, free disk space, or local windows logs, you should look into the DPM agent's logs if you got an indication that the error resides on the production server. The logfiles reside in the `C:\%ProgramFiles%\ Microsoft Data Protection Manager\DPM\Temp` catalog. The logfiles will log all the processes that are used within the communication between DPM server and DPM agents. On the DPM agent side, the logfiles you will find are as follows:

- `AgentBootstrapperCurr`
- `DPMACCurr`
- `DPMRACurr`

The DPM server logs

On the DPM server side, the logfiles reside in the `%ProgramFiles%\Microsoft DPM\ DPM\Temp` catalog. The logfiles are as follows:

- `AgentBootstrapperCurr`
- `AMServiceActivityCurr`
- `AMServiceAudit`
- `DPMAccessManagerCurr`
- `DpmBackupCurr`
- `DPMCLI0Curr`
- `DPMCLI9Curr`
- `DPMRACurr`
- `DPMRoleConfiguration0Curr`
- `DPMUI0Curr`
- `DpmWriterCurr`
- `LAAgentCurr`
- `MSDPMCurr`

These logfiles are very detailed and describe everything that goes on with the DPM server in readable form. Microsoft uses these files to track errors with DPM installations. The logfile that you can initially look into is the `DPMRACurr` logfile on both the DPM agent and DPM server side. This logfile logs all the processes for the remote agent and, if the DPMRA service has encountered an error, it will be stated in the logfiles as **WARNINGFailed** or **Error**.

Upgrading scenarios

When you are facing an upgrade scenario there are some things you must be aware of. Always have a local dump of the DPM database DPMDB. This is achieved by using the cmdlet `DPMBACKUP.EXE`. If anything goes wrong with the upgrade, you can always restore your DPM server using the previously dumped DPM database.

The upgrade of DPM is very easy. You can upgrade from DPM 2010 to DPM 2012 just by running the installation process initiated from the DPM media and following the wizard.

You cannot upgrade from DPM 2006 or DPM 2007 to DPM 2012. If you would like to benefit from the new features of DPM 2012 you should create a co-existence environment of DPM 2007 and DPM 2012.

Summary

In this chapter we looked at DPM and its architecture. We covered the important key features and underlying technologies in the operating system such as VSS, change journal, DPMDB, and file filter, among others. Additionally, we covered the new GUI and looked at some of its new key features.

In the next chapter, we will cover backup strategies and how to design them for use in the real world.

2
Backup Strategies

This chapter will make you understand why you should back up data such as system states, system drives, and so on. It will also provide you with the tools to define your **Service Level Agreement (SLA)**, protection groups, and guidelines to determine what data is really critical for your company.

Before you start protecting your company data, you must understand the importance of backup. A lot of administrators back up unnecessary data because they don't have a clear strategy of what data to select and how critical that selected data is to the company. Instead of planning a strategy, defining the internal and/or external SLA, the company invests in more storage hardware to host their backed-up data.

Please note that this chapter should be read before you start to plan your DPM installation to give you a good understanding of your environment.

This chapter will cover the following topics:

- The definition of data
- Microsoft's approach
- Service Level Agreements
- Recovery Point Objectives, Recovery Time Objectives, and Recovery Level Objectives
- What data should be back up
- The primary approach
- The next step
- Verification of your backups

The definition of data

It is important to understand the definition of and purpose of a company's data. The information that is stored in a file, SQL or Exchange server is to be seen as the company's heartbeat.

Your role as a backup administrator is very important to your company; it is your job to restore and verify that the the company's data and the services it represents. When a SQL database is corrupt or the content in a mailbox is missing, the end users will contact the backup administrator as their services are missing, not the data. If the sales department cannot place orders anymore since the system is not responding, it is your job to get it back on track. The end users don't care that their orders are stored in a SQL database or a flat file; they don't care if the latest patch didn't apply successfully. Their service is missing. In those situations, it is a good idea to have a restore strategy in place, one that is well defined from the perspective of getting the service for the end users online.

Microsoft's approach

The classification process of your services and data will influence the design of your **protection groups**. Protection groups should be seen as a backup schedule.

Microsoft has three different approaches for deployment scenarios for DPM and these scenarios will affect the design of your protection groups:

- The first approach is for smaller companies that have just a few servers and Windows workloads. The idea is to create a protection group for all the servers and apply the same backup schedule to all of them. This approach is a quick way to backup, but it isn't the approach you should use. It is important to differentiate the backup schedules for your Windows workloads or type of data since they are probably not equally important.

- The second approach is more effective. You create one protection group per Windows workload, which means that you will have one protection group for SQL, one for Exchange, one for SharePoint, and so on. This approach will give you more control over the backup of your Windows workloads since you can differentiate the backup schedules.

- The third approach is the enterprise approach, which you should definitely consider. The idea is to classify your data and services in your domains or forests and create a protection group that is influenced from your company's RPO, RTO, and RLO. This approach will give you full control of what data or function are backed up with each backup schedule.

Service Level Agreements

A Service Level Agreement (SLA) is the document that defines the strategic choices taken for the company's restore scenarios. The process of defining an SLA is time consuming and will take a lot of planning, analyzing, and research, along with several strategy meetings within the company.

The purpose of an SLA is to determine what the company defines as acceptable downtime and/or data loss. The SLA also states how quickly services need to be online and operational for internal or external systems or end users.

The statements made within the SLA define classes of data made for the the company's services, which should be mapped to different Windows workloads. An example of different classes is as follows:

- Platinum
- Gold
- Silver
- Bronze

The members of the Platinum group are the most important and members of the Bronze group are the least important.

Recovery Point Objectives, Recovery Time Objectives, and Recovery Level Objectives

In the initial planning stage, your restore strategy will always come down to how fast you are able to get the company's services back online. To determine this, there are several tools or techniques that are used to identify the company's maximum downtime or data loss during a catastrophic failure or disaster.

The best tools for you to use are the **Recovery Point Objectives (RPO)**, **Recovery Time Objectives (RTO)**, and **Recovery Level Objectives (RLO)**.

For a long time those tools have been the first choice to determine the maximum data loss and downtime for companies. When it comes for defining your restore plans, there are some things that should not be left to chance. Having a well-planned strategy based on the RPO, RTO, and RLO will ensure you make a great start.

Recovery Point Objectives (RPO)

The RPO defines the maximum amount of data that could be lost if you restore from your most recent backup.

For companies, it is important to have a backup schedule that will meet the need for restoration. With DPM, you will define how frequently recovery points should be created during the process of creating or modifying a protection group.

Recovery Time Objectives (RTO)

The RTO defines how much downtime a company or organization could manage or tolerate. There isn't an average value for the RTO; in most cases it is defined in different ways for different Windows workloads such as Exchange, SharePoint, files, and so on.

The main idea is to plan the company server environment so the RTO value can easily be met. For example, if you have a RTO of zero, you must apply a clustered server environment as a minimum requirements for those Windows workloads that represents the services.

Recovery Level Objectives (RLO)

The RLO defines the level of SharePoint to restore in your SharePoint farm, farms, or file server data.

Depending on the RPO and RTO for the SharePoint workload, the RLO may vary. You could have a RLO that states that company data must be restored at farm level for one kind of scenario and another RLO for individual items such as sites, lists or documents.

What data should we back up?

All data that is in any way critical to your company should be backed up. It is your challenge as backup administrator to define how critical or important a specific company service that uses a Windows workload is.

The initial step starts with classifying your company data. The classification is the first building block that will become your restore plan or SLA. The more accurate the classification task, the more effective the restore scenarios will be in real-world situations.

Classification of data

The most important part of the work is to always verify the services that the data represents has for the company. This might mean that you need to talk to the programmer that has developed that special application, the end users, or head of the marketing department, and so on. You many also need to categorize the actual servers that are associated with the different departments in your company.

Initial tasks

The first thing you need to do to do is to create a list, either manually or automated via scripts, of all of your servers. It doesn't matter if you have 20 servers or 20,000 servers, this job must be done:

	A
1	Servername
2	
3	SRV001
4	SRV002
5	SRV003
6	SRV004
7	SRV005
8	SRV006
9	SRV007
10	SRV008
11	SRV009
12	SRV010
13	SRV011

When you have that list ready, the next step is to verify whether the servers are `Physical or Virtual`. This is important due to the frequency of the recovery point creation in DPM:

	A	B
1	Servername	Physical or Virtual
2		
3	SRV001	P
4	SRV002	V
5	SRV003	V
6	SRV004	V
7	SRV005	P
8	SRV006	P
9	SRV007	P
10	SRV008	V
11	SRV009	V
12	SRV010	V
13	SRV011	V

If you have `Hyper-V` as your primary strategic virtual platform, you have a huge advantage when it comes to managing your disaster recovery scenarios. If you also have a physical DPM server it can actually start your Hyper-V servers by mounting the VHD from the replica volume associated with that data source.

Next, you will need to list the Windows workloads or applications that are present on each server:

	A	B	C
1	Servername	Physical or Virtual	Windows Application
2			
3	SRV001	P	SQL
4	SRV002	V	SharePoint
5	SRV003	V	Exchange
6	SRV004	V	File
7	SRV005	P	
8	SRV006	P	Exchange
9	SRV007	P	SQL
10	SRV008	V	Exchange
11	SRV009	V	
12	SRV010	V	Hyper-V

It is important that you know whether your Windows workloads are clustered or not. Are you using DAG for your Exchange environment? Is your `Hyper-V` solution High Availability (HA) enabled with CSV? Type that information as seen in the following screenshot:

	A	B	C	D
1	Servername	Physical or Virtual	Windows Application	Cluster
2				
3	SRV001	P	SQL	X
4	SRV002	V	SharePoint	
5	SRV003	V	Exchange	
6	SRV004	V	File	
7	SRV005	P		
8	SRV006	P	Exchange	X
9	SRV007	P	SQL	X
10	SRV008	V	Exchange	X
11	SRV009	V		
12	SRV010	V	Hyper-V	X
13	SRV011	V	Hyper-V	X

The next step is to identify which servers are domain controllers. If you have multiple domains or forests, it is important to keep track of the Active Directory database `NTDS.dit`:

	A	B	C	D	E
1	Servername	Physical or Virtual	Windows Application	Cluster	Domain Controller
2					
3	SRV001	P	SQL	X	
4	SRV002	V	SharePoint		
5	SRV003	V	Exchange		
6	SRV004	V	File		
7	SRV005	P			X
8	SRV006	P	Exchange	X	
9	SRV007	P	SQL	X	
10	SRV008	V	Exchange	X	
11	SRV009	V			X
12	SRV010	V	Hyper-V	X	

Once you have a basic overview of the servers running in your domain or forests, the next step is to work through all the servers representing your services.

Server technologies

Working through the server technologies representing the services is quite time consuming but you will find the result very satisfying. This work will aid you in:

- The configuration of your protection groups
- The number of protection groups
- The size needed for the DPM disk pool
- The number of DPM agents that need to be deployed
- The number of DPM servers that need to be deployed

The initial step will be configuring your protection groups. A protection group name should give a good understanding of what it is protecting and also give a hint as to how the configurations are made.

There are two different approaches regarding how to design your protection groups:

- Windows workload approach
- Enterprise approach

Windows workload protection group design

The Windows workload protection group design will reflect your Windows workload servers present in your domain or trusted domains. It is quite straightforward; you create unique protection groups for your SQL, SharePoint, domain controllers, system drives, volumes, and so on. This isn't very hard to accomplish; just keep in mind how you configure the backup schedule for the Windows workloads. You do not want multiple backups running on the same server if the server can't deliver enough performance or resources. If your servers hosting the services that can't deliver enough resource, separate the Windows workloads by using different backup schedules.

Enterprise protection group design

The Enterprise protection group design will really give you an overview of your protected data.

Initially you will need to define the company's RTO and RPO for every Windows workload representing your different services. Don't forget the RLO for your SharePoint environment.

To get started in this example, you need to define four different classes:

- Platinum
- Gold
- Silver
- Bronze

Please note that the number of protection groups in the end will probably be more than four. This is the first classification of your company or organization data, that will be broken down in more detail later on.

The Platinum class

The Platinum class contains the company's most critical services or data. Without this service or data the company is really lost.

A company's **Enterprise Resource Planning (ERP)** system resides in most cases within this group. The ERP is really the heart of the company and contains services for the CRM system, **Supply Chain Management (SCM)**, **Human Resources (HR)**, and so on.

The RTO for this class is often less than one hour acceptable downtime. RPO can vary but the value is very low and in some cases zero.

The Gold class

The Gold class contains data or services that are critical to the company but not as critical as the members of the Platinum group.

Here you will find file shares for system resources, or critical databases for the company's SQL server, and so on. The Exchange workload could also be present in this group.

This group has a RTO of two hours of acceptable downtime.

The Silver class

The Silver class is important to the company's services but not as important as the Gold or Platinum class. You can find static file server data or databases within this group.

If a member should fail the RTO for this group, it is four hours of accepted downtime.

The Bronze class

The Bronze class represents services that are not critical in a company. If your company loses the service, the administrators can easily set up a new server hosting the service.

The primary approach

When it comes to backing up your environment, it is critical that you have a good understanding of the server platforms that are present, and what service, these platforms deliver within your company or organization.

Non-Windows application servers

In many environment, you will run into different server technologies, but you can always be sure that there is a way to perform a backup. Most importantly you will be able to perform a fully supported restore.

Generic data source protection

A new feature within DPM 2012 is the generic data source protection. This can back up Windows applications that could leverage the VSS technology. This means that you will be able to make differential backups and support restore scenarios for Windows workloads that have not yet been defined within the DPM definition of protected workloads.

Local services

If the generic data source protection feature does not work, you can always rely on the local services. For those companies who do not use SQL or Exchange as their primary choices, there is still a possibility to get that company service protected with DPM.

Let's take Oracle for example. The strategy is to perform local dumps of the Oracle databases to an NTFS formatted volume, managed by an operating system that has a DPM agent installed. DPM will then be able to fetch those dump files and store them at the DPM server side.

The Windows workloads

When it comes to the Windows workloads you will always have a supported and fully optimized backup, restore, and disaster recovery scenario with DPM.

The initial task when it comes to managing your Windows workloads is to verify where you can use **Bare Metal Restore (BMR)**. BMR is a disaster recovery function that will back up your system state and system drive on physical servers, then make that restorable to different physical hardware.

BMR can also be applied in a Hyper-V environment. The difference here is that BMR is the same as protecting your entire virtual server this is called **host-level backup**. This gives you the ability to restore your virtual servers to another Hyper-V host if your primary host or cluster crashes.

Secondly, as an addition to the BMR backup of your virtual servers, you should install a DPM agent on your virtual server to perform **guest-level backup**. This means that you backup the SQL or SharePoint that is installed on the virtual OS.

The next step

After you have classified your company data, you should move on to designing your protection groups.

By now you should know which services and data are critical, and classify them into the groups: platinum, gold, silver and bronze.

Protection group names

One thing that is very important is the name standard of your protection groups. It should reflect the company classification of the RTO, RPO, and RLO.

If you have a protection group with an RTO of 4 hours, RPO of 1 hour, and a synchronization frequency of 15 minutes, the name for that protection group should be "RTO 4 hours / RPO 1 hour / Sync 15 min".

This means that the members of that group must be up and running within 4 hours, a recovery point should be created every hour, and between those points, the block-level changes are synchronized every 15 minutes.

It doesn't matter if you mix different kinds of data sources within the protection group. Bear in mind though that a data source can only be associated with one protection group. The idea is to always let the classification work decide which services should be members of a given group.

Member of the protection group

Keep in mind that DPM will use underlying technologies within the operating system when it comes to making a backup of your company services and data. You must be clear what services resides on which disk or volume.

When you perform a backup of your SQL database, you could back up the volume that the SQL database resides on at the same time due to the different VSS writers. However, this is not a good approach since your volumes hosting the SQL database will never have the same RTO or RPO as you actual SQL data. The SQL databases have a higher priority than the actual physical volume.

Verification of your backups

When you have the classification of your company's services and data, and protection group design up and running, you have come to the final step. Now it's time to restore the services and data.

The most important thing to consider as a DPM administrator is to be able to verify the data or services that have been backed up. This actually means that you must be comfortable with restoring Active Directory or your Exchange environment and so on.

Restore training

When it comes to restoring your company services or data, you must be self-confident that you can manage the job. You must know the different restore options regarding the different Windows applications and how long the actual restore job will take.

The best way of knowing is to practice different restore scenarios within a lab environment.

The verification process

When you know how to restore different Windows applications, it is time to put your knowledge to the test.

The verification process is the most important stage since this is where the SharePoint admin and DBA verify that the data you have backed up with DPM is restorable.

In DPM, you can restore the production data to an alternative location, and let the other admins verify that the data you have restored is the data they require.

Summary

In this chapter we found the tools that should be used to classify you company or organization's data. We also walked through the different designs of protection groups and explained the RPO, RTO, and RLO. We explained the SLA and how you could start off your work by initially designing your SLA.

Working tightly together with other administrators within your company or organization is most important during the classification process. The classification process is a time-consuming piece of work, but will define the company's primary approach to how important different services are.

In the next chapter, we will cover the DPM server management tasks.

3
DPM Server Management Tasks

This chapter is designed to provide you with the tools and tips for managing your DPM server. After reading this chapter you will have a lot of knowledge about the common DPM management tasks, such as automated DPM installation, storage pool migration, custom reporting, and DPM third-party add-ons.

Automated installation of DPM

The DPM unattended installation is a great way to make sure that all your DPM servers are installed with the same settings and configurations. In order to perform and automate the installation, you need to create an answer file with a .ini extension; in our case we will call it DPMSetup.ini. This file will include all the information needed for completing the installation, either installing DPM with its own SQL or when SQL is hosted remotely.

```
1   [OPTIONS]
2   UserName = <A user with credentials to install DPM>
3   CompanyName = <Name of your company>
4   ProductKey = <The 25-character DPM product key in the format xxxxx-xxxxx-xxxxx-xxxxx-xxxxx>
5   SqlAccountPassword = <The password to the DPM$ account>
6   # ProgramFiles = C:\Program Files\Microsoft Data Protection Manager
7   # DatabaseFiles = D:\Data\DPMDB
8   # IntegratedInstallSource = D:\Install #<Location of the DPM setup files>
9   # YukonMachineName = RemoteSQLServer <Name of the SQL Server computer>
10  # YukonInstanceName = MSSQL <Name of the instance of SQL Server that Setup must use>
11  # YukonMachineUserName = Domain\Adminuser <User name that Setup must user>
12  # YukonMachinePassword = DomainAdminPassword <Password for the user name Setup must use>
13  # YukonMachineDomainName = Domain.local <Domain to which the SQL Server computer is attached>
```

If you are installing the DPM database on a remote SQL Server you need to uncomment the code from line **9** to **13**.

At the elevated command prompt use the following command:

```
start /wait setup.exe /i /f <path>\DPMsetup.ini /l <path>\dpmlog.txt
```

In the previous command, `<path>` is the location for your answer file.

Migrating a DPM server to a new hardware

Let's say that you have a current DPM server (for example, DPM01), and you decide to move it to a different server (for example, DPM02). You must perform the following steps:

1. Perform the following task on DPM01:
    1. Back up the DPM database using the DPM command `DPMbackup -db`, the backup file will be located at `Microsoft System Center 2012\DPM\DPM\Volumes\ShadowCopy\DatabaseBackups\DPMDB.bak`.
    2. By adding `-targetLocation`, in the command, this will override the default location to the specified location on the local computer. If the DPM database is hosted remotely, use the SQL Server to get a full backup.
    3. Note the DPM version number. To do this, in the ribbon bar, click on **About DPM**.
2. In Active Directory, remove DPM01.
3. Perform the following tasks on DPM02:
    1. Ensure that the fully qualified domain name (FQDN) of DPM02 is the same as it was for DPM01. (If not, rename the server.)
    2. Install DPM 2012 on the new hardware.
    3. Install all DPM updates, so the DPM02 version number matches the version number for DPM01.
    4. Restore the DPM data base using the DPM command `DPMSync-RestoreDB -DBLoc` (this is the location and name of the database that has been backed up in the previous step).

5. Move the DPM01 storage to DPM02, you can do so using the PowerShell script provided with DPM in the `bin` folder, `MigrateDatasourceDataFromDPM.ps1`.

6. After successfully restoring the DPM database, run the `DPMSync -Sync` command in order to synchronize the database.

7. Perform a consistency check for all the data sources.

How to calculate storage for DPM

It is always important to plan how much disk space you will need for your DPM server. The storage for DPM varies based on the workloads and retention period for each workload protected by the DPM server. As you have learned from the previous chapters, DPM must allocate two different spaces on the storage pool — the **replicas** and **recovery** points — for each data source, and must allocate space on the protected file servers or workstations for the change journal. The following table shows how the DPM calculates the default allocation:

	Replica volume	Recovery point volume
Files	(DS x 3) / 2	((DS size x RR x 2) / 100) + 1600 MB
Exchange	DS x (1 + LG) / (alert threshold - .05)	(4.0 x RR x LG x DS) + 1600 MB
SQL Server data	DS x (1 + LG) / (alert threshold - .05)	(2.5 x RR x log change x DS)+ 1600 MB
Virtual server data	DS x 1.5	(DS x RR x 0.02) + 1600 MB
Hyper-V	DS x 1.5	(DS x RR x 0.1) + 1600 MB
System state	(DS x 3) / 2	((DS x RR x 2) / 100) + 1600 MB
Windows SharePoint Services data	Total size of all databases / (alert threshold - .05)	Total size of all databases / (alert threshold - .05)

Following are the attributes of the previous table:

- **DS**: This specifies the data source size
- **RR**: This specifies the retention range in days
- **LG**: This specifies the change rate on the database or storage group in question, for example, 6 percent for Exchange and SQL Server data and 10 percent for Windows SharePoint Services data
- **Alert threshold percent**: This specifies the threshold for the alert associated with replica growth, typically 90 percent

DPM calculates the default allocated space following the previous rules. We recommend adding five percent extra for the calculated value, and to do so, right-click on the protected data source and select **Modify Disk Allocation**, and enter the new value.

Creating custom reports in DPM

One of the biggest weaknesses in DPM is its reporting capabilities. DPM doesn't offer an easy way to create custom reports, so in this section we will explain how to create a custom report using the reporting services.

DPM Report Views

Microsoft has included a bunch of SQL views in the DPM database by default. They have included them so that the DPM administrators can create some custom reports. These Custom Report Views for DPM can be found at http://technet.microsoft.com/en-us/library/hh757766.aspx. (This URL also describes what type of data each view will provide you for your report.) The following screenshot shows what the views look like and where they are stored in SQL Management Studio:

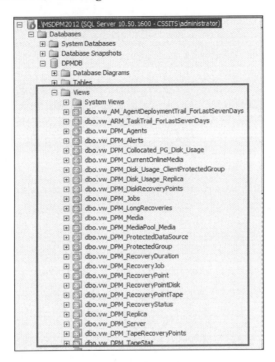

Building a custom DPM report

In order to create a custom report, you need to access the reporting service on a DPM server as follows:

1. Go to http://DPMserver.domain.local/Reports_MSDPM2012/.
2. Create a folder for your custom reports.

3. Click on **New Folder** in the SRS site.

4. Give it a name and click on the **OK** button.

Create a new folder in Home.

Name: Custom DPM reports

Description:

☐ Hide in tile view

[OK]   [Cancel]

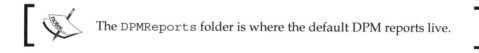 The DPMReports folder is where the default DPM reports live.

5. Now, click on the new folder that you created.

6. Then, click on **New Data Source**. We need to create a connection to the SQL DPM database. This is the typical string to your data source:

```
Data Source="DPMServerNameMSDPM2012";persist security info=False;
Initial catalog=DPMDB"
```

7. Use the settings as shown in the following screenshot. You also need to make sure that either the account you are using has permissions to access the DPM database or else you need to provide the credentials of an account that has the proper access. Click on **OK** when you are done.

Home > Custom DPM reports

SQL Server Reporting Services
New Data Source

Name: CustomDPMDataSource

Description:

☐ Hide in tile view
☑ Enable this data source

Data source type: Microsoft SQL Server

Connection string: data source="DPM-01\MSDPM2012";persist security info=False;initial catalog=DPMDB

Connect using:

○ Credentials supplied by the user running the report

Display the following text to prompt user for a user name and password:

Type or enter a user name and password to access the data source

☐ Use as Windows credentials when connecting to the data source

● Credentials stored securely in the report server

User name: DPMR$DPM-01

Password: ••••••••

☑ Use as Windows credentials when connecting to the data source

8. Now you can build a report. Click on the **Report Builder** button, and this will launch the report builder application.

9. In this example we are going to create a chart-based report. In the **Getting Started** wizard, click on **Chart Wizard**, as shown in the following screenshot:

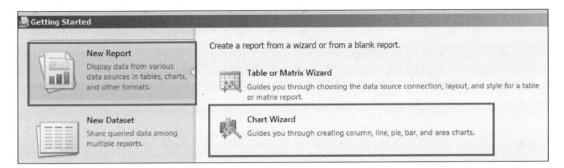

10. Select the data source that we created earlier (CustomDPMDataSource) and click on **Next**.

11. The following screenshot illustrates how to access the DPM SQL views to generate a report for the computer protected by this DPM server:

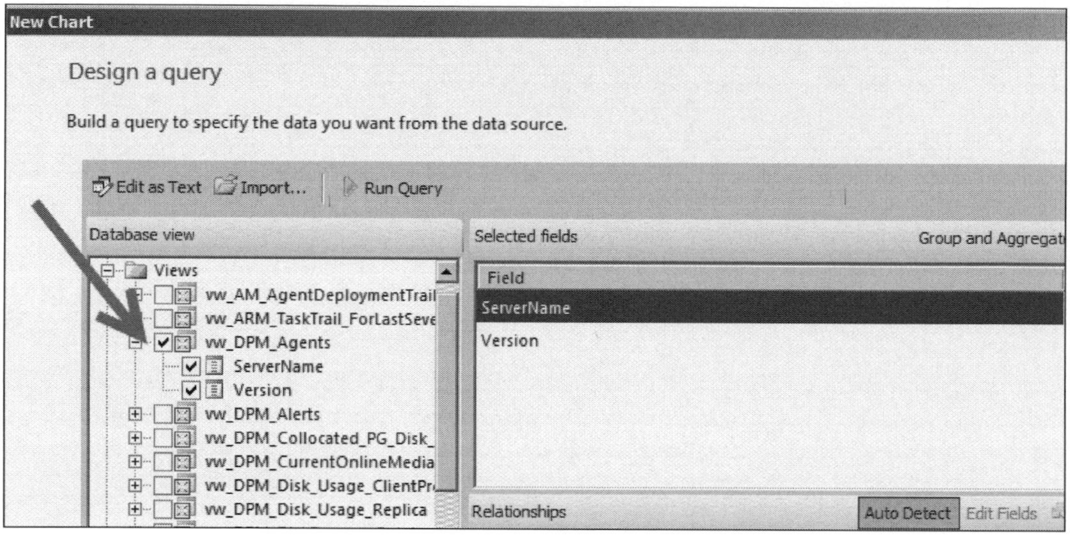

12. After choosing the chart type and the display (column), click on **Next**. The **Available fields** area contains the data that you can add to your chart. To add a field, just drag a field from the **Available fields** area to **Categories**, **Series**, or **Values**, and then click on **Next**.

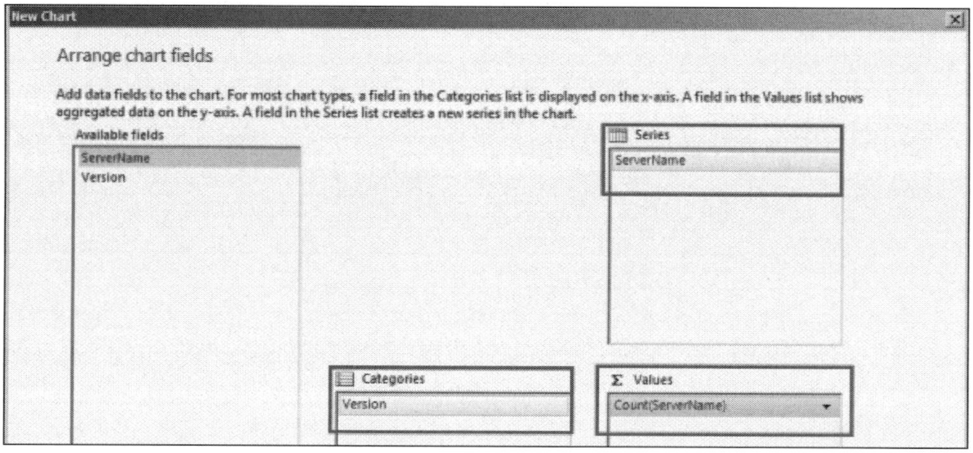

13. Then, choose your chart display. Click on **Finish** and then **Run** to generate the report. You will then see the finished report with the live data, as follows:

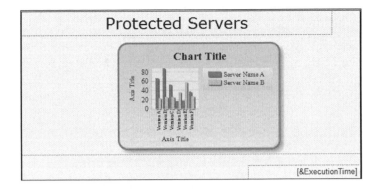

14. In order to reuse this report again, make sure to save it in the custom report folder that you created earlier.

Create custom DPM reports using Prism for DPM

In the previous section, we demonstrated how to create a custom report using SQL views. If you find that this approach is cumbersome and difficult, your other alternative is to use **Prism**.

Bocada has developed Prism to improve DPM report capability. They partnered with Microsoft to create two default DPM-specific reports in addition to the DPM default reports. These reports are as follows:

- **Recovery point summary**: This provides a summary of the number of non-expired recovery points, date of the last non-expired recovery point, and the average recovery point in range for all the clients being protected
- **Recovery point status**: This lets you see the various successes or failures of your daily recovery points

These default reports will also help you learn more about the following on your DPM server(s):

- Determine the status of all recovery points by protection group
- View recovery targets (disk or tape)
- Filter by recovery point status, for example, Best, Worst, and All
- Recovery Point Trends

- Determine if there are systemic problems in the environment
- Understand the load on each DPM server
- Fine tuning of schedules and resource utilization — view utilization by data size across assets and over time, to fine-tune scheduling windows and trigger levels

Prism also has a health-check report for your DPM that you can access. It helps you to answer questions about your DPM such as the following:

- How are the backup jobs trending?
- How long do the backup jobs run?
- How much data is being written to the DPM servers?

The health check can be used for easier troubleshooting of your DPM server, providing a summary of the failure's cause, and the ability to drill down to see the original error message. Another example is that Prism shows all the recovery jobs for a client in a single view with the ability to drill down into job details. This is illustrated in the screenshot:

Changing the SQL Server instance used by DPM

Installing the DPM database on a remote SQL Server has its advantages and disadvantages. One of the advantages is that the DPM database will be maintained by the same maintenance plan as all other databases hosted on the remote SQL Server, so you don't need to maintain a DPM database using different procedures; on the other hand, if you have a connectivity problem between the DPM server and the SQL Server hosting the DPM database, then the backup will be affected. Then comes the time when you may need to move the database, either because you have to upgrade the SQL hardware, or just simply because you have been told to move the server.

In this section, we will explain the required steps to move the DPM database:

1. Note the version number of the DPM server as described earlier.

2. Back up the DPM database using the `DPMbackup -db` DPM command, the backup file will be located at `Microsoft System Center 2012\DPM\DPM\Volumes\ShadowCopy\Database Backups\DPMDB.bak`.

3. Uninstall DPM and choose to retain data on the remote SQL Server.

4. Run `sqlprep.msi`, which is located on the DPM product DVD in the `SCDPM\SQLPrepInstaller\` folder.

5. Install DPM and choose a new instance of the SQL Server, making sure that the user account you will be using to run the SQL Server service and the SQL Server Agent service has *read* and *execute* permissions to the SQL Server installation location.

6. Restore DPMDB to the new instance of SQL Server. Copy the saved `DPMDB.BAK` to the local SQL Server (that is, `C:\DPMbackup`).

7. Run `DpmSync -RestoreDb -DbLoc C:\DPMBackup\DPMDB.bak -InstanceName <Sql_server\instancename>`.

8. On the DPM server, run `Dpmsync -sync`.

9. For all the data sources, run a consistency check to validate the replicas.

Moving the DPM server to a new domain or renaming a DPM server

There are a lot of dependencies based on the hostname of the DPM server, therefore you cannot rename a DPM server or move it to another domain, because of the following reasons:

- DPM internally stores the machine name in its DPM database, which is referred to in code at various places.

- The DPM scheduled jobs are stored as XML strings, which contain references to the original DPM machine name. Thus, changing the actual machine name of DPM can lead to undefined behavior.

Adding disks to the storage pool

After attaching the new storage to the DPM server, the new disk will not be seen in the **Disks** tab in the management task area on the DPM Administrator Console. To add the disk to the storage pool, click on the **Management** section, and then click on the **Add** button. Now select the disk that you want to add to the storage, then click on **Add**. DPM will start initializing and joining the disk to the storage pool, as shown in the following screenshot:

After you select the disk and click on **Add**, DPM will display the storage pool disk, as shown in the following screenshot:

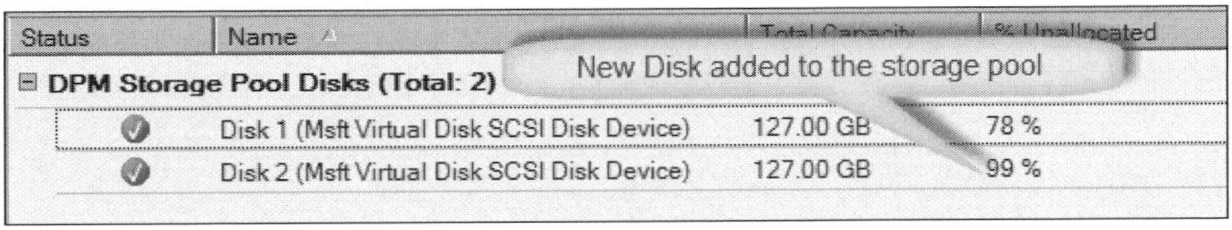

Removing a disk from the storage pool

The DPM storage pool comprises one or more disks. If it happens that you have a faulty disk or your SAN administrator asked you to move or replace the current disk from your DPM storage to another set of disks, then you have to migrate the data to a new disk and decommission the current disk.

In this section, we will explain how to migrate a data source from one disk to another using the MigrateDatasourceDataFromDPM command:

1. Attach the new disk to the DPM server. The disk will be unknown until it gets added to the DPM storage pool.

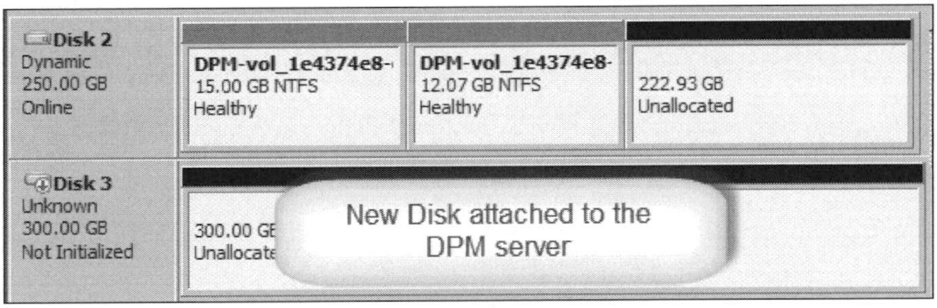

2. Add the new disk to the DPM storage pool. DPM will take care of the disk management, so you don't need to format and initialize the disk.

3. In the DPM command shell, run the following command to display the disk(s) in the DPM server:

```
Get-DPMDisk [-DPMServerName] <DPMServerName>
```

In order to use the migration PowerShell command you must use a variable name to save the array of returned items. In our case we are using $disk as a variable:

```
$disk =Get-DPMDisk-DPMServerName
```

4. In this example, after the first command we will notice that there are three disks listed; note the NtDiskId value:

   ° The disk with the NtDiskId value of 1 is hosting the Windows operating system

   ° The disk with the NtDiskId value of 2 is the current faulty disk that needs to be replaced (source)

   ° The disk with the NtDiskId value of 3 is the new disk that has been added to the storage pool (destination)

5. Now we are going to use the PowerShell command to migrate the storage. The syntax for the command is as follows:

```
MigrateDatasourceDataFromDPM.ps1 -DPMServerName<DPM Server Name>
-Source $disk[n] -Destination $disk[n])
```

Here n is the element index in the $disk array, for example, $disk[0] is the disk with the NtDiskId value of 2, $disk[1] is the disk with the NtDiskId value of 1, and $disk[2] is the disk with the NtDiskId value of 3.

So the variable needed here is the source disk $disk[0] and the destination disk will be $disk[2]. The final command will look like the following:

```
MigrateDatasourceDataFromDPM.ps1 -DPMServerName DPM-01 -Source
$disk[0] -Destination $disk[2]
```

The command may take some time depending on the number and size of the volume on the source disk(s). As soon as it is completed the prompt will return.

6. Since we have migrated disk 1 to disk 2, disk 1 will no longer be shown in the DPM storage pool, and will not be used any further for DPM.

7. After migration, the replicas will be placed in an inconsistent state and you will need to run a synchronization job with consistency check for each of the data sources that were located on that specific disk. The command causes the replica to be in an inconsistent state, therefore, you need to run a synchronization job with consistency check.

8. The original disk from where the data was migrated, is not chosen for hosting any *new* backups, however the recovery points located on the source disk can be used for restoration until the recovery points are expired.

9. You must retain your old disks until all the recovery points on them expire. After the recovery points expire, DPM automatically deallocates the replicas and recovery point volumes on these disks.

Replacing a disk in the storage pool

Replacing a disk in the DPM storage pool is a similar process to removing a disk from the storage pool. As described earlier in this chapter, it involves the following steps:

1. Migrate the data from a suspect disk to a temporary storage using the MigrateDatasourceDataFromDPM PowerShell script command.

2. Add a new disk to the DPM storage pool.

3. Migrate the data from the temporary storage to the new storage using the `MigrateDatasourceDataFromDPM` command.

4. Remember that when the `MigrateDatasourceDataFromDPM` command is executed the disk (source) doesn't show in DPM storage again.

DPM network bandwidth and control traffic

The network-bandwidth-usage throttling restricts the network bandwidth used by DPM during backup jobs. The throttling helps to ensure that DPM is not using all the bandwidth and there is bandwidth available for other applications, and it depends on QoS.

The network-bandwidth-usage throttling has a great advantage in the sense of limiting the amount of network resources consumed during backup, especially over the WAN. However, the trade-off is that the backup time will be increased until the synchronization job completes.

The network-bandwidth-usage throttling is configured on the *agent* level, so you should think about setting the throttling in the function where the maximum amount of data is to be transferred. For example, if you establish a limit of 25 percent of a 512 Kbps connection, then the protected server in that protection group will send the data at a rate no bigger than 128 Kbps.

Enabling the network-bandwidth-usage throttling

The following are the steps for enabling the network-bandwidth-usage throttling:

1. In the DPM Administrator Console, click on **Management** on the navigation bar.
2. Click on the **Agents** tab.
3. In the **Display** pane, select a server.
4. In the **Actions** pane, click on **Throttle computer**.
5. Click on **Enable network bandwidth usage**.

You can configure the bandwidth throttling based on the day and period of the backup. Let's say that your peak hours are between 9 AM and 5 PM from Monday to Friday, so you can define this period as working hours and throttle the bandwidth for DPM to use the minimum bandwidth.

Network bandwidth usage can be limited by **Group Policy**. If the DPM bandwidth usage limit, either by itself or in combination with the limits of other programs, exceeds the Group Policy reserved bandwidth limit, the DPM bandwidth usage limit might not be applied.

Enabling the network-bandwidth-usage throttling for multiple DPM agents at once

The following are the steps for enabling the network-bandwidth-usage throttling for multiple DPM agents at once:

1. In the DPM Administrator Console, enable throttling on an agent.

2. In the DPM server or remote SQL instance server, open up SQL Management Studio.

3. In SQL Management Studio, run the following query on the `tbl_AM_InstalledAgent` table to find out the settings and the GUID ID of the agent you just enabled throttling on.

```
SELECT  [InstallID], [ServerId], [AgentID], [OSType],
[RebootRequired], [Deleted], [DeletedDateTime], [ClusterID],
[Enabled], [PatchID], [IsThrottled], [WorkHoursTransmissionRate],
[NonWorkHoursTransmissionRate], [ThrottlingSettings], [OSVersion],
[ServerAttributes], [IsServerOS], [ApprovedPatchByAdmin] FROM
[DPMDB].[dbo].[tbl_AM_InstalledAgent]
GO
```

The results should look similar to the following screenshot:

4. Then, in the right-hand side you see the **IsThrottled** column, notice the row that has a value **1** in it.

IsThrottled	WorkHoursTransmissionRate	NonWorkHoursTransmissionRate	ThrottlingSettings	OSVersi
1	0		0	<?xml version="1.0" encoding="utf-16"?> <Thro...	6.1.760
2	1	256	512	<?xml version="1.0" encoding="utf-16"?> <Thro...	6.1.760
3	0	0	0	<?xml version="1.0" encoding="utf-16"?> <Thro...	6.1.760
4	0	0	0	<?xml version="1.0" encoding="utf-16"?> <Thro...	6.1.760

5. Copy the **InstallID** value into the following query and run this against the tbl_AM_InstalledAgent table.

```
DECLARE @w int
SET @w = (SELECT [WorkHoursTransmissionRate] from tbl_AM_
InstalledAgent WHERE InstallID = '2083CDAA-2872-4D2D-BAEA-
ADF033021EB9⊠)
DECLARE @n int
SET @n = (SELECT [NonWorkHoursTransmissionRate] from tbl_AM_
InstalledAgent WHERE InstallID = '2083CDAA-2872-4D2D-BAEA-
ADF033021EB9⊠)
DECLARE @t nvarchar(max)
SET @t = (SELECT [ThrottlingSettings] from tbl_AM_InstalledAgent
WHERE InstallID = '2083CDAA-2872-4D2D-BAEA-ADF033021EB9⊠)
UPDATE [DPMDB].[dbo].[tbl_AM_InstalledAgent]
SET
[IsThrottled] = 1
,[WorkHoursTransmissionRate] = @w
,[NonWorkHoursTransmissionRate] = @n
,[ThrottlingSettings] = @t
GO
```

6. This method helps you to throttle multiple agents in DPM, however, it is not supported by Microsoft. That does not mean this will not work, it simply means that it has not been tested by Microsoft and therefore cannot be supported. Use this at your own risk.

Working with DPM SQL self-service

DPM 2010 introduced a great feature that allows database administrators to recover/backup the databases, protected with DPM, without compromising access to the DPM server. In order to use the DPM self-service recovery you need to perform the following actions:

1. Install the application from the DPM media at `SCDPM\DpmSqlEURInstaller`.

2. In your DPM server click on **Protection**, and then click on **Self service recovery** to configure the self-service recovery tool.

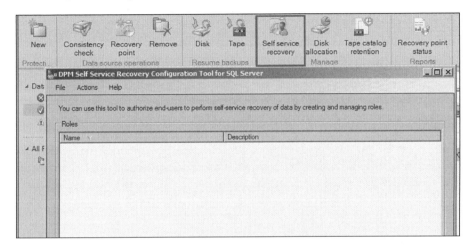

3. In order to use the tool, you need first to configure roles, so click on the **Create role** button, then follow the wizard. In the **Security Group** section, enter a security group that includes the database administrators, then click on **Next**.

4. In the **Specify Recovery Items** window, you need to specify which databases this group will have access to. If you leave the database name field empty, that means this group will have access to all the databases hosted on the SQL Server instance specified in the **SQL Server Instance** field, as shown in the following screenshot:

5. In the **Specify Recovery Target Locations** window, users by default are not allowed to override the original database.

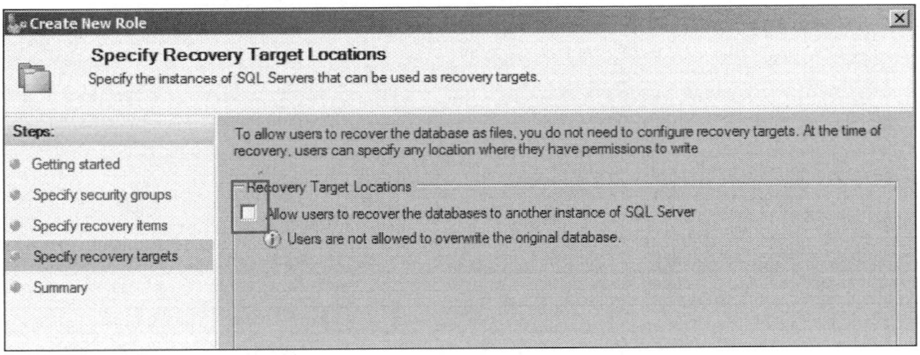

If you enable the checkbox to allow users to recover from another database you will be prompted to specify which server and the recovery location on the server.

6. When starting the Data Protection Manager self-service recovery tool for the first time, we need to connect to the DPM server, as shown in the following screenshot:

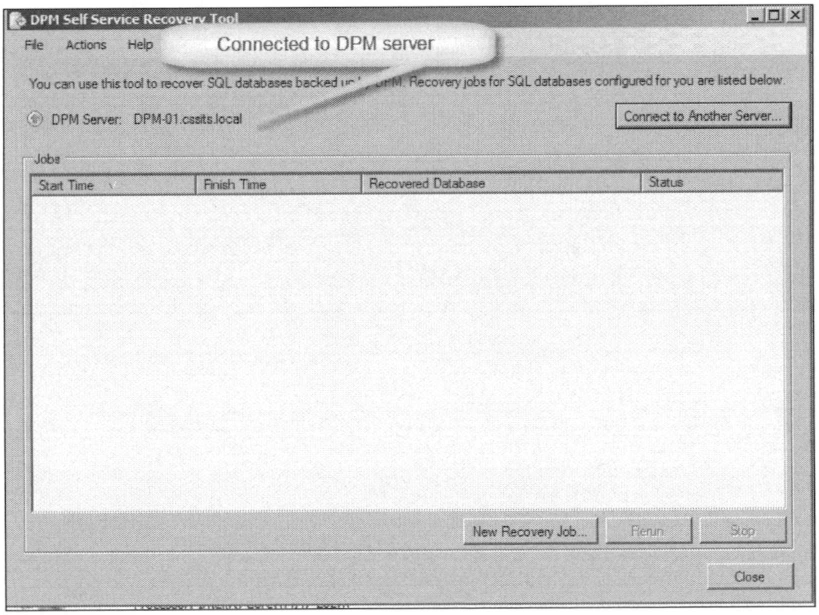

7. Click on **New recovery Job...**, and follow the recovery wizard to select the recovery place and the security options.

8. After you click on **Recover**, you will see an information message pop up to confirm that the recovery job has been completed.

For sure DPM self-service recovery tool adds great flexibility for the database owners to perform self-service recovery of protected SQL Server databases that they own without needing to access the DPM server or an intervention by a DPM administrator.

Working with third-party tools to deduplicate DPM data

One thing missing in DPM 2012 is deduplication, and with Crunch from BrightSTOR, you can accomplish the deduplication and save a lot of space on your DPM storage.

Crunch for DPM is optimized to interoperate with the unique storage workloads produced by DPM 2010 and 2012, when protecting Hyper-V, Exchange, SQL, SharePoint, and shared/networked storage (NAS and CIFS) servers. Coupled with Crunch for DPM, Microsoft's DPM can finally offer "bullet-proof" data protection with market-leading data storage efficiency:

- Crunch for DPM is supplied as a software download in Microsoft VHD format that is installed on the same physical server that acts as your Microsoft DPM 2010 or 2012 server

- A single Crunch for DPM Virtual Appliance can manage *12 containers* of physical storage capacity, each of which can be up to 4 TB in size (total of 48 TB of physical capacity)

- Thin provisioning ensures that physical capacity additions can be performed gradually and incrementally

- 32 GB of system memory in the Hyper-V server (or 8 GB of RAM supplemented by 32 GB of dedicated SSD storage) are recommended for optimal operation

- Throughput may be limited by constraints of the server and storage hardware you are using in your DPM system

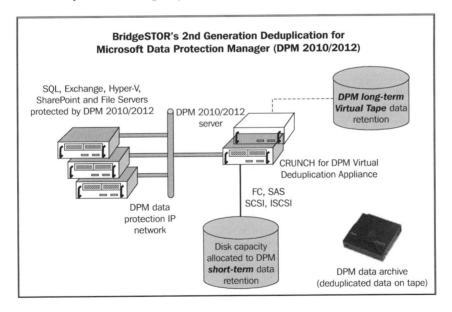

Summary

In this chapter, we covered common DPM management tasks. After reading this chapter, you should have a better understanding of working with DPM storage pool migration, creating custom reports, automating DPM installation, managing bandwidth in DPM, and using a third-party tool to perform deduplication of DPM storage pools. In the next chapter, we will learn about monitoring and managing the DPM's performance.

4
Monitoring and Managing the Performance of DPM

In this chapter, we take a look at monitoring your DPM server using standard Windows tools and **System Center Operations Manager** (**SCOM**). We will also explore how to remotely and centrally manage DPM. Finally we take a look at setting up and using role-based access in DPM through the SCOM console. Following are the topics we will cover in this chapter:

- Publishing the DPM event logs
- Monitoring DPM with SCOM
- Monitoring DPM without SCOM
- Using the new DPM central console
- Configuring remote administration of DPM
- Configuring and using role-based access in DPM

Publishing the DPM event logs

The first step to monitoring your DPM server is to make sure you publish the DPM alerts to the Windows event viewer. DPM alerts are not published to the event viewer by default. Once you publish DPM's alerts you can then monitor DPM from a monitoring tool such as SCOM. SCOM goes beyond monitoring your DPM server. You can use SCOM to help manage your DPM server and we will go into this further in later sections of this chapter. To publish the alerts follow these steps:

1. Go to the DPM Administrator Console.
2. Click on **Action** in the menu bar of the DPM Administrator Console, and select **Options**.
3. Click on the **Alert Publishing** tab.

4. Click on the **Publish Active Alerts** button.

5. Click on **OK**.

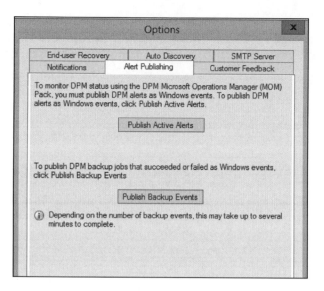

This will send your DPM alerts to the Windows event viewer on your server and SCOM can access them from there or a third-party system's monitoring tool. You will find the alerts in Windows **Event Viewer (Local)** under **Applications and Service Logs**. You will see **DPM Alerts** and **DPM Backup Events** listed in the following screenshot:

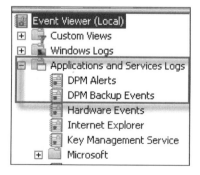

 If you want backup alert events and you want them to be monitored by SCOM you need to publish them as well.

There is a difference between DPM alerts and DPM backup events. DPM alerts contain information about the status of a DPM server. DPM backup events contain information about DPM backup jobs.

Now your DPM alerts are published to the event viewer and can be picked up by SCOM or other third-party monitoring tools.

Monitoring DPM with SCOM

SCOM is a cross-platform and service-oriented data center monitoring system. SCOM will provide insight into the overall health of an IT environment. It is used to monitor the state, health, and performance of large amounts of servers, applications, and clients. SCOM also provides alerting around availability, performance, configuration, and security. SCOM has the ability to monitor the Windows and Linux-based computers along with networking devices. The real power of SCOM comes into play through extending its capabilities via **management packs (MPs)**. MPs define how SCOM will monitor specific systems.

By using SCOM to monitor your DPM you will be able to:

- Centrally monitor multiple DPM servers having the ability to see the data protection and health status of them along with the computers and data sources they protect
- Manage multiple DPM servers from a central console (SCOM)
- Utilize role-based access (RBA) to DPM servers for administrators
- View the state of all roles on DPM servers
- View resource usage and performance trends on DPM servers
- Diagnose root causes of problems and resolve them on a remote DPM server

Now that we have talked about monitoring DPM with SCOM let's take a look at configuring this and importing the DPM management packs.

The following are the DPM management packs:

- `Microsoft.SystemCenter.DataProtectionManager.2011.Discovery.mp`
- `Microsoft.SystemCenter.DataProtectionManager.2011.Library.mp`

They can be found on the DPM media at `<DPMMEDIA>\SCDPM\ManagementPacks\en-US`.

To import the DPM management packs follow these steps:

1. Open the SCOM console.

2. Select **Administration** from the bar.

3. Select **Management Packs**.

4. Click on **Import Management Packs...** from the **Actions** menu.

5. Click on **Add** and select **Add from disk...**.

6. Browse to the DPM management packs mentioned previously on the DPM media.

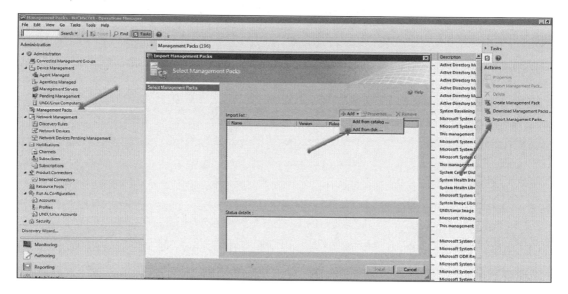

7. Once the DPM management packs are listed click on **Install**.

 When you import the management pack, Windows displays a warning about the write actions. This is an expected warning, and you can click **Yes** to continue.

8. Click on **Close** when it is done importing both management packs.

Now your DPM servers will be discovered and can be monitored in SCOM. We will discuss the DPM central console in a later section helping you better understand how DPM can be monitored and managed in SCOM.

Monitoring DPM without SCOM

It is recommended that you monitor DPM with SCOM. With System Center 2012, the suite is purchased as a whole, therefore you would automatically have a license for SCOM. This, in itself, is a strong reason to use it for monitoring your DPM server. Let's state some key monitoring features that are not available without SCOM. The key monitoring features include role-based access and management of multiple DPM servers from a central console, along with better control over DPM notifications. With that being said, DPM can be monitored without SCOM and we are going to discuss these methods in this section. The methods for monitoring DPM without SCOM are more of a manual de-centralized way to monitor. These are the methods available:

- Manually check the event viewer for any health issues
- Use the DPM administrator console to view the DPM operations directly
- Use the DPM reports to view the usage and health trends
- Use the standard built-in OS performance counters

Monitoring DPM operations through the DPM Administrator Console provides you with the following functionality:

- The **Monitoring** task area
    ○ Alerts (critical, warning, and informational)
    ○ Backup job statuses (successful jobs, failed jobs, and jobs in progress)
    ○ When backup jobs are scheduled to run
    ○ Amount of data that was transferred by the synchronizations
    ○ Length of time for consistency checks

- The **Management** task area
    ○ Status of the storage pools
    ○ Status of the tape libraries
    ○ Status of the DPM agents
    ○ Communication with the protected servers
    ○ DPM licensing
    ○ Disk space allocation such as what is used and what is free
    ○ How many disks are in the storage pool
    ○ The health of each disk
    ○ What data sources are on each disk

- The **Protection** task area
  - ° State of the protection groups
  - ° State of the protected members in a protection group
  - ° State of replicas
  - ° Disk allocation
  - ° Latest recovery point
  - ° Oldest recovery point
  - ° Total number of recovery points
  - ° Replica path in storage pool

Items can be monitored through the DPM reports and alerts. You can receive e-mail notifications about any protected computer alerts such as:

- DPM: Information
- DPM: Warning
- DPM: Critical
- DPM: Recovery
- DPM: Resolved

 Having all alerts turned on will flood your inbox with e-mails. It is recommended from experience to only set e-mail notifications on critical alerts.

You can also receive reports via e-mail on a schedule or you can go and view the reports manually. DPM reporting is typically used for usage and trend data, not for real-time monitoring. It is used to give you an overall view of the state of your DPM overtime. The default reports that are available are:

- **Disk Utilization**: Summarizes disk capacity, disk allocation, and disk usage in the DPM storage pool.

- **Recovery**: Provides details about recovery items and statistics of recovery jobs for tracking performance.

- **Recovery Point Status**: Provides the recovery point status of all selected data sources. If at least one good recovery point is present in the specified recovery point window, the status is shown as green. If no recovery point is present in that time window, then that time window is left blank.

- **Status**: Provides status of all recovery points for a specified time period, lists recovery jobs, and shows the total number of successes and failures for recovery points and disk-based and tape-based recovery point creations. This report shows trends in the frequency of errors that occur and lists the number of alerts.

- **Tape** Management: Provides details for managing tape rotation. This report lists all libraries that are below the free media threshold. The data is collected per library and aggregated for all libraries.

- **Tape Utilization**: Provides trends in tape utilization to assist in capacity planning and making decisions about allocating additional tapes.

Any of those reports can be put on a schedule to e-mail you or a distribution list. To schedule and set them up to be e-mailed, simply highlight the report in the lower pane. Click on **Edit** next to both **Schedule:** and **E-mail:** to configure your settings:

Details:	**Disk Utilization Report**
Description:	Summarizes disk ca
Schedule:	None Edit
E-mail:	0 subscribers Edit
History:	0 copies available

Custom reports can be created and used if the default reports are not sufficient. The process for doing this was covered in *Chapter 3, DPM Server Management Tasks*.

You can monitor the DPM alerts and the DPM backup events in event viewer on the DPM server.

Remember everything you can monitor and manage through the DPM console is on that single DPM server and has to be checked manually. Because monitoring and managing DPM this way is manual, it is recommended that you or your team establish a schedule for your monitoring tasks. This will help you to be proactive in maintaining your DPM server. You will stay aware of the trends and will be able to quickly troubleshoot and resolve issues. Here is a suggested schedule from Microsoft on maintaining your DPM:

Interval:	Sources to check:	Look for:
Daily	Critical and warning alerts	Replica issues, synchronization and recovery point creation issues, agent issues, jobs waiting for tape, and backup failures
	E-mail notifications	
	Status report	
Monthly	Reports	Trends and patterns that might indicate problems or potential issues
	Status	
	Tape management	
	Disk utilization	
As Needed	Recovery job status	Recovery job failures

Trends in your DPM server's performance counters that could indicate your DPM server is having a problem might include:

- Memory available overtime less than 50 megabytes (MB) indicates low memory on a DPM server

- If the processor is 95 percent used for more than 10 minutes on a continuous basis, this indicates very high CPU usage on the DPM server

- Disk queue length larger than 80 requests for more than 6 minutes indicates possible excessive disk queue length

Using the new DPM central console

DPM 2012 comes with a centralized console for managing multiple DPM servers. Some large organizations have many DPM servers and managing 20 to 30 DPM servers by remoting into each DPM server is not a viable option. This central console is actually integrated into a console that a lot of System Center administrators are already used to working with. Central console is integrated into SCOM. The DPM central console works on SCOM 2007 R2 and SCOM 2012.

Enabling the central console is pretty straightforward. The steps are deploying SCOM, running the DPM install from your DPM disc, and installing the central console on the SCOM server.

Installing the DPM central console

Now let's go through this process step-by-step. Some prerequisites are as follows:

- The SCOM agent needs to be installed on each DPM server that will be accessed.
- This registry key needs to be added on each of the DPM servers you plan to access with the central console [HKEY_LOCAL_MACHINE\SOFTWARE\ Microsoft\Microsoft Operations Manager\3.0\Modules\Global\ PowerShell] "ScriptLimit"=dword:0000000f.

 This registry key is used to control script execution behavior for the Windows PowerShell scripts run from an operations manager module. This key controls how many hosted Windows PowerShell scripts are allowed to run globally.

- Restart the health service (display name: System Center Management) on your SCOM server.
- The DPM management packs need to be already imported on the SCOM server. We completed this step in the previous monitoring DPM with the SCOM section. The management packs are:
    - Microsoft.SystemCenter.DataProtectionManager.2011. Discovery.mp
    - Microsoft.SystemCenter.DataProtectionManager.2011. Library.mp

 If you plan to manage DPM 2010 servers with the central console you also need to apply the SCDPM 2010 Interoperability Hotfix for Centralized Management hotfix. You can download it from the following link: http://www.microsoft.com/en-us/download/details. aspx?id=27218

The DPM central console can be installed either on the SCOM server or on client computers that have the SCOM console installed.

The central console supports the following operating systems:

- Server operating systems
  - ° Windows Server 2008 R2 SP1

- Client operating systems
  - ° Windows Vista
  - ° Windows 7

 DPM does not support installing central console on Windows XP.

The DPM central console can be installed in one of the following three ways:

- **Server and client components**: Server and client components will allow you to monitor the DPM servers on which the operations manager agent is present and use the scoped DPM Administrator Console.
- **Server components**: Server components will allow you to monitor DPM servers on which the operations manager agent is present but you cannot use the scoped DPM Administrator Console.
- **Client components**: Client components will allow you to use the scoped DPM Administrator Console but you cannot monitor DPM servers.

If you have the DPM protection agent installed on a computer and you are going to install the DPM central console on it, you cannot install central console client features.

In this section, we are going to cover the steps for installing the server and client components on the SCOM server:

1. Copy the DPM 2012 media to your SCOM server.
2. Launch the DPM setup and select the DPM central console.
3. Accept the license agreement and click on **Next**.
4. Select **Install Central Console server-side and client-side Components** and click on **Next**.

5. It then goes through the **Prerequisites** check. Click on **Next** when you're done.

6. Review the **Installation settings** option and click on **Next**.
7. Select your **Microsoft Update Opt-In** option and click on **Install**.
8. Once the install is completed, click on **Close**.

Once the install is done you will have the central console in SCOM, the remote administration console, and the DPM Management Shell.

Overview of the DPM central console

Installing the central console also enables another new feature of DPM. This feature is the scoped DPM console. The scoped console helps in troubleshooting for the administrator through SCOM. With the scoped console, if alerts are raised in SCOM, you can click the **Troubleshoot** button that brings you to the DPM console, which only shows the data sources, backup jobs, disks, and agents that are affected by this particular issue. Once the incident is resolved from the scoped console you can test the backup with a single click before you resume the entire backup job.

The DPM central console is accessed via the SCOM console. You have to open SCOM to access the DPM console. Once you have SCOM opened, navigate to the **Monitoring** wunderbar, then expand **System Center 2012 Data Protection Manager**. Initially you may think this is nothing more than a DPM management pack in SCOM. It is more because of what you can do now in the console and that it integrates directly with the remote DPM administration console on the SCOM server. The DPM central console was designed to monitor actionable DPM alerts relating to replica creation, synchronization, and recovery point creation. The DPM management pack was designed to filter out alerts that do not require an action, such as a replica creation job in progress. In the DPM central console there are well-organized alert and state views focusing on certain aspects of DPM's health. The following screenshot and list of features will give you an idea of what you can do with the DPM central console:

1. **Monitoring**

   Monitoring is where we can access the DPM central console and monitoring components consisting of DPM **Alert views** and **State views**.

2. **Alert views**

   Alert views provide an overview of all DPM-related alerts and also an overview of the two categories. These two categories are **Backup alerts** and **Infrastructure alerts**. **Backup alerts** show alerts related to backup issues such as recovery point creation, replica synchronization, and disk backup. **Infrastructure alerts** show alerts related to DPM's infrastructure such as disks, tapes, protected computers, and the DPM server itself.

3. **State views**

   State views show the health state per DPM component. You can view the status of **DPM servers**, **Protection Groups**, **Protected Servers**, **Disks** in the storage pool, **Tape libraries**, and more.

4. **Main Pane**

   When you click on an item (**Alert views** and so on) in the left-hand pane (under **Monitoring**) the main contents of the item will be shown in the Main Pane at the center of the console. For example, in the previous screenshot we have selected **Protection Groups** under **State views** on the left-hand side and to the right in the main pane it shows the protection groups we have. You can click on any of the protection groups and you will notice the information in the detail view changes and the options on the right-hand side change as well.

   Let's take a look at what would be shown for **Disks** under **State views**:

Click on **Disks** under **State views** to show the actual disks being used in DPM.

Notice in the Main Pane it now shows the storage we have in our DPM storage pools along with the total and free space. Also notice on the right-hand side the available tasks are different and are labeled as **DPM Disks Tasks**. Notice how the tasks available to us change again if we re-select **Protection Groups** under **State views** on the left-hand side.

5. **Detail View**

   The **Detail View** panel gives you more specific information about the object you have selected in the Main pane. This data varies depending on what the object is. For a disk in the storage pool it will tell you how much space is free. For a protection group it will give you the group ID along with the type of protection it has. Here are some screenshot examples of how this data changes when we select a protection group, a disk, and a tape library.

   This is an example of what would be shown when **Protection Group** is selected:

Detail View

Protection Group properties of SharePoint

Display Name	SharePoint
Full Path Name	DPM2012.buchatech.com\DPM2012\DPM2012**SharePoint**
Protection group id	617a0ded-7e26-4007-9f3f-8d87f7903fb5
Protection group name	SharePoint
DPM server	DPM2012.buchatech.com
Protection type	Short-term using disk
Collocated	False

This is an example of what would be shown when a DPM disk is selected:

Detail View

DPM Disk properties of ROCKET IMAGEFILE SCSI Disk Device

Display Name	ROCKET IMAGEFILE SCSI Disk Device
Full Path Name	DPM2012.buchatech.com\DPM2012\DPM2012**ROCKET IMAGEFILE SCSI Disk Device**
DPM server	DPM2012.buchatech.com
Total space (GB)	915
Free space (GB)	654
NT disk id	1d29d27d-b3ed-46a1-8efd-84ebda9cbe03

This is an example of what would be shown when a tape library is selected:

Detail View

DPM Tape Library properties of Firestreamer Media Changer

Display Name	Firestreamer Media Changer
Full Path Name	DPM2012.buchatech.com\DPM2012\DPM2012**Firestreamer Media Changer**
Library id	5070bd2e-023e-4e7c-8a91-46bea92ae141
Attached to computer	DPM2012.buchatech.com
Number of drives	5
Number of slots	200
Number of IE ports	0
Library serial number	L0CHGR165C0813918AE111A9ED00155
Product id	Firestreamer Media Changer
Vendor id	Cristalink Limited
DPM server	DPM2012.buchatech.com
Global library id	
Library type	TapeLibrary

6. DPM related tasks

   DPM related tasks appear on the right-hand side pane under **Tasks** and
   Navigation. The name of the DPM-related tasks changes depending on
   the object that is selected in the main pane. Some of these items can run
   directly from the central console in SCOM, others may require the DPM
   Administrator Console. If an item requires the DPM Administrator Console
   when you click on it, the remote DPM Administrator Console will open
   up directly to the action that needs to be performed. Let's look at how this
   changes when we click on a few different objects. This is an example of what
   tasks you would see when viewing **Protected Servers**.

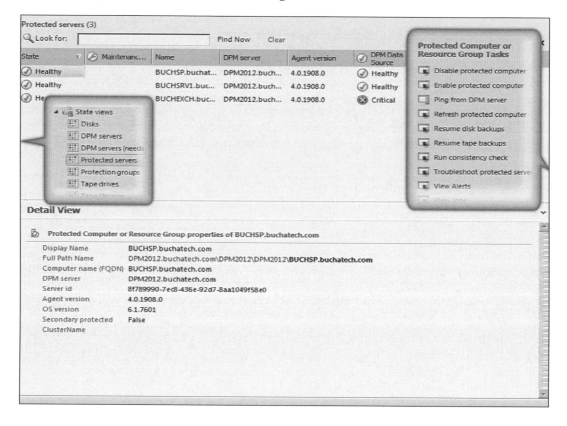

This is an example of what tasks you would see when viewing **DPM Disk Tasks**:

This is an example of what tasks you would see when viewing **DPM Server Tasks**:

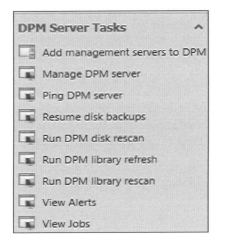

This is an example of what tasks you would see when viewing **SharePoint** workload.

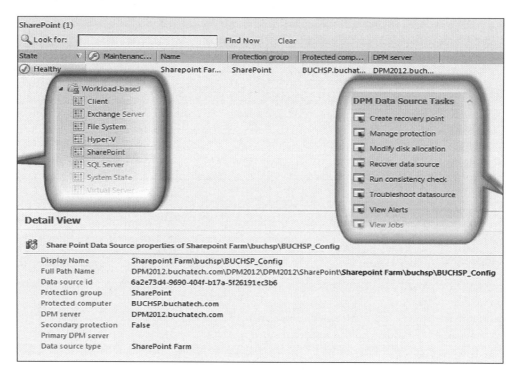

After seeing the DPM related task's that should give you a better understanding of why these are part of what makes the central console more than just another management pack. With each object you have specific things you can do that are related to that object, without having tso open up the DPM Administrator Console, be it on the DPM server or remote. Some of the items are being able to recover data right from this console and the ability to enable or disable a protected computer. You may have also noticed from the screenshot that many of the DPM related tasks have a selection for troubleshooting. This is what gives you the scoped troubleshooting through the DPM central console.

That sums up the DPM central console. This new console gives administrators a single management interface to DPM and is essential in environments with multiple DPM servers.

Configuring remote administration of DPM

One of the new features of DPM 2012 is that you can install the DPM Administrator Console on other servers or workstations for remote administration of your DPM 2012 and even DPM 2010 servers without having to log on to the DPM server. The cool part is that you can manage existing DPM 2010 servers. This is done through applying a hotfix to your DPM 2010 server and installing the console on your workstation or server from the DPM 2012 software.

In this section we are going to walk through setting this up, using the following steps:

1. Navigate to the DPM 2012 install and choose **32BIT** or **64BIT** depending on what your workstation or server is:

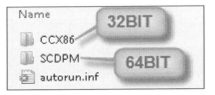

2. Launch the DPM 2012 install on your local workstation.
3. Select **DPM Remote Administration** to begin.
4. Accept the license agreement and click on **OK**.
5. Click on **Next** on the **Welcome** screen.
6. Click on **Next** to continue.
7. Let the **Prerequisite check** run and then click on **Next**.
8. Review your install settings and click on **Next**.

9. Choose to allow or not allow Windows updates to update your DPM console and click **Install**.

10. Click on **Close** when the install is done. Now the DPM 2012 console is installed. You will see new DPM icons on your desktop as follows:

11. Click on the DPM icon and then type in the name of your DPM 2010 server as follows:

The DPM Administrator Console should come up and connect to your DPM 2010 server.

You will notice that the interface for the DPM 2010 Administrator Console has been enhanced. It has a newer look much like DPM 2012 but everything is still located in the same place so that you will know how to find what you need.

That is all there is to installing the new remote administration console and using it to manage your DPM 2010 and DPM 2012 servers.

Configuring and using role-based access in DPM

Role-based access (RBA) is another new feature of DPM 2012 that will ease the lives of DPM administrators. RBA has been around in other System Center and Microsoft products but is new to DPM. RBA, as its name itself states, allows you to give specific access to other administrators based on their role.

Things to know about RBA are that this feature is enabled through the central console and works from SCOM only. For example, if an administrator logs directly onto the DPM server and uses the DPM admin console they will be able to see everything in DPM. Another item to know about RBA is that it has task-based security. For example, a user could be locked out from being able to recover data but could still view the data.

The built-in security roles and their descriptions that come in DPM RBA are as follows:

Role	Description
DPM Reporting Operator	Can create, modify, and view scheduled or on-demand reports.
DPM Read-Only Operator	Can view all DPM configuration, jobs, and alerts.
DPM Tier-1 Support	Can view all alert and job information. Can perform basic jobs such as re-running a failed job.
DPM Tape Admin	Can perform all tape-related actions.
DPM Tier-2 Support	Can perform all tasks of tier-1 support and additionally can troubleshoot problems.
DPM Admin	Can perform all actions.
DPM Recovery Operator	Can only perform recovery of data protected by DPM.
DPM Tape Operator	Can perform only lightweight tape-related operations such as running tape inventory, cleaning dives, and so on.

Let's look at how you would install RBA for DPM on your SCOM server and access it.

 DPM RBA cannot be set up until the DPM central console has been installed on the SCOM server.

Setting up RBA is straightforward. Here are the steps:

1. Open an elevated command prompt on your SCOM server.

2. Navigate to `%INSTALLDRIVE%\Program Files\Microsoft DPM\bin\`.

3. Run `DefaultRoleConfigurator.exe`.

    You will then see the default roles added:

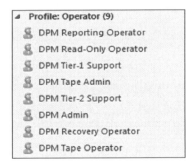

4. To see the roles open your SCOM console, and then click on **Administration | Security | User Roles**.

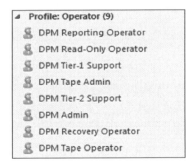

To apply a role to another administrator you need to add that administrator to a DPM RBA role. To add users to a role, right-click on the role you want to modify and select **Properties**:

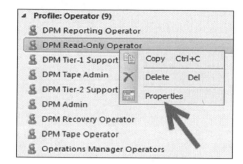

5. Click on **Add** and search for the user in the Active Directory.

6. Click on **OK** twice and the user will now be assigned to that role as follows:

That's all there is to setting up DPM RBA and working with DPM RBA in SCOM. As you can see this is a straightforward process.

Summary

In this chapter we had a chance to review the pros and cons of using SCOM to monitor and manage DPM versus manually monitoring and managing your DPM server using tools on the server itself. We looked at the process of installing the DPM central console, DPM remote administration console, and DPM RBA. In the next chapter, we will dive into the workload protection specifically on the general Microsoft workloads such as file servers, system state, bare metal backups, and much more.

5
Workload Protection

In this chapter, we will dive deeper into protecting workloads with Data Protection Manager. There are two types of workload protection. The first workload group is Microsoft workload protection and the second one is non-Microsoft workload protection. Microsoft workload protection is for things like server system states and Active Directory. The non-Microsoft workloads are other technologies, such as Linux servers and VMware. Microsoft workloads are supported directly within DPM and non-Microsoft workloads are typically not, but there are known ways to protect them with DPM that are known to work. In regards to the non-Microsoft workloads, you won't be able to call Microsoft if you run into issues unlike with their Microsoft counterparts. We are going to give more insight into these scenarios so you can evaluate your options. We will cover the following topics in this chapter:

- Working with BMR and troubleshooting common issues in DPM
- Working with system state protection and troubleshooting common issues in DPM
- Protecting domain controllers
- Restoring Active Directory
- Working with the Active Directory Recycle Bin
- Generic data source protection in DPM
- Protecting Oracle with DPM
- Protecting Linux with DPM
- Protecting non-domain/workgroup computers with DPM

Working with BMR and troubleshooting common issues in DPM

Bare Metal Restore (BMR) is a feature used to cover your disaster recovery scenarios for physical servers. Since virtualization for companies in any customer segment is getting more and more established, the number of actual physical servers is decreasing. This will mean that those servers that are still physical will generally hold a quite important function for these companies, so protect yours with a sophisticated feature such as BMR.

BMR was first introduced in DPM 2010 and was the successor to the SRT feature in DPM 2007. Both features aim to achieve the same purpose, to be able to protect the entire system drive and system state as a single data source.

The BMR function gives the DPM administrator the ability to restore an entire system from scratch. This means that if you have a BMR backup and your physical server crashes, you can restore that server operating system and system state on a new piece of hardware.

Many people tend to get the idea that BMR can be used in a V2P migration scenario, but, this is not supported. If you would like to perform a V2P migration, you should use the System Center Virtual Machine Management software and specific tools.

Supported operating systems

The BRM feature only supports operating systems from 2008 onward. This means that you can't use BMR in a Microsoft-supported way to manage your Windows Server 2003 operating system if you still have those.

If you haven't successfully upgraded or haven't found the convincing motive to upgrade your Windows Server 2003 operating system, you still have one way to accomplish a BMR feature, and this is achieved by carrying out a P2V migration to Hyper-V. This will give you the ability to take online and offline snapshots of your virtual server.

How to backup BMR files

When creating or modifying a protection group, you have the possibility to make BMR backups of installations of Windows Server 2008 or newer. The BMR files resides within the `System Protection` criteria, expand it and you will see the BMR feature.

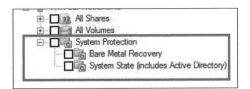

The BMR files will include the system state of the server and the system drive within the same replica, and also the recovery point volume. This means that you can't separate the system state backup from the BMR backup within two different protection groups.

This is because the protection uses VSS and only one data source can reside in one protection group.

Performing a BMR restore

When the day comes where you must restore your physical server using BMR, you can be quite relaxed, most of the job will be done for you.

The restore operation is made up of the following steps:

1. You must restore the BMR from your DPM server to a share that can be accessed on the network.

2. Secondly, insert the media for your Windows Server 2008 or R2 and choose to repair the server.

3. The next step is to choose **Restore your computer using a system image that you created earlier** and click on **Next**.

4. You may receive an error message but this can be ignored. In the **Re-image your computer** section, choose **Select a system image**.

5. On the **Select the location of the backup for the computer you want to restore** window, click on the **Advanced** button.

6. Click on the **Search for a system image on the network** option.

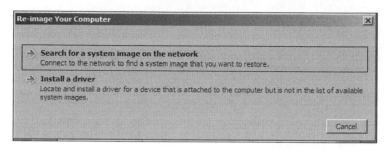

7. Type in the UNC path where you shared the restored BMR files in step 1 and click on the **OK** button.

 A good location for the restored BMR files is a share on the DPM server. It's important to share them.

8. On the **Select the location of the backup for the computer that you want to restore** window, you will see the system image that resides within the BMR backup. Click on **Next** to continue.

The restore process will take some time, and your server may restart a few times after the restore completes.

Troubleshooting BMR

One of the most common issues with BMR protection is free disk space. Since the BMR protection will include both the system state and the system drive of the server OS, it is critical that you have enough free space on your system drive.

Reading the alerts in the DPM console will also give you a hint of what is wrong. A new great feature for troubleshooting scenarios is the troubleshooting feature within the central console.

The local system and applications log also contains good troubleshooting information.

Working with system state protection and troubleshooting common issues in DPM

System state is important to back up considering the critical content of it. The system state includes the following:

- For member servers
  - Boot files
  - COM+
  - Registry
  - System files within the Windows system catalog

- For domain controllers
  - Active Directory domain services (NTDS)
  - System volume (SYSVOL)

- For certificate services
  - Certificate service database

- For clustered servers
  - Cluster service metadata

- For servers with IIS
  - IIS meta catalog

What is included in the system state will depend on the installed applications and whether the server is physical or virtual. If your server resides as a Hyper-V guest within a Hyper-V cluster, it's more likely that you will restore the entire virtual server instead of just the system state, considering the virtual server isn't a domain controller.

The restore of a system state is made in two steps:

1. Restore the system state files from the DPM server to the actual server or a NTFS share.

2. On the server that will actually have the system state restored, use wbadmin.

Restoring the system state from the DPM server

The first step is to restore the system state files, which can be placed on the DPM server or another accessible NTFS share within your environment.

After the files are restored it is important that you share the right folder; in the book's example the system state files are restored locally on the DPM server. Open the restored files and you will see a catalog with the structure name DPM_date_time. Open the catalog and share the subcatalog called DPM_Recovered_At_date_time. Share the catalog with the shared name systemstate. Finally, make sure everyone is able to read the catalog.

The next step is to start using the wbadmin tool.

Using the wbadmin tool

The wbadmin is the command-line tool for Windows Server Backup that you will use to restore system states. Before you start using wbadmin there are two things you must do:

1. You must put the server in **Directory Service Restore** mode if the server is a domain controller.

2. You must have restored your system state files from the DPM server.

To put a server in a Directory Service Restore mode, open an elevated command prompt and type bcdedit /set safeboot dsrepair. Now the server will start in safe mode and you must log on locally.

After you have logged on locally to the server, you will want to restore your system state. Open an elevated command prompt; the first thing you must do is verify the details of backups recoverable from your shared folder. Type `wbadmin get versions -backuptarget:\\nameofyourdpmserver\systemstate` and you will get the different versions that are recoverable. The important thing to keep track of is the version identifier.

After you have identified the version you want to restore, you need to type in the following text:

```
Wbadmin start systemstaterecovery -version:01/11/2012-13:00 -
backuptarget:\NAMEOFYOURDPMSERVER\systemstate
```

Hit Return and the restore process of your system state will start.

You will be prompted with two questions, answering yes to all of them will continue the restore process of the system state. The first question is `Do you want to start the system state recovery operation?`; answering `yes` will prompt you with a warning regarding restoring a system state over the network. Answer `yes` to the second question, `Do you want to continue?` and an informational note appears. Once again, answer `yes` to the question and the restore process will start.

It will take a while and `wbadmin` will give you output regarding the process. When the restore operation is finished, `wbadmin` will ask you to restart your server. Your restore of a system state is now done.

Protecting the domain controllers

The most important thing to protect that resides on a domain controller is the system state. When protecting a domain controller with DPM, the VSS writer that enumerates information from the domain controller will let you know that you are protecting an Active Directory. The Active Directory database called `NTDS.DIT` is located in the system state backup of a domain controller.

By checking the checkbox next to **System Protection**, you will also protect the Active Directory of your domain.

Restoring Active Directory

When restoring Active Directory data from a system state backup to the `NTDS.DIT` file you must use `ntdsutil.exe`. Before you can use the executable you must have put the domain controller in a Directory Service Restore mode and restored system state data that you would like to manage. Restore the system state files from the DPM server and then use the `wbadmin` tool on the domain controller to restore data into the `NTDS.DIT` file. In the last step you will be asked to restart your server, but *don't do this yet*.

Open a new command prompt and type `ntdsutil`. Now you must set the instance by typing `activate instance NTDS` and hit *Enter*. You will be prompted that the active instance is now NTDS. Now you must define which type of restore you would like to perform. In this example, we will perform an authoritative restore, so type `authoritative restore` and hit Return.

Next, we will restore a deleted user account using `Restore object`. Type in the distinguished name (DN) for that user. `Restore object "CN=John Doe,DN=contoso,DC=COM"` and hit Return.

The restore of the deleted user account of the user `John Doe` will now start. You will be prompted with a window asking if you would like to do `Authoritative Restore`, click on the **Yes** button and the restore will continue. After a while you will be prompted that the Authoritative Restore completed successfully.

You can now restart your domain controller and the deleted user account is now present again in the Active Directory, showing that the outbound replication of Active Directory data has propagated to all other domain controllers.

Working with the Active Directory Recycle Bin

Active Directory Recycle Bin was introduced in Windows Server 2008 R2. It allows you to preserve and recover accidentally-deleted Active Directory objects. Recovered objects are restored back to the logical state they were in before deletion. The Recycle Bin maintains link-valued and non-link-valued attributes of deleted Active Directory objects. This means an object that is logically deleted is not really gone, but stored in a deleted objects' container that you can restore from, much like the **Recycle Bin** that has been in Windows for years. The Active Directory Recycle Bin is not a direct part of DPM but it is an important part of protecting your infrastructure data, so it is a good tool. The data in the Active Directory Recycle Bin is protected as a part of system state on domain controllers by DPM. In this section, we are going to show you how to enable the Active Directory Recycle Bin feature and how to restore a deleted Active Directory object.

To enable the Active Directory Recycle Bin feature, on a domain controller open **Active Directory Module for Windows PowerShell** and run the following command:

```
Enable-ADOptionalFeature -Identity <ADOptionalFeature> -Scope
<ADOptionalFeatureScope> -Target <ADEntity>
```

You can restore the deleted objects by using the `Get-ADObject` cmdlet, then pass them via pipeline to the `Restore-DObject` cmdlet. Just follow these steps:

1. First display the deleted objects using **Active Directory Module for Windows PowerShell** by running the following syntax:

   ```
   Get-ADObject -ldapFilter:"(msDS-LastKnownRDN=*)" -
   IncludeDeletedObjects
   ```

2. Within **Active Directory Module for Windows PowerShell** run the following syntax:

   ```
   Get-ADObject -Filter {String} -IncludeDeletedObjects |
   Restore-ADObject
   ```

Generic data source protection in DPM

A new feature that was presented in the release of DPM 2012 was the **generic data source protection**. DPM has defined Windows applications that it can protect by using the Windows applications' VSS writer on the production servers.

For those Windows applications that do not have a defined protection within DPM, you will now be able to protect them with DPM using the generic data source protection.

There are two ways of accomplish this. If the Windows application can leverage a VSS DPM, you can use that VSS and perform a full application backup consisting of the following:

- Express-full backup
- Delta replication
- Consistency check

You will be able to restore your Windows application data to the original location or restore as files to a network location.

One example of a Windows application that could leverage VSS but does not have a defined protection within DPM is **System Center Virtual Machine Manager (SCVMM)**. You can employ generic data source protection and manage SCVMM from DPM.

If the Windows application can't leverage a VSS, you can still back it up by using XML support, though you will only be able to perform an express-full backup.

A prerequisite consideration regarding generic data source protection is that the application is running on a Windows operating system and that it is a Microsoft application.

Non-Microsoft workload protection in DPM

Being able to protect non-Microsoft workloads in DPM has always been in demand among the DPM community. Many environments have workloads such as Linux, VMware, and Oracle. These workloads often run on critical line-of-business applications so they need to be protected. Even with the release of DPM 2012, many non-Microsoft workloads still cannot be protected natively. In this section, we are going to discuss some methods that can be used to protect some of these workloads with DPM.

Before we dive into the methods of protecting these workloads, there is a third-party solution that can be used with DPM to protect these non-Microsoft workloads. This third-party solution is called **EVault for DPM (EDPM)**. EDPM can protect Linux, VMware, IBM i, IBM AIX, HP-UX, Sun Solaris, Novell Netware, and Oracle databases. When you use EDPM you do not need to use the methods described in this chapter, because EDPM supports protection of these workloads natively. This means that you simply install an agent, select the workload for protection, and then start backing up the data. EDPM is an appliance that is a combination of DPM and EVault. You can learn more about this at http://www.evault.com.

Now let's dive into protecting non-Microsoft workloads with DPM.

Protecting Oracle with DPM

DPM has not natively supported the protection of Oracle database with previous versions and still does not support it with DPM 2012. However, the new feature of generic data source protection can protect Oracle. This can be done because Oracle has released a VSS writer. The other way to protect Oracle with DPM is to simply use Oracle's RMAN utility to back up and store the database as an offline file and let DPM pick up that offline file. This is much like the VMware's protection process from earlier in combination with the pre and post backup scripts.

Protecting Oracle using RMAN and pre/post scripts with DPM

Oracle's native **Recovery Manager (RMAN)** utility. The RMAN utility performs backup and recovery on your Oracle databases. The RMAN client is automatically installed with the database and is typically located in the same directory as the other database executables. When you use RMAN it will produce the backup of your database and you can use DPM to back up that backup. This adds extra steps to the backup and recovery process but it is a workaround for protecting Oracle with DPM.

You can script RMAN because it has command-line capability, and use the DPM pre and post scripts to kick off the RMAN backups before DPM protects the copy of the backup that RMAN created. Visit the following link for more info about RMAN:

```
http://docs.oracle.com/cd/B28359_01/backup.111/b28270/rcmquick.
htm#BABJAGIB
```

Protecting Oracle as a generic data source with DPM

The Oracle database functions as a writer that is integrated with VSS-enabled applications. The Oracle VSS writer is installed automatically as part of the database. You can use VSS-enabled software such as DPM to back up and restore an Oracle database even when it is online. In this case DPM is the VSS requestor and Oracle is the VSS writer.

You need to register the generic data source in VSS. You will then need to register your Oracle database that you want to protect so that DPM can see it. Do this by registering the database SID with the Oracle VSS writer.

1. Install the DPM agent on the protected computer (the server that is running Oracle).

2. On the protected computer install VSS writer into the desired SID. For example, `C:\>oravssw ORACLEDPMDB /i:IDOFSID /user:DOMAIN\ YOURUSERNAME /password:********`.

3. On the protected computer, run `C:\>vssadmin list writers`.

4. Copy the writer ID listed against your SID.

5. On the protected computer run `Set-DPMGlobalProperty -RegisteredWriters @('VSSWriterID') -DPMservername <NAMEOFYOURDPMSERVER>`.

6. On your DPM server, create or modify a protection group and select the Oracle VSS writer (SID and the object under it).

You will now be protecting Oracle with DPM. From the recovery in DPM you should see:

- **All tablespaces**: This includes all tablespaces in a snapshot
- **Control file**: This contains the snapshot location of the control file for a database running in ARCHIVELOG mode

 If an Oracle database is in ARCHIVELOG mode then a shadow copy can be created when the database is open or closed.

- **Flash recovery area**: This includes all backup files and archived logs in the Flash recovery area in the VSS snapshot
- **Server parameter file**: This contains the location of the server parameter file, if the instance is using one

Protecting Linux with DPM

Protecting Linux with DPM is something that many DPM administrators in the community have wanted to do natively in DPM for a while. With DPM 2012 this is still not possible natively. However, there are still ways to protect Linux servers with DPM. Here are the main options:

- If Linux is running as a virtual machine on Hyper-V, you can protect the VM—this come with some limitations. DPM treats this as a legacy operating system VM, and the VM is shutdown momentarily while DPM gets a backup of it. This also does not give you granular control of what to protect. With this approach it is the entire server or nothing.
- For granular protection of Linux with DPM, you will need to use a technology called **Samba**. Samba is an open source suite that runs on a Linux server. It can provides a seamless file and print services for SMB and CIFS clients. This means that Linux shares can be accessed from Windows computers and Windows shares can be accessed from Linux computers. The method here is to use Samba as a gateway, moving the data you need to protect from your Linux server onto a Samba share on a Windows server, and let DPM pick up the data from there. An example of this in real-world use is a cron (equivalent to task scheduler in Windows), which runs a MySQL backup and places the backed-up database on a Windows share via Samba, and then DPM protects the data in that share, in turn protecting the backed-up MySQL database.

As you can see, the options are limited when it comes to protecting Linux data with DPM. The methods are not pretty but if you really need to protect your Linux data you can make it happen.

Protecting non-domain/workgroup computers with DPM

DPM can protect computers that are in workgroups or other domains. This comes with some limitations and takes some know how to set. We will cover both in this section. First let's look at what is supported and what is not supported in the following table:

	Workgroup	Non-domain
Files – Basic - All server and client SKUs	Supported	Supported
Files – Clustering	Not applicable	Not supported
System state – Windows Server 2003, Windows Server 2008, Windows 2008 R2	Supported	Supported
SQL Server – Basic – SQL Server 2000, SQL Server 2005, SQL Server 2008	Supported	Supported
SQL Server - Mirroring	Not supported	Not supported
SQL Server - Clustering	Not applicable	Not supported
Hyper-V – Basic – Windows Server 2008, Windows 2008 R2	Supported	Supported
Hyper-V – Clustering	Not applicable	Not supported
Hyper-V – Cluster Shared Volume	Not applicable	Not supported
Exchange – Basic – Exchange Server 2003, Exchange Server 2007, Exchange Server 2010	Not applicable	Supported
Exchange Server – Clustering	Not applicable	Not supported
Exchange Server – CCR	Not applicable	Not supported
Exchange Server – LCR	Not applicable	Supported
Exchange Server – SCR	Not applicable	Not supported
Exchange Server – DAG	Not applicable	Not supported
Microsoft SharePoint Server	Not supported	Not supported
Portable computers	Not supported	Not supported
Bare Metal Recovery	Not supported	Not supported
End-user Recovery	Not supported	Not supported
DPM Disaster Protection of workgroup / untrusted domain computers	Not supported	Not supported
Secondary protection for workgroup / untrusted domain computers	Not supported	Not supported

When protecting a workgroup or non-domain computer, DPM uses Windows NTLM authentication, using a local user account that was specified during the installation of the DPM agent on the protected computer.

 This account does not need to have administrative rights on the local protected computer.

To protect non-domain/workgroup computers you need to manually install the DPM agent on the computer locally. You then need to run the `SetDpmServer` command on the protected computer with the `-isNonDomainServer` switch. You will be asked to provide credentials to the local protected server. DPM will use these credentials when communicating with the protected computer.

Some other requirements of protecting workgroup and non-domain are as follows:

- A direct connection between the DPM server and the protected computer such as VPN, site-to-site VPN, DirectAccess, or MPLS
- The following type of data traffic and ports need to be open for DPM and the protected computer in order to communicate:
  - On an untrusted computer make sure it has DCOM enabled. If this is not enabled, you will receive errors because DPM will not be able to use the local user account from the protected computer.
  - DCOM – Port 135 file transfers
  - WINSOCK
- NTLM v2 is the recommended authentication method between the DPM server and the protected computer as it is more secure

A few other key things to watch out for when protecting a non-domain/ workgroup computer:

- To protect a computer that is running Windows XP, you must first disable the `ForceGuest` registry key, otherwise the NTLM authentication will fail while attaching the computer. To turn this off modify the following registry key from 1 to 0 on the XP computer (`HKEY_LOCAL_MACHINE\SYSTEM\ CurrentControlSet\Control\Lsa`):
  - ° `ForceGuest=1`: Use this value to force guests on
  - ° `ForceGuest=0`: Use this value to force guests off

- The majority of workgroup computers are accessible only by using a NetBIOS name, therefore when you install the DPM agent you need to use a value for DPMServerName as a NetBIOS name.

- Firewall considerations.

Follow these steps to protect a workgroup or non-domain computer:

1. On the protected computer, run `DPMAgentinstaller.exe` to install the agent. You can find this on the DPM setup DVD or you can copy it from the DPM server at `%systemdrive%\Program Files\Microsoft System Center 2012\DPM\DPM\ProtectionAgents\RA` to the protected computer.

2. Run `SetDpmServer` and specify the local user credentials that will be used for authentication:

   ```
   SetDpmServer.exe -dpmServerName <NAMEOFDPMSERVER>
   -isNonDomainServer -userName <NAMEOFUSER>
   ```

3. Now you need to attach the protected computer on the DPM server. Run the following command to accomplish this:

   ```
   Attach-NonDomainServer.ps1 -DPMServername <NAMEOFDPMSERVER>
   -PSName <NAMEOFPROTECTEDCOMPUTER> -Username <NAMEOFUSER> -Password
   <PASSWORDTOBEUSED>
   ```

Now you should be able to protect the workgroup/non-domain computer through DPM.

From time to time, you may need to change the password of the local account you used when the DPM agent as installed on the protected computer. The following syntax can be run on the protected computer to make sure that DPM has the updated password:

```
SetDpmServer.exe -dpmServerName <NAMEOFDPMSERVER>
-isNonDomainServer -updatePassword
```

Summary

In this chapter, we covered the basics of Microsoft workload and non-Microsoft workload protection. You should now be more familiar with the different workload protections including BMR, system state, protecting domain controllers, Oracle, VMware, and generic data source protection. In the next chapter, we will focus on application workload protection with DPM, and will learn about the workloads DPM is aware of that can be protected natively.

6
DPM-aware Windows Workload Protection

In the previous chapter, we covered workload protection with DPM. This included general Windows server workloads such as Active Directory (AD), bare metal restore (BMR), system state, and many more. In the previous chapter, we also covered general non-Microsoft server workloads such as VMware and Linux.

In this chapter we will cover more Microsoft workloads. The difference between the previous chapter and this chapter is that, in this chapter we will cover Microsoft application workloads that DPM is aware of. What we mean by DPM being aware of certain workloads is that DPM understands what specific application the data that is being protected belongs to. In this chapter, we will also cover content of Service Pack 1 features that have been added to DPM 2012. For example, when you protect SharePoint with DPM, it is aware that you are protecting SharePoint and can automatically protect the necessary data to ensure a good backup of your SharePoint farm. Another DPM aware workload is SQL. DPM knows how to work with and protect SQL data. After you have read through this chapter, you should have a good knowledge of what it takes to back up some of the critical workloads in your environment.

In this chapter, we will cover the following topics:

- Protecting SQL with DPM
- Protecting SharePoint with DPM
- Protecting Exchange with DPM
- Protecting Hyper-V with DPM
- DPM scale-out protection
- Protecting deduplicated volumes
- Protecting Windows clusters with DPM

Protecting SQL with DPM

Almost every application nowadays runs a SQL database on the backend. Some examples are SAP, SharePoint, CRM systems, financial systems, web applications, and even management suites such as System Center products. Many of the previously mentioned applications and other lines of business applications run on top of Microsoft SQL Server. This makes SQL Server high on the list of critical applications in most IT environments today. As an administrator, it is critical that we ensure the SQL data is protected, as businesses often depend on the data stored in these databases. This leads us to the discussion around DPM and SQL protection, and why DPM is a top choice for protecting your Microsoft SQL Servers.

DPM has been engineered to provide the best protection for Microsoft SQL Servers. The Microsoft DPM and SQL product groups teamed up when the protection of SQL for DPM was designed. Having those two product groups collaborate in the design of protection is a very good assurance that DPM is a great option for SQL protection. DPM supports protecting the following Microsoft SQL versions:

- Microsoft SQL Server 2005
- Microsoft SQL Server 2008
- Microsoft SQL Server 2008 R2
- Microsoft SQL Server 2012

The following are some quick facts about Microsoft SQL protection and DPM:

- DPM can provide data recovery at database level
- DPM can protect up to 2,000 databases
- DPM has self-service recovery for database administrators
- DPM can protect SQL Server's highly available database configurations
- DPM provides automatic SQL instance-level protection

Note that the DPM 2012 SP1 can protect SQL 2012 **AlwaysOn**.

For DPM 2012 deployments pre-release SP1, to protect SQL 2012 ensure that the SQL 2012 instance you are protecting does not have the **AlwaysOn** feature enabled, and also ensure that the **SQL NT AUTHORITY\SYSTEM** account has SysAdmin rights on the SQL 2012 instance.

Here is an overview of how DPM protects SQL under the hood. DPM works directly with SQL Server VSS. DPM creates a baseline copy of the SQL data at the block level without interrupting the database access. After the initial backup, the DPM agent and SQL Server VSS writer work together to identify and backup only the changed blocks since the baseline. This is known as an express-full backup. The SQL transaction logs are synced with DPM at regular intervals and this can be run as often as every 15 minutes. These are typically run between express-full backups. The SQL log will be committed and internally truncated after each incremental (synchronization) backup. SQL will not truncate logs after express-full backups. Setting up the protection for SQL with DPM is one of the easiest workloads to configure protection for. When you set up protection for other workloads such as SharePoint, you need to install the DPM agent and perform some manual configurations on the SharePoint's web frontend before DPM can protect it. With SQL protection, you do not have to perform additional steps like you do with SharePoint or Exchange. Basically when you install a DPM agent on a SQL server, DPM automatically knows that SQL is on that server and you can simply add protection for it. To configure protection for your SQL Server perform the following steps:

1. Install the DPM agent on your SQL Server.
2. Go to the DPM Administrator Console, then click on the **Protection** bar.
3. Click on either the New Protection Group icon or on the **Actions** menu.
4. Select **Create protection group** or **Modify protection group** if you already have one created.
5. Expand the server running SQL.
6. Expand the SQL instance and select the SQL database/s you want to protect.
7. Step through the rest of the wizard.

Now your SQL data will be protected.

> Note that when you check the box next to the SQL instance, DPM adds **(Auto)** next to the SQL instance name. This means that the automatic SQL database protection is turned on. The next time a database is added to the instance it will be automatically protected. DPM won't automatically remove any deleted database from the protection group. This is known as the automatic SQL protection. Keep in mind that after this is configured it will happen after the next express-full backup.

The following are the options that are available to you when you go to recover your SQL data:

- Recover all protected SQL Server data
- Recover a specific database to its original location
- Recover a specific database to an alternate instance
- Recover database files to a network folder
- Recover database files to own tape in a DPM library

Protect SQL Server 2012 AlwaysOn

With DPM SP1 you can now protect SQL Server 2012 AlwaysOn. SQL Server 2012 AlwaysOn is a high-availability feature for SQL. It consists of **Availability Groups**. DPM 2012 SP1 can protect databases that are part of an Availability Group.

DPM protection for AlwaysOn is much like protecting a Hyper-V cluster. When creating a protection group in DPM 2012 SP1 Availability Groups will be shown under Cluster Group. To set up the AlwaysOn protection, you need to install the DPM agent on each SQL 2012 instance in the Availability Group. When you go to add a database to a protection group, DPM runs a query to see if the database is a part of an Availability Group. When a failover happens DPM automatically detects this and continues the protection of the database(s).

When protecting SQL 2012 AlwaysOn you have two options. The first is to protect an entire Availability Group. When you protect an entire Availability Group, all databases in that group will be protected and when new databases are added to the group they will automatically be added to protection within DPM as well. The second option is to simply protect individual SQL databases that are a part of a SQL Availability Group. Using the second option requires an administrator to manually add any new databases in an Availability Group to DPM protection.

 For more information about SQL 2012 AlwaysOn visit
http://technet.microsoft.com/en-us/sqlserver/
gg490638.aspx.

Remote SQL Server 2012 SP1

DPM 2012 SP1 has added the support of hosting your DPM database on SQL 2012.

In this section, we are going to walk through what it takes to host your DPM database on SQL 2012. There are some things that need to be configured to get this to work properly. Let's step through the process now:

1. Go ahead and set up SQL 2012 with the following features, as shown in the following screenshot:

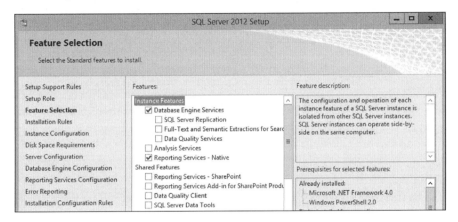

Be sure to select SQL **Reporting Services - Native**, as this is required.

2. Run SQL under a service account.

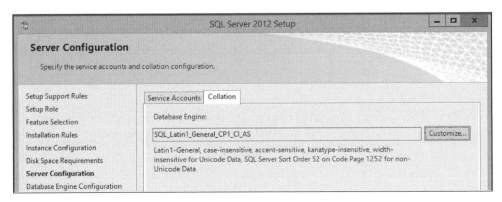

3. For SQL access, add the account that will be used for SQL administration and the account that will be used to install DPM.

4. Select default settings for SQL Reporting Services.

5. From the DPM install, launch **DPM Remote SQL Prep**.

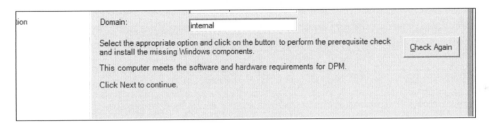

6. On the DPM server, start the installer and select **Use an existing instance of SQL Server** and enter administrative permissions for the remote SQL Server.

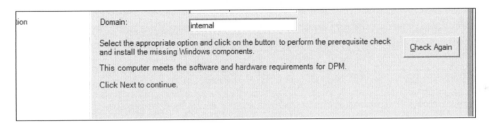

7. The installer will state that it needs the requirement to proceed.

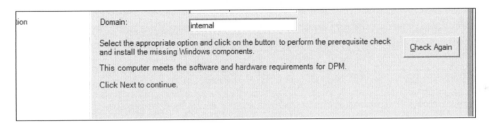

8. Location for database is grayed out as the database is on the remote SQL instance.

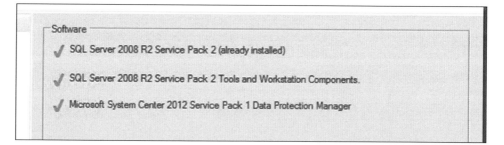

9. Add credentials for the SQL Server Reporting Services user.

10. The installer will skip the SQL Server install and jumps directly to tools and workstations.

Now you can place your DPM 2012 database on SQL Server 2012.

SQL self-service recovery

In DPM, you have what is called the DPM self-service recovery tool (SSRT). This feature gives your SQL DBAs (database administrators) the ability to recover SQL databases on their own without contacting the DPM administrator to perform the recovery for them.

For this feature to work the following tasks need to be performed:

- Configure self-service recovery in DPM
- Configure end users (SQL DBAs) with permissions to recover the databases
- Install the self-service recovery tool on the SQL DBA's computer

Configuring self-service recovery in DPM

In this section we are going to walk through the steps to configure self-service recovery in DPM:

1. Open the DPM Administrator Console, then in the Data Protection Manager Console, navigate to the **Protection** bar.

2. Click on the **Self service recovery** icon on the top toolbar.

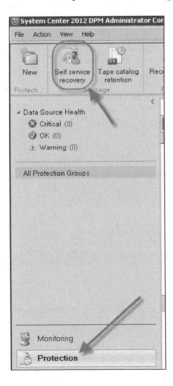

3. Now the **Configuration** tool will open, click on the **Create Role...** button. It will create a security role that you will add Active Directory groups or users to. This is how you will give access for SQL self-service recovery to your SQL DBAs.

4. After you click on **Create Role...**, a wizard will open up. In this wizard select the users/groups, choose the SQL instance and databases the role has access to, and select a staging area that the databases can be recovered to.

5. Now you can give the role a name and description, then add a group of users or specific user you want to have access. Note that you can add multiple users or groups here. Click on **Next** when you're done.

Specify a name which will be used to uniquely identify this role.

Role Name   `DBA`

                Example: SQL Admins

Description   `SQL DBAs`

Security Groups

Specify the security groups that represent the set of SQL Server users that will be included in this role.

Security Group
buchatech\sqldba

                                                                       Add   Remove

6. On the next screen, add the SQL instances and databases you want this role to have access to. Click on **Next** when you're done.

Specify the SQL server databases and instances of SQL Server that you want users of this role to be allowed to recover.

To allow all databases in an instance of SQL Server, clear the text in the Database Name column for that instance of SQL Server.

SQL Server Instance	Database Name
SQL1	DB1

When selecting the recovery targets you will see that you cannot overwrite the original database. You have two options here either specify a path that the DBA can recover to or leave it blank to give the DBA the option to recover to any path they have access to.

To allow users to recover the database as files, you do not need to configure recovery targets. At the time of recovery, users can specify any location where they have permissions to write

Recovery Target Locations

☑ Allow users to recover the databases to another instance of SQL Server

ⓘ Users are not allowed to overwrite the original database.

To restrict where the end users can put the recovered files on the SQL Server, specify a path below. To allow end users the flexibility to specify any path, clear the text in the Recovered Files Path column for that instance of SQL Server.

Installing the DPM self-service recovery tool (SSRT) on a client computer

Now let's look at the process of installing the recovery tool on the SQL DBA's computer. Before an end user can install the SSRT on their computer, they need to have .NET Framework 3.5 and administrative privileges on their computer.

1. Launch the SSRT tool here from the install media (`DPMInstallationMedia\CCX86\DpmSqlEURInstaller\ DPMSQLEur_x86.msi` or `DPMSQLEur_x64.msi`).

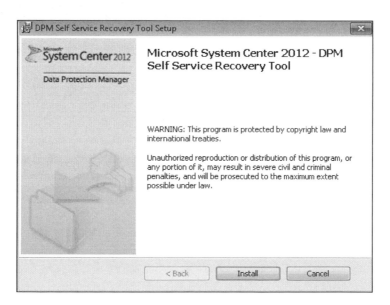

2. Click on **Install** to start the installation.

3. When the install action finishes, click on **Finish**.

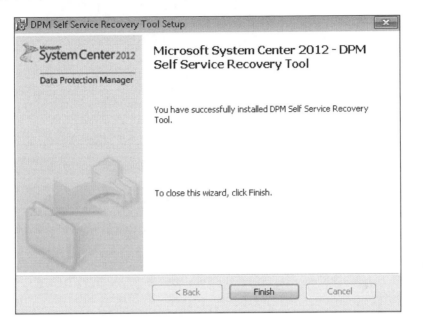

4. To start the DPM SSRT tool, click on **Start | All Programs | DPM Self-Service Recovery Tool**.

Protecting SharePoint with DPM

SharePoint has had steady growth since its first version and continues to expand in many organizations at an increasing rate. SharePoint has quickly become a line-of-business application that workers depend on from day to day, putting it high on the list of applications that needs to be protected. DPM is a great choice as a tool for protecting your SharePoint environments. In this section we are going to discuss setting up SharePoint protection, what DPM protects by default, and how to go above and beyond the default protection.

The following are some of the features that DPM provides for your SharePoint protection:

- Optimized item-level recovery for SharePoint farms through faster recovery. With DPM 2012 SharePoint, recoveries are staged locally on the DPM server giving SharePoint administrators really fast recoveries. A restore of a 1 MB document takes less than 20 seconds in DPM 2012.

- DPM is aware that it's backing up SharePoint. This means that it knows about all the transactions that are occurring during backup and therefore you get a more consistent backup of the data.

- DPM can also protect SharePoint search.

- DPM automatically protects new content of the databases when added to your SharePoint farm.

- DPM is light with low I/O when it is backing up SharePoint, getting only the changes during protection (meaning your production environment will not take a performance hit).

- DPM will let you perform item-level restores of SharePoint objects such as SharePoint site collections, SharePoint sites, documents, lists, and other objects.

- Starting with the release of SharePoint 2010 a recovery farm is no longer required to perform restores. DPM takes full advantage of this feature so that you can perform a restore without a recovery farm, right from DPM to your SharePoint.

In the following sections we will dive deeper into SharePoint protection with DPM.

Configuring SharePoint protection

Configuring protection for SharePoint in DPM 2012 is much the same as it was with DPM 2010. It requires that the DPM agent be installed on your SharePoint server(s) and then manually configuring the SharePoint VSS writer to report back to the DPM server about your SharePoint servers. Configuring this protection is a two-step process; it consists of installing and making some configuration changes on the SharePoint server(s) and then adding the proper protection on the DPM server. The following are the steps to protect your SharePoint environments with DPM:

1. Install the DPM agent on your SharePoint web frontend.

2. On the SharePoint web frontend, open up an elevated command prompt.

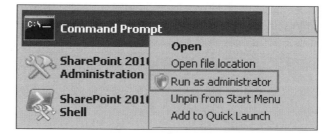

3. Change the directory to C:\Program Files\Microsoft Data Protection Manager\DPM\bin, as shown in the following syntax:

   cd C:\Program Files\Microsoft Data Protection Manager\DPM\bin

4. Type ConfigureSharepoint -EnableSharePointProtection and press *Enter*.

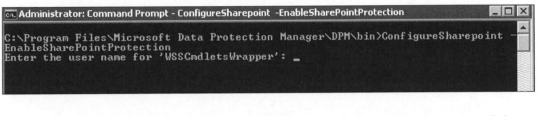

5. Enter the user name and password of a farm administrator account and then press *Enter*.

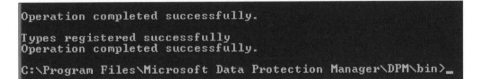

6. When completed, you will see a message confirming that it has successfully completed.

```
Operation completed successfully.

Types registered successfully
Operation completed successfully.

C:\Program Files\Microsoft Data Protection Manager\DPM\bin>_
```

 If your SharePoint farm administrator password changes, you will need to run ConfigureSharePoint -EnableSharePointProtection again to update the DPM backup with the proper credentials.

That covers it on the SharePoint side. Now we need to go back to our DPM server and finish up. Here is what needs to be done on the DPM server:

1. Go to the DPM Administrator Console.

2. Click on the **Protection** bar.

3. Click on either the **New Protection Group** icon  or on the **Actions** menu, select **Create protection group** or **Modify protection group** if you already have one created.

4. Expand the server running SharePoint.

5. Expand **SharePoint** and select the SharePoint configuration.

```
☐ 🗃 SharePoint
   → ☑🗃 BUCHSP\SQLSP\SharePoint_Config
☐ ☐🗃 System Protection
```

6. Click on **Next** in the following five windows if no further protection group configuration changes are required.

7. Click on **Update Group** or **Create Group** to add your SharePoint to the protection group.

Now you should be able to see the SharePoint protection group and what will be protected. What's included by default for protection are the content databases, the SharePoint_Config and SharePoint_AdminContent* databases.

The default protection is perfect for most basic SharePoint farms. However, if you have a heavily customized or more complex SharePoint deployment you may need to protect more. By default, DPM SharePoint protection does not explicitly include other components you may have in your SharePoint farm. This leads us into the next section where we will describe what else would be good to protect around your SharePoint.

It is common practice in SharePoint deployments to run the SQL instances on **SQL Aliases**. DPM is SQL Alias aware. So, if you are running your SQL Servers on SQL Aliases, then this is not a problem for DPM. It does, however, require an extra step in configuration. To configure DPM for SQL Aliases, after you have already run `ConfigureSharePoint -EnableSharePointProtection`, run the following syntax:

```
ConfigureSharePoint -ResolveAllSQLAliases
```

Doing this will resolve SQL instances and any mirrored instance to a corresponding SQL Server. That's it! Now your DPM will protect SharePoint even if it is running on a SQL Server Alias and/or is mirrored.

Protecting all SharePoint components

DPM protection for SharePoint was designed to be controlled by the SharePoint VSS writer service, therefore, DPM by default protects what is recommended by the SharePoint VSS writer as "required for backup". The decision of what needs to be protected or not is actually made by the SharePoint VSS service. From DPM's perspective, it is protecting everything that it needs to protect (the content databases and the configuration databases). This may or may not fit certain SharePoint environment protection needs.

Keep in mind this default protection is by design; typically the DPM team will design protection of workloads around the recommendations of the Microsoft product group responsible for the workload that DPM is protecting. For example, when DPM protects Exchange or SharePoint this protection has been designed to fit supported scenarios. Now there is some confusion around protecting SharePoint because if you view the instance on which SharePoint lives, you will notice several other databases that DPM is not backing up. Some of these databases belong to service applications, while others are system databases needed for SharePoint. These system databases are generic and are sometimes not critical to backup. Following are the databases that may have been created out of the box for SharePoint 2010 Enterprise:

- `Application_Registry_Service_DB_GUID`
- `Bdc_Service_DB_GUID`
- `Managed Metadata Service_GUID`
- `PerformancePoint Service Application_GUID`
- `Search_Service_Application_CrawlStoreDB_GUID`
- `Search_Service_Application_DB`

- `Search_Service_Application_PropertyStoreDB_GUID`

- `Secure_Store_Service_DB_GUID`

- `SharePoint_AdminContent_GUID`

- `SharePoint_Config`

- `StateService_GUID`

- `User Profile Service Application_ProfileDB_GUID`

- `User Profile Service Application_SocialDB_GUID`

- `User Profile Service Application_SyncDB_GUID`

- `WebAnalyticsServiceApplication_ReportingDB_GUID`

- `WebAnalyticsServiceApplication_StagingDB_GUID`

- `WordAutomationServices_GUID`

- `WSS_Content`

- `WSS_Logging`

A complete list of SharePoint 2010 database names and what they are for is listed at `http://technet.microsoft.com/en-us/library/cc678868.aspx#Section1`.

In a scenario of a complete SharePoint farm failure, you would need to restore the databases that are included from the DPM backup of SharePoint. Note the generic databases are not included in the DPM SharePoint backup but they would be regenerated by re-running the SharePoint configuration wizard. Please note that this would bring your farm back, however, you would still lose configurations within these databases. Some of these configurations would include Business Connectivity Services (BCS) applications, Search Configuration, Use Profile data, and so on.

Now let's look at the other components beyond the content databases and generic databases that you would want to protect as a part of your SharePoint backup. Here are the other components you should protect in addition to what DPM protects by default:

- Databases for service applications
- SharePoint customizations (some customizations are packaged as the `.wsp` files; contact the developers for information on what needs to be backed up)
- Third-party add-ons (contact the add-on vendor for information on what needs to be backed up)

- IIS
    - ○ `Web.config` that contains any custom policies and permissions
    - ○ The website files (typically in the `C:\inetpub` directory but can be moved; you as a SharePoint administrator should know if they have been moved)
    - ○ Metabase (this can be protected explicitly or through a system state backup)
- The 12\14\15 hive (`%COMMONPROGRAMFILES%\Microsoft Shared\Web Server Extensions\12` or `14` or `15`); 12 is for SharePoint 2007, 14 is for SharePoint 2010, and 15 is for SharePoint 2013.
- Global assembly cache (GAC) (`%WINDIR%\Assembly`)
- Logfiles
- Search indexes

In addition to this list, you could also run your SharePoint farm as virtual machines (VMs) and protect at the VM level or, alternatively, you could protect your SharePoint servers using the BMR method.

Note that protecting search indexes will utilize large amounts of storage. Only protect this if it is absolutely necessary. Keep in mind that search indexes are data that can be rebuilt after recovering everything else. When working with SharePoint ILR in DPM, the power behind ILR comes from the SharePoint VSS writer that is working with DPM.

Here is what happens to make ILR possible: after you run `configuresharepoint.exe` a process called `GatherWriterMetadata` is run by the SharePoint VSS writer service on the SharePoint farm. This gathers metadata about the data sources in the SharePoint farm such as where the data lives, what parts of the data live where, and what type of data it is. This information comes from the SharePoint configuration database. It is enumerated into a writer metadata document and eventually pushed back to the DPM server. By making DPM aware of all of this data, it knows how to locate each item in the farm when you need to restore. This is what gives you the ability to restore individual items from a SharePoint farm.

> DPM 2012 SP1 enables the ability to protect SharePoint 2013. There are no new requirements for protecting SharePoint 2013 with DPM 2012 SP1. The process for enabling protection for SharePoint 2013 is the same as it is for SharePoint 2007 and SharePoint 2010.

How to protect a multi-tenancy SharePoint deployment

In multi-tenancy you will typically have a web application with multiple site collections with the site collections belonging to different customers. This web application and associated site collections will share service applications but the data in the service application will be partitioned. This all needs to be protected. You can do what you would normally do to protect SharePoint with DPM. The only thing you need to do differently in this scenario is to make sure that you are protecting all service applications.

The following is a list of the service applications that can be partitioned in SharePoint 2010 for multi-tenancy:

- User Profiles
- Managed Metadata
- Business Connectivity Services
- Search
- Secure Store
- Word Automation
- Project

Protecting the service applications consists of protecting the following:

- Active Directory (customer accounts are typically split into separate OUs; AD is critical to protect)
- The service application databases (the list of multi-tenant service applications that is previously listed)
- IIS (system state or BMR of the SharePoint servers is recommended)
- The SharePoint hive (it is used to store SharePoint data that is not stored in its databases; some data that is stored in the SharePoint hive includes templates and logs)
- Any custom solutions deployed in the farm

How to protect RBS with DPM

RBS stands for **remote BLOB storage**. This is a standard set of APIs that are used to store and retrieve BLOBs outside of a SQL database where a dedicated BLOB store is desirable for various reasons. RBS is typically used to store large files such as video, large images, and more. This is being used more and more in SharePoint environments that host video and other media content. A technology called FileStream is used with SQL for RBS. FileStream is a SQL Server 2008 feature to store BLOB content on to a filesystem. Third-party RBS providers are also available.

DPM 2012 supports protecting RBS. When DPM 2012 protects an RBS-enabled content database, DPM will back up everything including BLOB data. When an RBS-enabled database is restored, the BLOB data will be restored as well. Even if you restore an RBS-enabled database to a non-RBS-enabled database, the BLOB objects will be restored into the content database. Protecting SQL databases through native DPM SharePoint protection is enough with DPM 2012 to protect RBS-enabled databases. This will act as normal and should give you ILR of SharePoint data.

How to protect claims authentication with DPM

DPM does not back up claims authentication natively. It protects the SharePoint admin content and the SharePoint configuration database natively. You can protect claims authentication with DPM, but this will require some manual setup from your end.

Without knowing the specific configuration in your environment we can only give a general idea of what to protect. This should get you going in the right direction to protect your claims-based authentication. You need to back up central administration and your web applications (this is already done by protecting the admin and config, and content databases), your identity provider (examples are SQL users (membership store DB), LiveID, and a SharePoint List), Security Token Service application, and IIS on the SharePoint web frontend and/or SharePoint application server (ASP.NET and other settings).

You will need all of those settings and may require some configuration after a restore.

How to protect search with DPM

Before you protect SharePoint search you need to make some configuration changes on the SharePoint server:

1. On the SharePoint web frontend open up an elevated command prompt and change the directory to `C:\Program Files\Microsoft Data Protection Manager\DPM\bin`. Its syntax is as follows:

   ```
   cd C:\Program Files\Microsoft Data Protection Manager\DPM\bin
   ```

2. Type `ConfigureSharePoint -EnableSPSearchProtection` and press *Enter*.

Now you can go back to the DPM server and add the `SPSearch` databases for protection on your protection group.

> DPM will perform express-full backup on the search databases during backups. DPM also performs a consistency check on the index files. During the consistency check, DPM will pause the index crawl and all background processes on that SQL instance. On SQL instances running more than just SharePoint databases, you can avoid performance issues by scheduling the search backup when no other SQL database backups are set to run.

Protecting Exchange with DPM

Mail conversations have been traditionally one of the most important functions for companies worldwide. To create and design an optimal protection that the DPM administrators can rely on is therefore crucial.

The design implementation for Exchange may also vary depending on the size of the Exchange environment and DPM needs to be designed in the correct matter according to the number of **Database Availability Group (DAG)** nodes or if the company uses just a single Exchange server installation.

Configure Exchange protection

The first step before you can start to protect anything with DPM is to deploy and attach a DPM agent to the Exchange server or all members of the cluster. Before and during the creation of the protection group, you have some specific configurations that you will need to consider:

- DPM agent deployment considerations
- DAG clusters

- Specify Exchange protection options
- Specify Exchange DAG protection

DPM agent deployment considerations

As mentioned, you must deploy and attach a DPM agent to all the nodes in the DAG before you can start to protect the Exchange environment. There are, however, some issues that you must consider: the first is the size of the DAG; one DPM server can protect 10,000 mailboxes. Secondly, if you have a DAG that is large in size, you should use more DPM servers and split the nodes of the DAG between multiple DPM servers.

DAG clusters

On the **Select Group Members** page, you should expand the domain that the DAG resides in, and then expand the DAG to be able to choose all the Exchange mailbox databases that reside within that DAG cluster.

If you don't have a DAG, you should just expand your Exchange server and the Exchange workload will appear.

Specifying the Exchange protection options

On the **Specify Exchange Protection Options** page, you specify if you would like the DPM server to run the Eseutil tool during the express-full backup of the Exchange databases.

If your DPM server uses a DPM disk pool, DPM will perform a consistency check of the Exchange data using the Eseutil tool on the data on the DPM server side. If you just use a tape drive, DPM will trigger the Eseutil tool on the Exchange server side.

For a DAG, you should just use the Eseutil on the logfiles, but for a standalone Exchange server, you should use the Eseutil tool for both the Exchange mailbox database and the logfiles.

If you would like DPM to use or trigger the Eseutil tool you must copy the eseutil.exe file and the ese.dll assembly from the <INSTALLDRIVE>\Program Files\Microsoft\Exchange Server\V14or15\Bin catalog on the Exchange server to the <INSTALLDRIVE>\Program Files\Microsoft Data Protection Manager\ DPM\bin catalog on the DPM server.

Exchange maintenance

For an Exchange environment to work optimally, it is important to perform Exchange maintenance on the Exchange data. Exchange maintenance consists of managing Exchange database defragmentation and also index purging.

While those maintenance tasks are performed on an Exchange server, it is important to disable the DPM agent on the DPM server side, as you don't want any protection jobs running during the maintenance. If your Exchange environment is clustered, you should disable all the DPM agents that reside within that cluster during the maintenance of the Exchange environment.

Specifying the DAG protection

On the **Specify DAG Protection** page, you will select the mailboxes to be protected using an express-full or copy backup. The DAG will not populate any information to DPM regarding which DAG mailbox databases are active or passive. You must know this before you create the protection group.

The active database will also use the logfiles and during the express-full back up the logfiles will be cleared.

If a database changes from active to passive, DPM will still be able to protect the DAG mailbox database.

Restore Exchange mailboxes

DPM can perform two different types of restore operations:

- Recovering Exchange server mailboxes
- Recovering Exchange server mailbox databases

Recovering Exchange server mailboxes

In earlier versions of DPM the ability to search for an explicit mailbox was introduced. A common misunderstanding is that the explicit mailbox is restored from the DPM server to the Exchange server; this is not the case. DPM will restore the entire mailbox database to an Exchange recovery database (RDB) if you are using Exchange 2010, or a recovery storage group (RSG) if you are using Exchange 2007.

After the restore operation has finished, you must use the **Exchange Management Shell (EMS)** for Exchange 2010 or the **Exchange Troubleshooting Assistant (ExTRA)** for Exchange 2007.

You will be able to restore the Exchange server 2010 mailbox databases to the following locations:

- Recover to an Exchange server database
- Recover to a network location
- Copy to tape

You will be able to restore the Exchange server 2010 mailbox databases to the following locations:

- Recover the database to its original location
- Recover the database to an alternate location
- Recover to an Exchange Recovery database
- Recover to a network location
- Copy to tape

How to protect a multi-tenancy Exchange deployment

For those companies that manage more than one domain within their Exchange environment, DPM will be able to protect the Exchange mailbox databases using the same design if the Exchange server was hosting just one domain.

There are no special considerations regarding the DPM design that differs from the standard DPM design considerations.

BMR protection technique of Exchange

Bare Metal Restore (BMR) was first introduced in DPM 2010 and provides the ability to restore an entire physical server to a new hardware. If you would like to use BMR to protect a physical Exchange server this could easily have been done but you need to consider two important things:

- Using the `-include` switch within the XML configuration to include all the other physical disks
- You still need to protect Exchange as an Exchange workload to be able to restore using the latest restore technique

Exchange 2013 protection

With the SP1 release also comes the support for protecting the Exchange 2013 workload. There are no major changes made on how you can protect an Exchange 2013 server or restore. You will continue using Recover Mailbox Databases and the Exchange PowerShell cmdlet.

To protect Exchange 2013 with DPM SP1, in addition to copying the `ese.dll` and `eseutil.exe` files to the DPM `bin` folder, you also need to install the Visual C++ redistributable for Visual Studio 2012 Update 1 (`vcredist`) on your Exchange server. You can download it from `http://www.microsoft.com/en-us/download/details.aspx?id=30679`.

Installing `vcredist` on your Exchange server loads components of Visual C++ libraries. The Visual C++ libraries are needed when an application that was developed using Visual Studio 2012 is installed on a computer that does not have Visual Studio 2012 installed. Without Visual Studio 2012 or the Visual C++ libraries, you will run into errors trying to protect Exchange 2013.

Protecting Hyper-V with DPM

Hyper-V is one of Microsoft's most important server platforms, as being able to virtualize the servers offloading the physical hardware and reducing the cost has always been of great interest to companies globally.

During the release of DPM 2012, Microsoft presented a new enhancement made for DPM 2012 protecting stand-alone Hyper-V servers, thus the backup process was made more efficient.

With the release of SP1, Microsoft also made it possible to protect CSV 2.0 clusters for Hyper-V 3.0. Since the cluster service was rewritten and optimized to use a parallel-node execution, it was possible now to protect Hyper-V clusters without using a VSS hardware provider. You can still do it, but since the optimization of Hyper-V and CSV 2.0, DPM will more easily read the changes made within a VM than before, as the actual changes are stored outside the VM's operating system for DPM to read.

Configuring Hyper-V protection with DPM

There are two ways of letting DPM protect Hyper-V:

- Host-level backup
- Guest-level backup

For host-level backup, a DPM agent is installed on the Hyper-V host and will protect the entire VM running on that Hyper-V host.

For guest-level backup, a DPM agent is installed within the VM operating system and is used to protect the workload present within that VM.

Protecting Hyper-V should be seen as protecting a physical server using BMR. The reason that you are doing backup of a VM is to easily be able to restore the entire function that the VM represents.

The best combination for protecting a Hyper-V environment is to combine the host-level backup and the guest-level backup. The host-level backup is more to be seen as a BMR, while the guest-level backup will protect the SQL or Exchange workload running within the VM.

A basic setup for a great Hyper-V protection is to create a recovery point every week for the VM and back up the workload present within the VM more frequently.

Protecting Hyper-V from DPM running in Hyper-V

From the DPM 2010 version onwards it was possible to run the DPM server as a virtual server. There are many great benefits of using a Hypervisor, but there are also some issues that you should consider.

Regarding the DPM disk pool, the best way is to use a pass-through disk for the DPM disk pool, if you are running the DPM server as a VM on Hyper-V. Also note that using VHDs in a disk pool for DPM is not supported.

How Hyper-V ILR works with DPM

A new feature with DPM 2012 is that it is now supported to perform an item-level recovery (ILR) of a VM, even if the DPM server itself is running as a VM.

DPM is able to perform an ILR by indexing the VHDs associated with the VM. One important thing to bear in mind is that DPM will only be able to restore flat files from the indexed VHD. You cannot restore a windows workload such as Exchange, SQL, or SharePoint.

Hyper-V 3.0

This section will cover the new features and functions released for System Center Data Protection Manager (DPM) supporting Hyper-V 3.0, released in the Windows Server 2012. The news for Hyper-V 3.0 related to DPM is:

- Clustered Shared Volume (CSV 2.0)
- Hyper-V servers using SMB storage
- Hyper-V replica
- DPM Scale-out protection

Clustered Shared Volume (CSV) 2.0

The former techniques used to back up a virtual server running on Hyper-V 1.0 or Hyper-V 2.0 were to pass a Volume Shadow Copy Service (VSS) request from the DPM server to the virtual host. The virtual host then passed the request to the VM and indexed the VHD file. All changes made were then passed to the DPM server.

DPM has, from SP1, made an optimization regarding the backup of virtual servers. DPM is now able to perform a 90 percent faster backup using a special mini driver filter called the DPM filter. The DPM filter is not new but how DPM interacts with the CSV 2.0 coordinator is highly optimized. All changes made within a virtual server are now accessible for DPM before it's actually written to the CSV 2.0 volumes. This gives DPM the advance of managing block-level changes fully optimized for the Hyper-V workload.

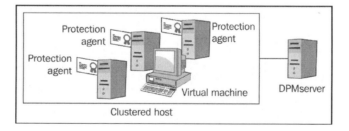

Protection of Hyper-V servers using SMB and Hyper-V Replica

The new SMB feature will make large-scale performance improvements for both business in the "small and medium" business segment and enterprise. SMB will interact with both SQL 2012 and the new Hyper-V role.

The first thing to do before you can start to protect your Hyper-V environment using remote SMB shares is to install the DPM agent on all servers using the SMB remote storage. This applies to all application servers in the cluster and also all nodes of the remote SMB file cluster. Next you need to add a custom cluster resource type so that DPM will be able to identify the cluster. As you are reaching the final steps you must enable the file server VSS agent service on all the nodes in the SMB file cluster.

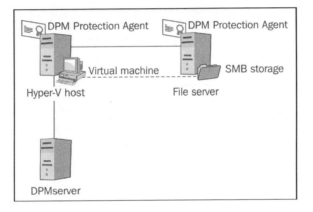

 All Hyper-V machine$ accounts should have full permissions on the specific remote SMB file shares.

Unsupported scenarios for SMB

There are cases where you must be accurate with your design so that you will keep your supported scenario for DPM. These cases are where:

- Some components of the virtual machine are placed on local volumes and others are on remote volumes
- IPv4 or IPv6 addresses for storage location file servers
- Recovery of the virtual machine using remote SMB shares

When it comes to DPM protecting Hyper-V Replica, DPM can protect Hyper-V servers using the new function Hyper-V Replica by protecting the primary node. It's not supported to protect the actual replica.

DPM scale-out protection

A new feature enabled in Service Pack 1 is the ability to interact with Windows Server 2012 scale-out protection. The purpose of using a scale-out protection is to make a DPM agent aware of multiple DPM servers.

The reason you would want to do this is to protect the virtual machines in a cluster on a node by different DPM servers. In the past if you wanted to protect a VM on a new DPM server you had to first remove protection of that VM on the first DPM server, and then add the protection for it on the second DPM server. Now the DPM agent can be attached to multiple DPM servers and can simply be added to a protection group on any of the DPM servers the DPM agent is aware of.

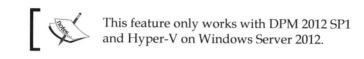 This feature only works with DPM 2012 SP1 and Hyper-V on Windows Server 2012.

This screenshot should give a better visual idea of how the new scale-out protection works:

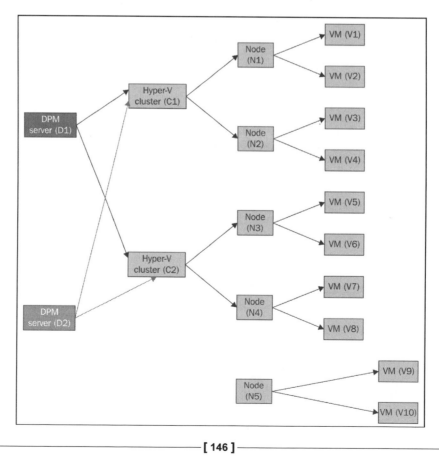

The VMs present on the cluster node **N1** to **N5** are aware of DPM server **D1** but also **D2**, and can be protected by either one of them, but not at the same time. Before SP1, there was a one-to-one relationship between a Hyper-V cluster and a DPM server. The one-to-one relationship between a Hyper-V cluster and a DPM server had a negative impact of scale, as the limiting factor in a Hyper-V cluster was the backup engine.

There are some limitations of the new scale-out protection for Hyper-V. These limitations are as follows:

- There is no support for DPM chaining.
- Your DPM 2012 needs to be a fresh install. The scale-out protection for Hyper-V on DPM servers that were upgraded to DPM 2012 is not supported.

Next we are going to look at what it takes to enable scale-out protection:

- You cannot protect the DPM server when the scale-out protection is used.
- The scale-out feature cannot be used across separate domains. All Hyper-V hosts need to be in the same domain.
- VMs on remote SMB shares are not supported.
- Using IPv4 or IPv6 for the storage location file is not supported.

Enabling the scale-out protection

To be able to make a DPM agent aware of multiple DPM servers, you need to use the SetDPMServer executable with the -add switch. The following is the process for enabling scale-out protection:

1. Push the DPM agent to the Hyper-V hosts from your first DPM server. For this book we will be using DPM01, DPM02, and DPM03.
2. Now, from the Hyper-V hosts, run this syntax for each additional DPM server you want to enable for scale-out protection:

```
setdpmserver -add -dpmservername dpm02
setdpmserver -add -dpmservername dpm03
```

Refer to the following screenshot for an example of what this should look like:

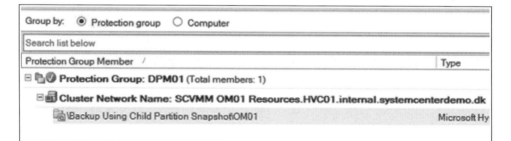

3. Now, from the additional DPM servers, attach the DPM agent to the Hyper-V hosts.

4. Once this has been done you will notice that all three DPM servers in our example are protecting the same virtual machine. Refer to the virtual machine protected on the **DPM01** server.

See the same virtual machine protected on the **DPM02** server.

See the same virtual machine protected on the **DPM03** server.

Protecting deduplicated volumes

Deduplication is a new feature in Windows Server 2012; it is applied on a volume and not to a selected file or folder. DPM supports protection for Windows Server 2012 volumes that have deduplication enabled. In order to protect deduplicated volumes, you must turn on the deduplication role on DPM server by running the following PowerShell command:

```
PS:/>importsystemmodules
```

```
PS:/>add-windowsfeature FS-Data-Deduplication
```

Once you have enabled the deduplication role on the DPM server, you are ready to protect any deduplicated volumes. It is really important to note that DPM doesn't perform any deduplication on its own storage pool.

Recovering volumes with deduplication

Recovering a volume with a deduplication is still the same as any volume, however, you need to be aware of the following points:

- You cannot recover a deduplicated volume to a non-Windows Server 2012 computer
- The destination to which you are recovering the volume must be empty and formatted
- You cannot recover a volume to its original location

Protecting Resilient File System

Resilient File System (ReFS) is a new filesystem that combats the bit rot; it relies on the NTFS code base. DPM 2012 SP1 seamlessly supports ReFS, and offers a similar experience as protecting the NTFS Volumes.

Protecting CSV 2

In Windows Server 2012, CSV 2.0 functionality has been significantly enhanced and this has allowed DPM to perform a true full backup using the block-level changes for Windows 2012 Hyper-V-clustered guests. At the same time it allows a parallel backup to the Hyper-V guests. Both improvements allow Microsoft to claim a 90 percent improvement to express-full backups.

Protecting Windows Clusters with DPM

DPM is cluster aware meaning that it will interact with the cluster services and be able to understand which servers are members of the cluster group.

Protecting file server clusters

System Center Data Protection Manager is easy to use to start protecting your file clusters. For DPM to start protecting your file clusters, it is important to deploy a DPM agent to all the file cluster nodes, and when that is done, you will be able to start protecting your file cluster.

In those cases where you would like to add a node to the cluster, DPM will issue an alert stating that the backup will fail until you have deployed a DPM agent to the new node present in the cluster.

If you would like to remove a node from the cluster, you will failover the clustered resource to another node present in the cluster, using the administration console for your clustering service. Using the same administration console, you remove the cluster node from the cluster, DPM will now identify the removed cluster node as a non-member of the cluster and present the DPM agent within the DPM console as an unprotected server.

Planned failover for file clusters

In those scenarios when you have server maintenance and you need to failover the cluster resource from one node to another, DPM will continue to protect the protected file cluster.

If you have planned and unplanned failover, DPM will need to perform a consistency check to be able to continue the protection for the file cluster.

Changing the resource group

If you move a DPM protected data source to a resource group, between resource groups, or out of a resource group, the DPM protection will fail.

To be able to continue the DPM protection, you need to stop the protection that uses the previously protected name and recreate the protection using the new name.

Protecting DHCP clusters

DHCP is a critical component of networks today. We hardly think about DHCP because on Windows Server it is stable and runs easily. With Windows Server, you have the option to cluster the DHCP service. Clustering DHCP gives you failover, but how do you backup DHCP in case your cluster completely fails? This is actually a straightforward process. DPM is not DHCP-cluster aware and it does not need to be, as the manual backup of it is very straightforward.

By default, Windows automatically creates a backup of the DHCP database every 60 minutes. Windows places the database in this location: `%SystemRoot%\System32\dhcp\backup`. The DHCP database is named `dhcp.mdb` and this is basically what you want DPM to back up. Protecting the `dhcp.mdb` file will contain everything you need to restore DHCP.

Now you may ask, can I change the automatic backup interval? Can I change the location that the backup is sent to? Can I even change the name of the backup? Are there other files I may need to backup?

The answers are yes, yes, yes, and yes. It is a good day in IT when all the answers are yes.

To change the location of the automatic backup interval, you would need to modify the `BackupInterval` key located in this path `HKLM\System\CurrentControlSet\Services\DHCPServer\Parameters` inside the registry on the DHCP server.

To change the location of the `dhcp.mdb` dump, you would need to modify the `BackupDatabasePath` key in the registry located in the same path.

To change the name it would be this key: `DatabaseName`.

Another file you could consider backing up with DPM, but which is not required, is the `J50.log`. This is a transaction logfile also located at `%SystemRoot%\System32\DHCP`, which is used to recover incomplete transactions in case of a server malfunction. You may want to also protect the system state of your servers in your DHCP cluster, but again this is not required.

To restore your DHCP, you would simply bring your DHCP server back online whether this is done by installing a new server and deploying DHCP or doing a system state restore and then restoring the latest dhcp.mdb file to it. The process would look like this:

1. Restore the %SystemRoot%\System32\DHCP\Backup directory.

2. Restore the DHCP database with the DHCP management console. This entails launching the DHCP console, right-clicking on the server you want to restore, and then clicking on **Restore**. Navigate to the DHCP backup folder and select the database.

 Note that during a restore the DHCP service will be offline, and therefore clients will not be able to contact the DHCP server.

Summary

You made it through this chapter, and now you should have a deeper understanding of protecting DPM-aware workloads such as Exchange, SQL, SharePoint, Hyper-V, CSV 2.0, de-duplicated volumes, and clustered services. Some sub-topics you should be more familiar with include protecting multi-tenancy SharePoint, protecting SharePoint search, protecting multi-tenancy Exchange, protecting SQL clusters, as well as some of the new features with DPM Service Pack 1.

In the next chapter, you will learn ways to protect DPM non-aware workloads such as DFS, Lync 2010, TMG 2010, Dynamics CRM, and many more.

7
DPM Non-aware Windows
Workload Protection

In previous chapters we covered both **Microsoft workload protection** and **non-Microsoft workload protection**. In this chapter, we are going to discuss DPM non-aware Microsoft workload protection. What is the difference, you may wonder? DPM non-aware simply means that the Microsoft workloads we will look at here cannot be natively protected by DPM. Yes, DPM can protect them but you typically need to set up the protection manually. This means knowing all the components of these workloads, in order to know what has to be protected to ensure successful restores.

When DPM can protect a workload natively, you simply go into DPM and select the data to protect and it will back up the components needed for a successful restore. An example of a Microsoft workload that DPM can protect natively would be a virtual machine running on Hyper-V. You simply select the virtual machine for protection and DPM will protect the VHD's, the virtual machine configuration and any snapshots of that virtual machine. DPM automatically knows to protect all of the virtual machines components because DPM understands Hyper-V. This understanding comes from the workloads Volume Shadow Copy Service; this is what is considered "DPM aware". In this chapter we will give you valuable insight into what components need to be protected for successful backups of DPM non-aware workloads.

DPM non-aware Microsoft workload protection includes the following:

- Protecting DFS with DPM
- Protecting Dynamics CRM with DPM
- Protecting Dynamics GP with DPM
- Protecting TMG 2010 with DPM
- Protecting Lync 2010 with DPM
- Protecting IIS

Protecting DFS with DPM

DFS stands for **Distributed File System**. It was introduced in Windows Server 2003, and is a set of services available as a role on Windows Server operating systems that allow you to group file shares held in different locations (different servers) under one folder known as **DFS root**. The actual locations of the file shares are transparent to the end user. DFS is also often used for redundancy of file shares.

For more information on DFS

Windows Server 2008:

`http://technet.microsoft.com/en-us/library/`
`cc753479%28v=ws.10%29.aspx`

Windows Server 2008 R2 and Windows Server 2012:

`http://technet.microsoft.com/en-us/library/`
`cc732006.aspx`

Before DFS can be protected it is important to know how it is structured. DFS consists of both data and configuration information:

- The configuration for DFS is stored in the registry of each server, and in either the DFS tree during standalone DFS deployments, or in Active Directory when domain-based DFS is deployed.
- DFS data is stored on each server in the DFS tree. The data consists of the multiple shares that make up the DFS root. Protecting DFS with DPM is fairly straightforward. It is recommended to protect the actual file shares directly on each of the servers in the DFS root.

When you have a standalone DFS deployment you should protect the system state on the servers in the DFS root, and when you have a domain-based DFS deployment we recommend you protect your Active Directory of the domain controller that hosts the DFS root. If you are using DFS replication it is also recommended to protect the shadow copy components on servers that host the replication data, in addition to the previously mentioned items. These methods would allow you to restore DFS by restoring the data and either system state or Active Directory depending on your deployment type.

Another option is to use the **DfsUtil** tool to export/import your DFS configuration. This is a command-line utility that comes with Windows Server that can export the namespace configuration to a file. The configuration can then be imported back into a DFS server to restore a DFS namespace. DPM can be set up to protect the DFS export. You would still need to protect the actual data directly.

An example of using the DfsUtil tool would be:

Run DfsUtil root `export \\domainname\rootname dfsrootname.xml` to export the DFS configuration to an XML file, then run DfsUtil root `import` to import the DFS configuration back in.

For more information on the DfsUtil tool, visit the following URL:

```
http://blogs.technet.com/b/josebda/archive/2009/05/01/using-
the-windows-server-2008-dfsutil-exe-command-line-to-manage-dfs-
namespaces.aspx
```

That covers the backing up of DFS with DPM.

Protecting Dynamics CRM with DPM

Microsoft Dynamics CRM is Microsoft's customer relationship management (CRM) software in the CRM market. Microsoft Dynamics CRM Version 1.0 was released in 2003. It then progressed to Version 4.0 and the latest one is 2011. CRM is a part of the Microsoft Dynamics product family. In this section we will cover protecting Versions 4.0 and 2011.

> Note that when protecting Microsoft Dynamics CRM on either Version 4.0 or 2011, you should keep a note of your update-rollup level some place safe, so that you can install CRM back to that level in the event of a restore. You will need to restore the CRM database and this could lead to an error if CRM is not at the correct update level.

To protect Microsoft Dynamics CRM 4.0, back up the following components:

- Microsoft CRM Server database
    - This is straightforward; you simply need to protect the SQL CRM databases. The two databases you want to protect are the following:
        - The configuration database: `MSCRM_CONFIG`
        - The organization database: `OrganizationName_MSCRM`

- Microsoft CRM Server program files
    - By default, these files will be located at `C:\Program Files\ Microsoft CRM\`.

- Microsoft CRM website
    - By default the CRM website files are located in the `C:\Inetpub\ wwwroot` directory.
    - The `web.config` file can be protected. It only needs protecting if it has been changed from the default settings.

- Microsoft CRM registry subkey
    - Back up the `HKEY_LOCAL_MACHINE\SOFTWARE\Microsoft\MSCRM` key.

- Microsoft CRM customizations
    - To protect customizations or any third-party add-ons you will need to understand the specific components to back up and protect.

- Other components to back up for protecting Microsoft CRM include the following:
    - System state of your domain controller.
    - Exchange server if the CRM's e-mail router is used.

To protect Microsoft Dynamics CRM 2011, back up the following components:

- Microsoft CRM 2011 databases
    - This is straightforward, you simply need to protect the SQL CRM databases. The two databases you want to protect are:
        - The configuration database: `MSCRM_CONFIG`
        - The organization database: `OrganizationName_MSCRM`

- Microsoft CRM 2011 program files
    - By default, these files will be located at `C:\Program Files\Microsoft CRM\`.

- Microsoft CRM 2011 website
    - By default the CRM website files are located in the `C:\Program Files\Microsoft CRM\CRMWeb` directory.
    - The `web.config` file can be protected. It only needs protecting if it has been changed from the default settings.

- Microsoft CRM 2011 registry subkey
    - Back up the `HKEY_LOCAL_MACHINE\SOFTWARE\Microsoft\MSCRM` subkey.

- Microsoft CRM 2011 customizations
    - To protect customizations or any third-party add-ons you will need to understand the specific components to back up and protect.

- Other components to back up for protecting Microsoft CRM 2011 include:
    - System state of your domain controller.
    - Exchange server if the CRM's e-mail router is used.
    - SharePoint if CRM and SharePoint integration is in use.

 Note that for both CRM 4.0 and CRM 2011, you could have more than one `OrganizationName_MSCRM` database if you have more than one organization in CRM. Be sure to protect all of the `OrganizationName_MSCRM` databases that may exist.

That wraps up the Microsoft Dynamics CRM protection for both 4.0 and 2011. You simply need to configure protection of the mentioned components with DPM. Now let's look at what it will take to protect another product from the Dynamics family.

Protecting Dynamics GP with DPM

Dynamics GP is Microsoft's ERP and accounting software package for mid-market businesses. GP has standard accounting functions but it can do more such as Sales Order Processing, Order Management, Inventory Management, and Demand Planner for forecasting, thus making it usable as a full-blown ERP. GP was once known as **Great Plains Software** before acquisition by Microsoft. The most recent versions of GP are Microsoft Dynamics GP 10.0 and Dynamics GP 2010 R2.

GP holds your organization's financial data. If you use it as an ERP solution, it holds even more critical data, and losing this data could be devastating to an organization. Yes, there is a built-in backup utility in GP but this does not cover all bases in protecting your GP. In fact, the built-in backup process only backs up the SQL database, and does not cover items like:

- Customized forms
- Reports
- Financial statement formats
- The `sysdata` folder

These are the GP components you should protect with DPM:

- SQL administrative databases: `Master`, `TempDB`, and `Model`
- Microsoft Dynamics GP system database (`DYNAMICS`)
- Each of your company databases
- If you use SQL Server Agent to schedule automatic tasks, back up the `msdb` database
- `forms.dic` (for customized forms) can be found in `%systemdrive%\Program Files (x86)\Microsoft Dynamics\GP2010\`
- `reports.dic` (for reports) can be found in `%systemdrive%\Program Files (x86)\Microsoft Dynamics\GP2010\`

Backing up these components with DPM should be sufficient protection in the event a restore is needed.

Protecting TMG 2010 with DPM

Threat Management Gateway (TMG) is a part of the Forefront product family. The predecessor to TMG is **Internet Security and Acceleration Server (ISA Server)**.

TMG is fundamentally a firewall, but a very powerful one with features such as VPN, web caching, reverse proxy, advanced stateful packet, WAN failover, malware protection, routing, load balancer, and much more.

There have been several forum threads on the Microsoft DPM TechNet forums asking about DPM protecting TMG, which sparked the inclusion of this section in the book. TMG is a critical part of networks and should have high priority in regards to backup, right up there with your other critical business applications. In many environments, if TMG is down, there are a good amount of users that cannot access certain business applications which causes downtime. Let's take a look at how and what to protect in regards to TMG.

The first step is to allow DPM traffic on TMG so that the agent can communicate with DPM. You will need to install the DPM agent on TMG and then start protecting it from there. Follow the ensuing steps to protect your TMG server:

1. On the TMG server, go to **Start** | **All Programs** | **Microsoft TMG Server**.

2. Open the **TMG Server Management** MMC.

3. Expand **Arrays** and then **TMG Server computer**, then click on **Firewall Policy**.

4. On the **View** menu, click on **Show System Policy Rules**.

5. Right-click on the **Allow remote management from selected computers using MMC** system policy rule. Select **Edit System Policy**.

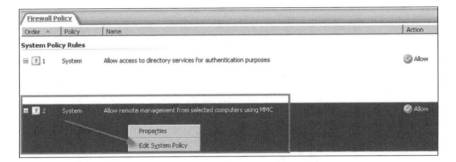

6. In the **System Policy Editor** dialog box, click to clear the **Enable this configuration group** checkbox, and then click on **OK**.

7. Click on **Apply** to update the firewall configuration, and then click on **OK**.

8. Right-click on the **Allow RPC from TMG server to trusted servers** system policy rule. Select **Edit System Policy**.

9. In the **System Policy Editor** dialog box, click to clear the **Enforce strict RPC compliance** checkbox, and then click on **OK**.

10. Click on **Apply** to update the firewall configuration, and then click on **OK**.

11. On the **View** menu, click on **Hide System Policy Rules**.

12. Right-click on **Firewall Policy**.

13. Select **New** and then **Access Rule**.

14. In the **New Access Rule Wizard** window, type a name in the **Access rule name** box. Click on **Next**.

15. Check the **Allow** checkbox and then click on **Next**.

16. In the **This rule applies to** list, select **All outbound traffic** from the
    drop-down menu and click on **Next**.

17. On the **Access Rule Sources** page, click on **Add**.

18. In the **Add Network Entities** dialog window, click on **New** and select **Computer** from the drop-down list.

19. Now type the name of your DPM server and type the DPM server's IP address in the **Computer IP Address** field. Click on **OK** when you are done.

20. You will then see your DPM server listed under the **Computers** folder in the
    Add Network Entities window. Select it and click on **Add**. This will bring
    the DPM computer into your access rule wizard. Click on **Next**.

21. In the **Add Rule Destinations** window click on **Add**. The **Add Network Entities** window will come up again. In this window expand the **Networks** folder, and then select **Local Host** and click on **Add**.

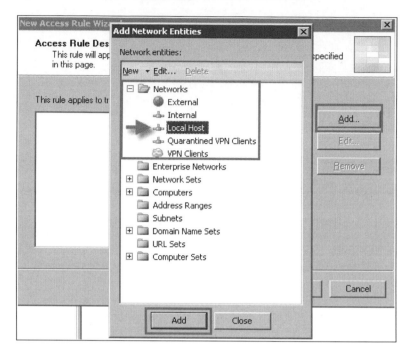

22. Now click on **Next**.

Your rule should have both the DPM server and Local Host listed for both incoming and outgoing.

23. Click on **Next**, leave the default **All Users** entry in the **This rule applies to requests from the following user sets** box, click on **Next** again.

New Access Rule Wizard		×
User Sets		
You can apply the rule to requests from all users. Or, you can limit access to specific user sets.		

This rule applies to requests from the following user sets:

   All Users   Add...

                           Edit...

                           Remove

                 < Back   Next >   Cancel

24. Click on **Finish**.

25. Right-click on the new rule (**DPM2010** in this example), and then click on **Move Up**.

26. Right-click on the new rule, and select **Properties**.

27. In the rule name properties dialog box (**DPM2010 Properties**), click on the **Protocols** tab, then click on **Filtering**.

28. Now select **Configure RPC Protocol**.

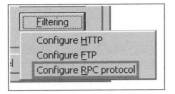

29. In the **Configure RPC protocol policy** dialog box, check the **Enforce strict RPC compliance** checkbox, and then click on **OK** twice.

Configure RPC protocol policy

Protocol

Define RPC protocol related rules

☑ Enforce strict RPC compliance

When this checkbox is not selected, the filter will
allow additional RPC type protocols, such as DCOM

OK   Cancel   Apply

30. Click on **Apply** to update the firewall policy, and then click on **OK**.

Now you will need to attach the DPM agent for the TMG server. Follow the ensuing steps to complete this task:

1. Open the DPM Administrator Console.
2. Click on the **Management** tab on the navigation bar.
3. Now click on the **Agents** tab.
4. On the **Actions** pane, click on **Install**.
5. Now the **Protection Agent Install Wizard** window should pop up.
6. Choose the **Attach agents** checkbox.
7. Choose **Computer on trusted domain**, and click on **Next**.

8. Select the TMG server from the list and click on **Add** and then click on **Next**.
9. Enter credentials for the domain account. The account that is used here needs to have administrative rights on the computer you are going to protect. Click on **Next** to continue.

Please specify username and domain for a domain account that has administrator rights on the computers which you wish to attach to the DPM server.

DPM uses the credentials to attach the protection agents.

User name:

administrator

Password:

••••••••

Domain:

buchatech.com

10. You will receive a warning that DPM cannot tell if the TMG server is clustered or not. Click on **OK** for this.

Microsoft System Center Data Protection Manager 2010

DPM could not identify if computer buchisa.buchatech.com is clustered. (ID: 405)

Agent installation on buchisa.buchatech.com can continue. To successfully protect clustered resources, you must install the DPM protection agent on all the members of the cluster. Review the error details and ensure that the Windows Management Instrumentation service is running and can be accessed remotely from the DPM server.

OK

11. On the next screen click on **Attach** to continue.

Next you have to install the agent on the TMG firewall and point it to the correct DPM server. Follow the ensuing steps to complete this task:

1. From the TMG server that you will be protecting, access the DPM server over the network and copy the folder with the agent installed in it down to the local machine. Use this path `\\DPMSERVERNAME\%systemdrive%\program files\Microsoft DPM\DPM\ProtectionAgents\RA\3.0\3.0.7696.0\ i386`.

2. Then from the local folder on the protected computer, run `dpmra.msi` to install the agent.

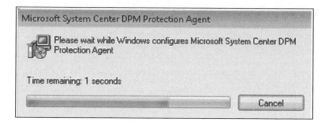

3. Open a command prompt (make sure you have elevated privileges), change directory to `C:\Program Files\Microsoft Data Protection Manager\ DPM\bin` then run the following:

   ```
   SetDpmServer.exe -dpmServerName <serverName>  userName <userName>
   ```

   Following is the example of the previous command:

   ```
   SetDpmServer.exe -dpmServerName buchdpm
   ```

4. Now restart the TMG server.

5. Once your TMG server comes back, check the Windows services to make sure that the **DPMRA** service is set to automatic, and then start it.

DPMRA	Helps back up and recover file and appl...	Manual	Local System

That is it for configuring DPM to start protecting TMG, but there are a few more things that we still need to cover on this topic.

With TMG backup you can choose to back up certain components of TMG, depending on your recovery needs. With DPM you can back up the TMG hard drive, TMG logs that are stored in SQL, TMG's system state, or BMR of TMG. Following is the list of components you should back up depending on your circumstances:

What can be included in TMG server backup:

- TMG configuration settings (exported through TMG)
- TMG firewall settings (exported through TMG)
- TMG logfiles (stored in SQL databases)
- TMG install directory (only needed if you have custom forms for things such as an Outlook Web Access login screen
- TMG server system state
- TMG BMR

None of the previous components are required for protection of TMG. In fact, protecting the SQL logfiles tends to cause more issues than it helps, as they change so often. These SQL log databases change so often that DPM will send an error when the old SQL databases no longer shown under protection. The logfiles are not required to restore your TMG. For a standard TMG restore, you will need to reinstall TMG, reconfigure NIC settings, import any certificates, and restore TMG configuration and firewall settings. For more information on backing up TMG 2010, visit the following page: `http://technet.microsoft.com/en-us/library/cc984454.aspx`.

DPM cannot back up the TMG configuration and firewall settings natively. This needs to be scripted and scheduled through Windows Task Scheduler, and then placed on the local hard drive. DPM can back up the .XML settings for TMG export from there. You can find the TMG server's export script at `http://msdn.microsoft.com/en-us/library/ms812627.aspx`. Place this script into a .VBS file, and then set up a scheduled task to call this file to run. This automates the export of your TMG server settings.

There is another way to back up the entire TMG server. This is a new type of protection, specific to TMG 2010. This protection is BMR and is available because TMG is now installed on top of Windows Server 2008 and Windows Server 2008 R2. Protecting the BMR of your TMG gives you the ability to restore your entire TMG in the event that it fails-configuration and firewall settings included. BMR will also bring back certificates and NIC card settings.

 Note that BMR of TMG restored on a virtual machine can't use its NIC card settings. It only on the same hardware.

Well that covers how to protect TMG with DPM. As you can see that there are some improvements through BMR, and if you do not employ BMR protection you can still automate the process of protecting TMG.

How to protect IIS

Internet Information Services (IIS) is Microsoft's web server platform. It is included for free with Windows Server operating systems. Its modular nature makes it scalable for different organization web server need. The latest version is IIS 8. It can be used for more than standard web hosting, for example as an **FTP server** or for **media delivery**. Knowing what to protect when it comes to IIS will come in handy in almost any environment you may work in. Backing up IIS is one thing but you need to ensure that you understand the websites or web applications you are running, so that you know how to back them up too. In this section, we are going to look at the protection of IIS.

To protect IIS, you should backup the following components:

- IIS configuration files
- Website or web applications data
- SSL certificates
- Registry (only needed if website or web application required modifications of the registry)
- Metabase

The IIS configuration files are located in the `%systemdrive%\windows\system32\inetsrv\config\` directory (and subdirectories).

The website or web application files are typically found in `C:\inetpub\wwwroot`. Now this is the default location but the website or web application files can be located anywhere on an IIS server.

To export SSL certificates directly from IIS, follow the ensuing steps:

1. Open the Microsoft IIS 7 console.
2. In the left-hand pane, select the server name.
3. In the center pane click on the server certificates icon.
4. Right-click on the certificate you wish to export and select **export**.
5. Enter a file path, name the certificate file, and give it a password.
6. Click on **OK** and your certificate will be exported as a `.pfx` file in the path you specified.

Metabase is an internal database that holds IIS configuration data. It is made up of two files: `MBSchema.xml` and `MetaBase.xml`. These can be found in `%SystemRoot%\system32\inetsrv\`.

A good thing to know is that if you protect the system state of a server, then IIS configuration will be included in this backup. This does not include the website or web application files, so you will still need to protect these in addition to a system state backup.

That covers the items you will need to protect IIS with DPM backup.

Protecting Lync 2010 with DPM

Lync 2010 is Microsoft's Unified Communication platform complete with IM, presence, conferencing, enterprise video and voice, and more. Lync was formerly known as Office Communicator. Lync is quickly becoming an integral part of business communications. With Lync being a critical application to organizations, it important to ensure this platform is backed up.

Lync is a massive product with many moving parts. We are not going to cover all of Lync's architecture as this would need its own book. We are going to focus on what should be backed up to ensure protection of your Lync deployment. Overall, we want to protect Lync's settings and configuration data. The majority of this data is stored in the Lync Central Management store. The following are the components that needs to be protected in order to back up Lync:

- Settings and configuration data
    - Topology configuration (Xds.mdf)
    - Location information (Lis.mdf)
    - Response group configuration (RgsConfig.mdf)
- Data stored in databases
    - User data (Rtc.mdf)
    - Archiving data (LcsLog.mdf)
    - Monitoring data (csCDR.mdf and QoeMetrics.mdf)
- File stores
    - Lync server file store
    - Archiving file store

These stores will be file shares on the Lync server, named in the format \\lyncservername\sharename. To track down these file shares if you don't know where they are, go to the Lync **Topology Builder** and look in the **File stores** node.

Note the files named Meeting.Active should *not* be backed up. These files are in use and locked while a meeting takes place.

- Other components as follows:
  - ◦ Active Directory (User SIP data, a pointer to the Central Management store, and objects for Response Group and Conferencing Attendant)
  - ◦ Certification authority (CA) and certificates (if you use an internal CA)
  - ◦ Microsoft Exchange and Exchange Unified Messaging (UM) if you are using UM with your Exchange
  - ◦ Domain Name System (DNS) records and IP addresses
  - ◦ IIS on Lync Server
  - ◦ DHCP Configuration
  - ◦ Group Chat (if used)
  - ◦ XMPP gateways if you are using XMPP gateway
  - ◦ Public switched telephone network (PSTN) gateway configuration, if your Lync is connected to one
  - ◦ Firewall and Load Balancer (if used) configurations

Summary

Now that we had a chance to look at several Microsoft workloads that are used in organizations today and how to protect them with DPM, you should have a good understanding what it takes to back them up. These workloads included Lync 2010, IIS, CRM, GP, DFS, and TMG. Note there are many more Microsoft workloads that DPM cannot protect natively, which we were unable to cover in this chapter.

For more information on other DPM non-aware Microsoft workloads you can protect with DPM visit `http://www.buchatech.com/2011/07/backing-up-applications-with-dpm/`, this list is maintained regularly by Steve Buchanan.

In the next chapter we will dive into managing tapes with DPM.

8
Managing Tapes in DPM

Tapes have been around for many years and will be around for a while yet. Starting with Service Pack 1 (SP1) for the System Center 2012 family, Microsoft's primary focus has been to move company data to the cloud (Azure). They are also pushing for cloud-based storage and placement of functions.

The cloud is *absolutely* where the company should put its data, but it is also worth looking into features such as Virtual Tape Libraries (VTL), which make life much easier for backup administrators. Azure and the backup portal is of big interest for the companies worldwide, both big and small companies, since it will assist the DPM administrators to place the backed-up production data in a highly-secured datacenter off-site.

How DPM manages tapes

System Center Data Protection Manager as formerly stated is focused on delivering a fully supported backup and restore operation for Microsoft workloads. It will provide you a fully supported and optimized restore operation for Microsoft workloads within your domain and give you a fast restore from tape.

How DPM writes information to tape

System Center Data Protection Manager can manage two different scenarios concerning long-term recovery goals. If your primary DPM server has no disk pool DPM, then you can write your data incrementally to the tape, but this is not the most common scenario, nor is it an optimal one. This scenario will however enable the DPM server to use the tapes as short-term recovery goals, by placing the data temporarily in the MTA scratch area.

The second, far more common approach will write a full copy of the backup to a tape. This is a more time-consuming process than the incremental approach, but from a restore perspective the "the most optimal" is like saying "the best" optimal one, since you do not need to assemble incremental data from a large number of different tapes.

Tape information

All the information regarding which tapes are associated to what data source and so on is stored in the DPM server's database (DPMDB). The DPM administrator has the ability to specify the tape catalog retention by clicking on **Tape Catalog Retention** in the **Protection** task area.

The DPM administrator can choose if the tape catalog should be pruned at the same time as the recovery points expire, or set its own prune catalog value.

If the DPM administrator sets a value for when DPM should prune the tape catalog, then that value can't be greater than the protection groups' retention time.

Within the **Tape Catalog Retention** window, the DPM administrator also has the option to choose when DPM shall trigger an alert regarding the size of the local database (DPMDB).

The DPM administrator can also create some maintenance tasks for the DPMDB database. If it grows very large the DPM administrator can perform a shrink operation within the local or remote SQL Management Studio.

Basic tape management tasks for DPM

There is some basic information that the backup administrator must know regarding where to find the key functions for tape management within the DPM console, and what commands are available.

Within the **Management** task pane, you will find all the necessary information regarding the tape solution that is attached to your DPM server. For the solution to work with your DPM server, there are some prerequisites:

- Microsoft signed drivers
- Vendor drivers that are tested with DPM
- Tape drives and media library changer is presented correctly within device manager

 The tape information is stored within the DPMDB database.

Tape commands for DPM

In the **Management** task area, the DPM administrator will find all the necessary information regarding the DPM server's tape solution. There are some commands that the DPM administrator must know for the tape management work.

By right-clicking on the tape drive or media library present within the console, a drop-down menu will be presented with the available commands for that specific unit.

The general tape and tape library commands will also be presented in the ribbon bar at the top of the DPM console.

Tape library commands

By right-clicking on a library, the DPM administrator will be presented with a list of the available commands for the management of the library attached to the DPM server, as shown in the following screenshot:

Inventory library

The **Inventory library...** function will perform an inventory check of the media library. The inventory can be made in two different ways:

- **Detailed inventory**: This will mount every tape within the tape library and reads what information is written to the tape
- **Fast inventory**: This will just read the barcode and update the information in the DPMDB database and the DPM console

Rescan

When performing a **Rescan** operation, the DPM server will try to find a newly-attached tape drive or media change library.

Refresh

The **Refresh** command will update any changes made to the already-attached tape drive or media change library.

Unlock library door

Before the DPM administrator can insert new tapes to the media library he or she must unlock the library door, which prepares the library for changing the tapes.

Rename library...

The DPM administrator has the option of specifying a name for the tape library. This is useful if a DPM server has multiple tape libraries attached, and the DPM administrator wishes to differentiate the primary tape library and the copy library.

Disable library

When performing a maintenance check for the library, the DPM administrator must put the library in disabled mode, so that the DPM server will not use the library for its long-term recovery goals.

Add tape (I/E port)...

For those libraries that have an I/E port, the DPM administrator can unlock the library door from the DPM server and place the tapes in the I/E port. And then from the DPM server choose **Add tape (I/E port)...**.

Clean

When managing a tape solution with DPM, it is important to clean your tape drives. If you have marked a tape within your library as a cleaning tape, DPM will automatically mount this tape and clean the drive marked for cleaning. In a standalone tape drive scenario, you can clean the tape drive or let DPM manage it.

Disable

From the DPM console, the DPM administrator has the option to disable a tape drive, which is useful in those scenarios where maintenance of the hardware is needed.

Protection group configuration

When the DPM administrator designs the protection group there are two sections within the protection group configuration to be considered:

- Specify long-term goals
- Select library and tape details

Specify long-term goals

In the process of creating or modifying a protection group, you will have two options for specifying the long-term recovery goals and backup schedule.

In the previous screenshot, under the **Specify long-term goals** step, you will see a **Recovery goals** section, where you have the ability to set up the retention range and the backup frequency for the recovery point schedule.

If you would like to create a more grandfather-father-son relation, you simply click on the **Customize** button and a new window will appear called **Customize Recovery Goal**.

In the **Customize Recovery Goal** window, you can define your recovery goals in terms of when DPM should write data to the tape.

You can use up to three different recovery goals and recurrence in days, weeks, months or years. You also have the ability to choose the number of backup copies.

At the bottom of the window, there is a special option that will let you decide what the DPM server should do if multiple recovery goals are scheduled to be on the same day. DPM will let the yearly backup run instead of the monthly backup, and if the month and week backup are be scheduled to run on the same day, then the month backup will run instead of the year backup. Best practice is to define your most frequently occurring recovery goal first, for example week and then go on with the month for the second recovery goal and so on. You can also let the DPM server create two copies if recovery goals clash, which is good for archiving purposes.

At the bottom you find the **Backup schedule** section, where you define the backup schedule for the protection group. You can modify the backup schedule by clicking on the **Modify...** button.

In the **Modify Long-Term Backup Schedule** window, you can define the backup schedule for the different recovery goals.

Select library and tape details

Since DPM is defined not only as a restore product but also as a disaster recovery product, there is some advanced configuration that can be made during the creation or modification of a protection group.

Companies using multiple sites can configure a copy library that can be used with the intention to copy data across multiple sites.

You can also compress or encrypt the data written to tape - but you cannot do both. For compression to be enabled, the tape drive must have the option to be able to compress data.

If the data written to tape is confidential or in some way sensitive, you have the option to encrypt the data using a local certificate that must be placed on the DPM server. Losing this certificate, however, will lead to the devastating situation of being unable to restore the data previously backed up data.

Co-location of data on tape

For those environments that have a large amount of data to be written to tape or an environment where the DPM server only has a standalone tape drive, you have the option to customize how DPM writes the protection groups to tape.

Using a tape library DPM will allocate one or more tapes per protection group, this could lead to unnecessary usage of tape and costs. The co-location function was first introduced in the 2007 version of DPM but now it has been optimized.

The optimized co-location feature lets the DPM administrator co-locate protection groups with different definitions of long-term recovery goals. This was not possible in the earlier versions, since the co-location function depended on long-term recovery goals being configured the same way.

If you navigate to the **Management** task area in the DPM console, you will find the new media co-location function by clicking on the **Optimize usage** option in the ribbon bar at the upper part of the DPM console.

Clicking on the **Optimize usage** button in the ribbon bar will show you a new window called **Tape Optimization Setup**. To be able to use the new co-location feature, you must start off by creating a new media co-location set by clicking on the **Create** button.

In the **Tape Optimization Setup** window you define a name for the media co-location set and choose which protection groups should be co-located to tape.

After naming the new media co-location set and choosing the protection group members, you should notice the lower part called **Select tape co-location details**. If this option is checked, protection groups with different long-term recovery goals cannot be co-located. If it's unchecked, backups with different retention periods will not be co-located. Uncheck this box and click on the **Advanced** button.

The advanced tape co-location options window will provide you with two values as follows:

- **Write period**: This defines how long a tape will be available for writing after it becomes off site ready
- **Expiry tolerance**: This defines the maximum period of time a recovery point can lie expired on an active tape

Co-locating tape and upgrading DPM

In previous versions of DPM, you enabled the co-locate function by setting a global variable for DPM in PowerShell. This global property has been removed from the DPM 2012 version.

This is important because when upgrading a DPM server that has co-location active, the PowerShell function will be deactivated. This means that after you have made your in-place upgrade, you must create your own media co-location set so that it continues to co-locate the data written to the tapes.

Standalone tape drives and tape libraries

There are many vendors in the market that produce great hardware for tape drives and tape libraries. Since it can be a hard task choosing the right type and vendor for your tape solution, Microsoft has created a sophisticated hardware compliant list (HCL) that covers all the supported standalone tape drives and media libraries that Microsoft themselves has verified as fully functional with DPM.

You can read the HCL at the following URL:

```
http://technet.microsoft.com/en-us/library/hh916523
```

In those cases where the hardware is not listed on the HCL URL, you can use the tape testing tool. More information could be found at the following URL:

```
http://technet.microsoft.com/en-us/library/jj733580.aspx
```

Standalone tape drives

System Center Data Protection Manager will also work fine just by using a stand-alone tape drive. If you plan to use a stand-alone tape drive and have more than one protection group, you should consider activating the co-location feature for tape optimization.

Tape libraries

System Center Data Protection Manager will provide you with a more optimal tape management solution if you are using a tape library. DPM will interact with the tape library and providing you with a fully manageable solution.

Virtual Tape Library (VTL)

If you are running DPM as a Hyper-V VM, you will not be able to use a stand-alone tape drive or a tape library with that DPM server, since the Microsoft Hypervisor can't mount the tape solution. This is a limitation of the Hyper-V role.

Many companies today have stopped using tapes as their archive solution and put their data in the Azure storage. The backup-to-cloud is a feature that was enabled in System Center's SP1.

If you need the granularity of tape (the grandfather-father-son relation), but the speed of disk for the protected production data you should consider using a Virtual Tape Library (VTL).

Firestreamer

There is one supported VTL solution for Microsoft, the **Firestreamer** software from Cristalink. It will provide you with a great VTL experience.

Since a VTL places tape files on a disk instead of tapes, you will have a great restore time and also an optimal granularity for the data that should use for the long-term recovery goals. You could also place your VTL library on removable storage for a smaller DPM installation.

You can read more regarding the Firestreamer software at the following URL:

```
http://www.cristalink.com/fs
```

Tape Library Sharing (TLS)

In a larger environment, where the tape libraries communicate using fiber channel (FC) technology, the DPM administrator could leverage the function of TLS. This feature allows multiple DPM servers to share one tape library, provided that the communication channel is FC.

The TLS feature depends on two things:

- Library server
- Library clients

The library server coordinates communications between the library clients, meaning the DPM servers that share the tape library which is attached to the library server.

One important thing to consider is that the DPM servers using the TLS feature will also share the DPM database. This makes it even more critical to keep backups of the DPMDB databases.

You should always be careful while upgrading the DPM servers that operates in a TLS solution, since this could be considered a cluster. When upgrading the DPM servers with major upgrades like service packs and so on, you must disable the TLS feature and re-enable it after the upgrade is complete.

Tape reports

As a responsible administrator for DPM solution, it is important to keep yourself updated with the actual status of the tape rotation or tape utilization. There are two specific reports that you should subscribe to and read on a regular basis:

- Tape management
- Tape utilization

The tape management report will provide you with the information regarding the tape rotation and free media thresholds. Note that the data is collected per library.

The tape utilization report lists the trends in tape utilization; you can use this report to inform your capacity planning.

Summary

In this chapter, we covered how System Center Data Protection Manager manages tapes and how DPM will write the data to the tape using different recovery goals. We spoke about different tape reports and introduced the TLS feature, and then also covered the encryption of data written to the tape. The new co-location feature was also covered that lets you write different protection groups with different long-term recovery goals to the same tape.

In the next chapter we will have a closer look at client-side protection.

9
Client Protection in DPM

There are many types of client backup solution. Some examples are: supplying end users with an external drive and asking them to copy data over; sync solutions such as redirecting folders to a server or using FTP; cloud-based backup such as Microsoft's SkyDrive or Dropbox; and centralized backup for the corporate servers controlled and maintained by an IT department. There are both pros and cons to each of the mentioned solutions. DPM offers a centralized backup solution for your client data and this is what we will focus on for this chapter.

In this chapter, the reader will be exposed to techniques of protecting client data with DPM. We will look at many aspects of client protection, from creating a plan and configuring DPM, to deploying the agent, end user self-service restores, and more. The following are the specific topics we will cover in this chapter:

- Creating a plan for backing up end user data
- Planning for off-site end user backup
- Configuring DPM and Active Directory for end user protection
- Installing an agent automatically and manually on a client computer
- Performing image-level backups of client computers with DPM
- Other resources for DPM client protection

Creating a plan for backing up end user data

In many of today's organizations, corporate policy dictates that all mission-critical data should be stored on central file servers. Even with this policy in place, client data does not always make it to the central file servers, resulting in data loss when a client computer fails. The client's computer protection is often a secondary consideration when it comes to disaster recovery plans. Depending on the user's willingness to place the data whether on file servers or local servers and the level of complexity for client computer configurations, it may be essential to consider client computer protection. There are many types of client protection solutions, but, in this chapter we will focus on centralized client protection with DPM 2012.

DPM 2012 allows you to protect client computers in a centralized fashion. DPM 2012 can protect desktops, laptops, and Windows 8 tablets as well as client computers that are on the network or remotely connected to the network. DPM administrators are able to centrally configure data protection for the desktops and laptops in their environment. Additionally, DPM administrators can give their end users the ability to define and manage their own backups. DPM 2012 enables end users to perform their own recoveries by leveraging the Previous Versions feature in Windows.

Now let's look at what items need to be considered when planning for client protection.

With client protection you want to consider all the items a user uses on a regular basis. Some common items of importance to end users include:

- Desktop
- Documents
- E-mail (if user has local PST files or not an Exchange user)
- IE favorites
- User profile

This list of items will vary across different organizations, so it is up to you when creating your recovery plan to determine what is important to backup. You will also need to determine what to exclude from the backups. End users often keep data that is not critical to the business on their computers. Some examples are music, pictures, and even video data. You may not want personal music files filling up the storage on your backup server, so it is equally important to map out what types of files will not be backed up.

There are certain types of data that DPM does not protect. You will need to plan around this list as well when planning what to protect. DPM does not support backups of the following:

- Hard links
- Reparse points
- Recycle Bin
- Paging files
- The System Volume Information folder
- Non-NTFS volumes
- Encrypted drives

Another item to consider when planning DPM client backup is that administrators can give end users the ability to choose what to back up on their client computer. The folders an end user would be able to select are in addition to the folders already specified in the backup policy. This feature allows the end user to have some control over their own backups, but, this could be a bad thing if the end user were to backup large amounts of data using up the disk space in the DPM storage pool so plan carefully for this feature. Administrators can put a maximum of GB/TB per user and block certain folders from being protected.

The client operating systems that DPM can protect are as follows:

- Windows XP with Service Pack 2 (SP2) or later
- Windows Vista or Windows Vista with Service Pack 1 (SP1)
- Windows 7
- Windows 8

All of the operating systems from the previous list are supported in both their 32-bit and 64-bit versions. The operating system of your client computers needs to be taken into consideration, as not all features are available on all of the operating systems. For example, restoring from previous versions of files and folders doesn't work on Windows XP, and is not supported on client computers running it.

As a part of client protection you will also need to plan your recovery goals. These goals should include but are not limited to:

- Disk
    - Retention range
    - Synchronization frequency
    - Number of recovery points

- Tape
    ◦ Backup schedule
    ◦ Type of backup
    ◦ Number of backup copies
    ◦ Tape labeling scheme

A single DPM server can protect up to 3,000 client computers. If you have more than 3,000 client computers, then more than one DPM server will need to be deployed.

There is a lot to consider when planning for end user protection. The end user protection will benefit the end users and ensure that the organization's data is secure, so take time on this activity to ensure it is done right.

Plan for off-site end user backup

Now that we have planned for client protection in general, let's look at what is involved when protecting clients off-site.

DPM can only protect off-site clients that are connected via VPN or **DirectAccess**. For off-site client computers that are intermittently connected, it is recommended that the client computers have a minimum network bandwidth of 1 megabit per second (Mbps). For client computers that are continually connected to the network, it is recommended they have a minimum network bandwidth of 256 kilobits per second (Kbps).

DPM supports the following VPN protocols:

- Point-to-Point Tunneling Protocol (PPTP)
- Secure Socket Tunneling Protocol (SSTP)
- Layer 2 Tunneling Protocol (L2TP)
- DirectAccess

The off-site protection also requires Internet Control Message Protocol (ICMP) through the network firewall. DPM is able to handle the protection of clients even on unstable connections.

DPM handles connection drops like this. If a connection goes down while DPM is synchronizing, then it will continue synchronization from the point where it dropped off. If the connection is dropped during a consistency check then DPM will retry the consistency check five minutes after the connection has dropped. If the connection is back within five minutes then it will continue the consistency check with no issues, otherwise DPM will mark the replica as inconsistent and alert will be created in DPM. The consistency will have to be manually kicked off again at this point once the connection is restored.

Another good resource when planning for off-site client protection is the following chart. This shows the amount of time it would take, at different network speeds, to transmit various amounts of data:

Data size	Network speed 1 Gbps	Network speed 100 Mbps	Network speed 32 Mbps	Network speed 8 Mbps	Network speed 2 Mbps	Network speed 512 Kbps
1 GB	less than 1 minute	less than 1 hour	less than 1 hour	less than 1 hour	1.5	6
50 GB	less than 10 minutes	1.5 hour	5	18	71	284
200 GB	less than 36 minutes	6 hours	18	71	284	1137
500 GB	less than 1.5 hours	15	45	178	711	2844

All values in this chart are in hours except where specified.

This chart gives you an idea of what you can expect in regards to performance over certain speeds when protecting clients over a WAN with DPM.

You can view this chart on TechNet along with more information at http://technet.microsoft.com/en-us/library/ff399619.aspx.

There has been much concern about protecting clients over slow WAN links and how to improve this and make it work. Some options are:

- On-the-wire compression
- Bandwidth throttling
- WAN optimization technology (technologies such as DPM acceleration by Riverbed have been tested to help improve the DPM traffic over slow WAN links)

On-the-wire compression in DPM reduces the size of data being transferred during replica creation and synchronization, although it does increase the CPU's load on the DPM server and the client computer that is being protected. On-the-wire compression is enabled at the protected client level. To enable this you need to take the following steps:

1. In DPM Administrator Console, click on **Protection** on the navigation bar.
2. In the **Actions** pane, click on **Optimize performance**.
3. On the **Network** tab, select **Enable on-the-wire compression**.
4. To apply your changes, click on **OK**.

On-the-wire compression can also be turned on via PowerShell, meaning that it can be scripted. This script to turn this on can be found at `http://www.scdpmonline.org/enable-on-the-wire-compression.aspx`.

Bandwidth throttling limits the amount of network bandwidth that DPM can use to create and synchronize replicas. Throttling can be used to make sure DPM does not eat up bandwidth on a network. It is enabled at the agent level and can be set to specific hours such as work hours and non-work hours. To enable throttling, perform the following steps:

1. In DPM Administrator Console, click on **Management** on the navigation bar.
2. Click on the **Agents** tab.
3. In the **Display** pane, select a server.
4. In the **Actions** pane, click on **Throttle computer**.
5. Click on **Enable network bandwidth usage**.

> Throttling is enabled on an agent-by-agent basis. There is no way in DPM or in the DPM Management Shell to enable throttling on multiple agents at once, which can mean a huge task if you need to enable throttling on hundreds or even thousands of DPM clients. However, there is a way to enable throttling on multiple agents at once. This process can be found at `http://www.buchatech.com/2012/07/how-to-enable-throttling-on-multiple-agents-in-dpm/`. Note that this is not officially supported by Microsoft.

Note that bandwidth throttling will not work over a DirectAccess connection due to a limitation in DirectAccess.

Riverbed can give LAN-like performance for protecting clients over a slow link WAN connection through its Steelhead appliance and software-based Steelhead that runs on the client computer. Riverbed addresses bandwidth constraints and the combined effects of latency and protocol inefficiencies through its **Riverbed Optimization System (RiOS)** technology. Riverbed has verified the following through DPM acceleration tests:

- 14 times faster replica recovery operations
- 41 times faster end user recovery operations
- 99 percent reduction in bandwidth utilization

For more information about Riverbed's DPM `http://www.riverbed.com/assets/media/documents/briefs/PerformanceBrief-Riverbed-MS-DPM.pdf`.

As you can see from this section, the two biggest challenges when protecting off-site clients are having a direct connection such as VPN and having good WAN speeds.

The best way to overcome these challenges are to ensure you have a good solid VPN solution in place (or use technology such as DirectAccess) and to meet the minimum WAN speed requirements.

Configuring DPM and Active Directory for end user protection

DPM 2012 client backup consists of backing up desktops and laptops. As a DPM administrator, you can configure the client and control what is backed up. You also have the option of letting the end users control their own backup.

The DPM client utilizes the Previous Versions feature that first appeared in Windows Vista. DPM creates a local copy of protected data and a remote copy on the DPM server. DPM can protect both 32 and 64-bit client computers. The following operating systems are supported by DPM client protection:

- Windows XP SP2 or later
- Windows Vista
- Windows 7
- Windows 8

Following are the step-by-step instructions to configure Active Directory and enable end-user recovery for DPM. There are two sets of steps, one for configuring Active Directory automatically and one for configuring it manually.

1. Log onto the DPM server with a domain account that has domain admin and schema admin privileges.
2. Open the DPM Administrator Console, go to the **Action** menu and click on **Options**.
3. Click on the **End-user Recovery** tab.

Note that the **Enable end-user recovery** box is grayed out, so you cannot check it.

4. Click on the **Configure Active Directory** button.

5. Select **Use current credentials** or **Enter credentials** and enter an account that has domain admin and schema admin privileges.

Configure Active Directory

Enter the credentials of a user with permission to update the Active Directory Schema.

○ Use current credentials

◉ Enter credentials

User name:

administrator

Password:

●●●●●●●●●|

Domain:

BUCHATECH

OK   Cancel

6. An informational alert will pop up letting you know your Active Directory is about to be extended. Click on **Yes** to continue.

Active Directory Configuration for Data Protection Manager   ✕

? This package will configure your Active Directory to support end-user recovery for Data Protection Manager. Do you want to continue?

Yes   No

7. Another informational alert will pop up letting you know the update may take some time. Click on **OK** to continue.

8. Once the configurations are complete, another window will pop up letting you know the update of Active Directory was successful. Click on **OK**.

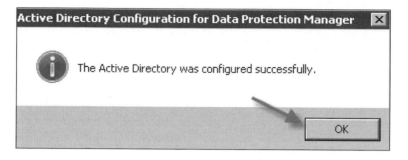

You will then go back to the DPM **Options** window on the **End-user Recovery** tab.

You will notice the **Enable end-user recovery** checkbox is now available to be checked.

9. Check the **Enable end-user recovery** checkbox and click on **OK**.

10. Another window will pop up, warning you that the changes do not take effect until after the next successful sync of your protection groups. Click on **OK**. Your DPM is now configured for end-user recovery.

Note that an error may pop up if your account does not have the proper permissions or the domain controller cannot be contacted.

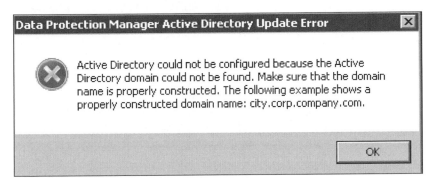

If this error comes up, click on **OK** and follow the next series of steps, which will will guide you through manually extending the Active Directory schema on the domain controller.

Manually preparing Active Directory for DPM

Following are the manual steps to configure Active Directory and enable end-user recovery for DPM:

1. Log onto your domain controller.

2. Click on **Start** and type in the path to your DPM folder on your DPM server, for example `\\DPMSERVERNAME\c$\program files\Microsoft DPM\ DPM\End User Recovery\`.

3. Double-click on the `DPMADSchemaExtension.exe` file, as shown in the following screenshot:

4. An informational alert will pop up letting you know your Active Directory is about to be extended for DPM end-user recovery. Click on **Yes** to continue.

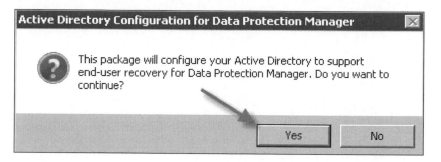

5. In the subsequent window, enter your domain name and click on **OK**.

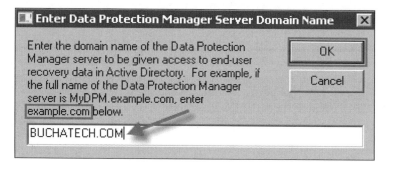

> Note that the actual domain name should be entered, not a subdomain. For example, do not enter BUCHDPM. BUCHATECH.com enter BUCHATECH.com only.

6. Leave the field blank as shown in the following screenshot and click on **OK**.

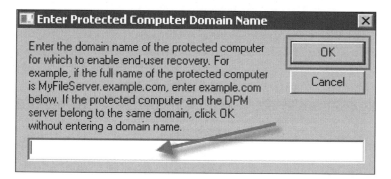

Note that you can leave this field blank as long as the DPM server and the domain controller are in the same domain. If you are on a separate domain you will need to enter the domain name that the protected servers live on. For example, only enter BUCHATECH.com.

7. Another informational alert will pop up, letting you know the update may take some time. Click on **OK** to continue.

    The window goes away and you won't see anything for a moment. All of a sudden a new window will pop up to notify that the Active Directory was successfully configured.

8. Now go back to the DPM server and open the DPM Administrator Console.

9. Go to the **Action** menu and click on **Options**.

10. Click on the **End-user Recovery** tab.

11. You will notice the **Enable end-user recovery** checkbox is now available to be checked.

12. Check **Enable end-user recovery** and click on **OK**.

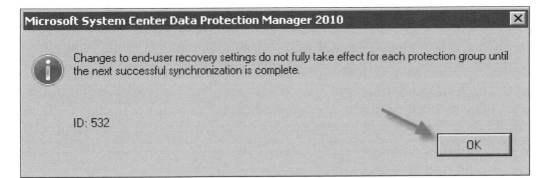

Now your DPM is configured for end-user recovery.

Note that the DPMADSchemaExtension tool makes the following changes to your Active Directory schema to support the following tasks for end-user recovery:

- Extends the schema
- Creates a container (MS-ShareMapConfiguration)
- Grants the DPM server permissions to change the contents of the container
- Adds mappings between source shares and shares on the replicas

Installing the agent automatically and manually on a client computer

In Data Protection Manager 2012, there are two ways to install the DPM agent on client computers. The first option is to automatic installation through the DPM Administrator Console and the second is a manual installation. There is also an option to script the install if you have a large amount of clients that you need to install the DPM agent on.

The agent can be installed on computers in the same domain as DPM, in a workgroup or even an untrusted domain. For more information on using DPM in workgroups or untrusted domains refer to *Chapter 10, Workgroups and Untrusted Domains*. In this section, we will walk through the steps to install the DPM agent automatically and manually.

Automatic install

Let's look at the steps for installing the DPM client on a client computer:

1. Go to the DPM server and open DPM Administrator Console.
2. Click on the **Management** tab on the navigation bar.
3. Now click on the **Agents** tab.
4. On the **Actions** pane, click on **Install**.
5. Now the **Protection Agent Install Wizard** window should pop up. Choose **Install agents**, and then click on **Next**.
6. Select the computer you want to protect from the list and click on **Add**. Click on **Next** to continue.

The computers listed are in the same domain as the DPM server. To add a computer from a different domain, type the fully qualified domain name. For example: machinename.domain.contoso.com

Computer name:

LANTERNVIRT.buchatech.com

Computer	Domain
BUCHEXCH	buchatech.com
BUCHISA	buchatech.com
BUCHSCE	buchatech.com
LANTERNVIRT	buchatech.com

Selected computers:

Computer	Domain

Add >

< Remove

Click Advanced to install an earlier version of the protection agent.

Advanced...

7. Enter a domain account and click on **Next**.

Note that this does not have to be the administrator account. The account that is used does need to have permission to install a Windows service. This can be done by giving the user local administrative access.

Please specify username and domain for a domain account th which you wish to install agents.
DPM uses the credentials to install the protection agents.

User name:

administrator

Password:

•••••••

Domain:

buchatech.com

8. Chose to restart manually later and click on **Next**.

You might need to restart the protected computer after installing the protection agent on a Windows Server 2003 or Windows XP operating system.

DPM will automatically detect whether a restart is required. If a restart is required, DPM can restart all protected computers after the protection agent installation is completed, or you can manually restart the computers at a later time.

Do you want DPM to restart the selected computers?

○ Yes. Restart the selected computers after installing the protection agents (if required).

◉ No. I will restart the selected computers later.

Note that after a DPM agent is installed the **volume filter** needs to be loaded. This is used by DPM to track and transfer block-level changes from the protected computer to the DPM server. The volume filter is not loaded until the protected computer is restarted after a DPM agent installation.

9. Click on **Install** to start the actual installation.

Tasks	
Task ▽	Results
Install protection agent on LANTERNVIRT.buchatech.com	Performing: 54%

You will see a **Success** or **Failure** status when the installation is complete, as shown in the following screenshot:

Tasks	
Task ▽	Results
Install protection agent on LANTERNVIRT.buchatech.com	Success

Manual install

To install the DPM agent manually on a client computer follow these steps:

1. On the client computer, access the drive of the DPM server via UNC or mapped drive.

2. Navigate to `\\DPMSERVERNAME\%systemdrive%\Program Files\Microsoft System Center 2012\DPM\DPM\ProtectionAgents\RA\4.0.1908.0\amd64`.

3. Launch `DpmAgentInstaller.exe` (32-bit) or `DPMAgentInstaller_amd64.exe` (64-bit).

 Note that the DPM agent can be installed in silent mode by running the installer from a command prompt with the following command switch: `DpmAgentInstaller.exe /q`

The DPM agent is now installed on the client computer, but still needs configuring. You will need to tell the DPM agent what DPM server to use and then attach the protected client on the DPM server.

Follow these steps to point the DPM agent to the DPM server:

1. On the client computer open an elevated command prompt.

2. Navigate to `%systemdrive%\Program Files\Microsoft Data Protection Manager\DPM\bin\`.

3. Run the `SetDpmServer.exe - dpmServerName YOURDPMSERVERNAMEHERE` command.

Running the previous command will also set the appropriate firewall rule in the Windows firewall to allow DPM communication to and from the DPM server.

Follow these steps to attach the protected client to the DPM server:

1. On the DPM server open up the DPM Management Shell.

2. Run the following `Attach-ProductionServer.ps1` file and you will be prompted for the following:

    ○ DPM server name (this is your DPM server)

    ○ Production server name (this is your client computer)

Scripted install

When the need arises to install the DPM client on a large amount of computers there is a way to script this out, so you only have to run it one time.

1. Create a list of the computers that you need to install the DPM agent on in a file called `computer_list.txt`.

2. Place this file in the `Bin` folder on your DPM server at `\\DPMSERVERNAME\%systemdrive%$\Program Files\Microsoft System Center 2012\DPM\DPM\bin`.

3. Copy the following script and place in a `DPMAGENTINSTALLSCRIPT.PS1` file. Give it a name such as `DPMAGENTINSTALLSCRIPT.PS1`.

```
---BEGIN DPM AGENT INSTALL SCRIPT---
param([string] $DPMServerName, [string] $PSFileList)

if(!$args[0])

{
    if(!$DPMServerName)
    {
        $DPMServerName = read-host "DPMServer:"
    }
}

    if(!$PSFileList)
    {
        $PSFileList = read-host "PSFileList:"
    }

    $UserName =  read-host "UserName:"
    $Pwd = read-host "Password:"
    $Domain = read-host "Domain:"

type $PSFileList | foreach -process {
    if (!$_.Equals(""))
    {
        .\Attach-ProductionServer.ps1 -DPMServerName
$DPMServerName -PSName $_ -Username $UserName -Password $Pwd
-domain $Domain

    }
}
---END DPM AGENT INSTALL SCRIPT---
```

4. Open the DPM Management Shell and run the `.PS1` script file you just created.

Now you should be able to go to the DPM console and see the computers the script installed the DPM agent on. There is one more way to deploy the DPM agent on client computers. You can use Microsoft System Center Configuration Manager (SCCM) to install and configure the DPM protection agent. Deploying software through SCCM is however outside of the scope of this chapter so we will not be covering these steps. To learn more about deploying software through SCCM refer to *Chapter 3, DPM Server Management Tasks,* or visit `http://technet.microsoft.com/en-us/library/gg699393.aspx`.

Performing image-level backups of client computers with DPM

DPM was designed to protect client data but not the entire machine. This means that DPM cannot get an image-level backup or system state backup. DPM, does a great job of protecting client data but there still is a real need in some environments to protect the client's computer as a whole. This is a need that comes up in the DPM community time and time again.

DPM 2007, DPM 2010, and DPM 2012 are not able to protect client's system state or image-level backups. In this section of the chapter, we are going to cover a workaround that will give you a complete image of a client's PC.

> Note that the workaround described in this chapter is not an officially supported solution for protecting entire client computers. What this means is the workaround does work but Microsoft will not give you support on this, if issues arise.

For Microsoft Windows XP clients, you can back up the system state of the machines to a network share or folder, and then have DPM pick it up from there.

Microsoft Windows Vista and Microsoft Windows 7 do not have a system state backup option, but they do have the **Complete PC Back up** tool. This provides an image of the computer, achieving a similar goal to system state. You can schedule to run the Complete PC Back up out to a folder or network share and then let DPM pick it up from there.

Again this solution is a workaround for when you need complete protection of your client computers with DPM.

Follow these steps to set this up on Windows 7:

1. Go to **Start | Control Panel | Backup and Restore**.

 Note that Windows backup has not been set up yet.

2. Click on **Set up backup**. The Windows Backup wizard will start. This can take a while to open so be patient here.
3. Once it opens, go ahead and click on the **Save on a network** button.

4. Put in your network share information and the credentials for this share. We recommend you create a central share somewhere, and have DPM pick up all the PC's backups from this same location all at once.

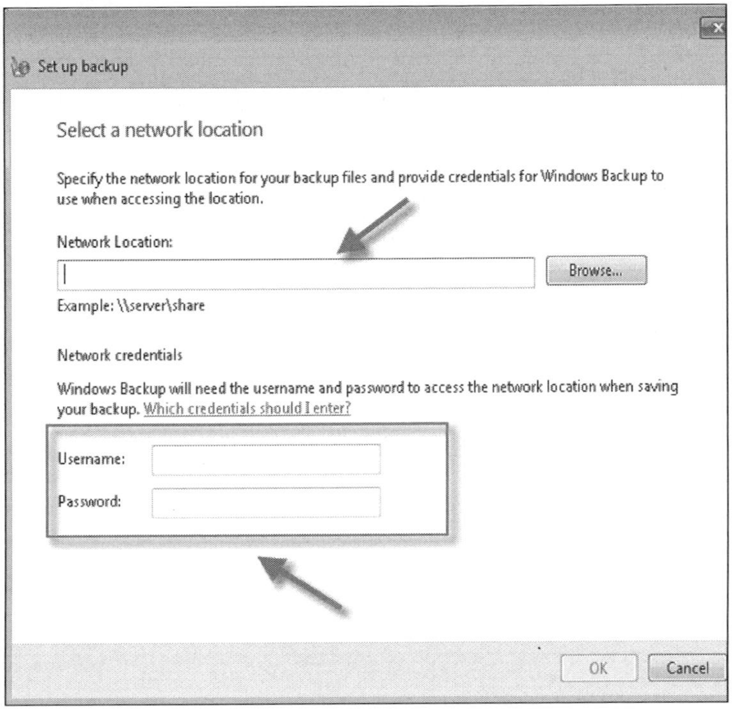

It will validate the share exists. If it is not set up yet you will get an error as shown in the following screenshot:

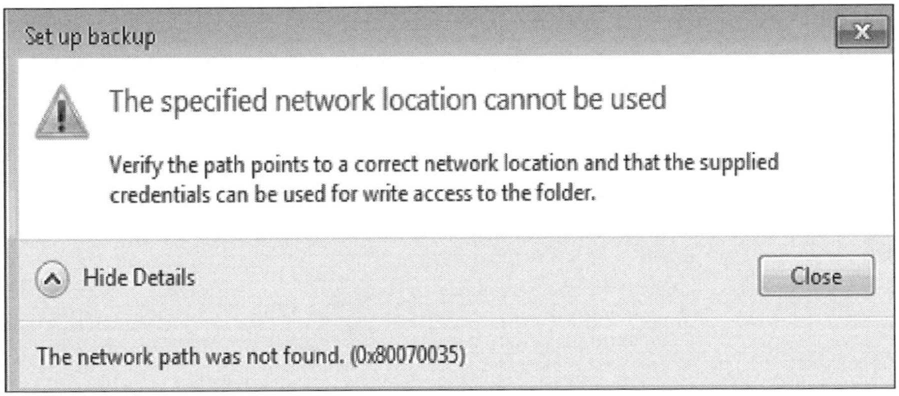

5. Once your share is validated it will pop you back to the previous window and you will see your share listed as **Backup Destination**. You need to select it and click on the **Next** button.

> Select where you want to save your backup
>
> We recommend that you save your backup on an external hard drive. Guidelines for choosing a backup destination
>
> Save backup on:
>
> | Backup Destination | Free Space | Total Size |
> | --- | --- | --- |
> | \\ \te re\ | 319.78 GB | 465.76 GB |
>
> Refresh   Save on a network...

6. Now you can choose what to backup. **Let me choose** and select system image along with any extra drives that need protecting. The system image is what is needed for a complete image of your computer. Make your selection and click on **Next**.

> What do you want to back up?
>
> ○ Let Windows choose (recommended)
>
> Windows will back up data files saved in libraries, on the desktop, and in default Windows folders. Windows will also create a system image, which can be used to restore your computer if it stops working. These items will be backed up on a regular schedule. How does Windows choose what files to back up?
>
> ⦿ Let me choose
>
> You can select libraries and folders and whether to include a system image in the backup. The items you choose will be backed up on a regular schedule.
>
> Next   Cancel

7. The following screenshot shows you what is being backed up. Click on **Change schedule** in the **Schedule** section to set when you want your backup to run.

Review your backup settings

Backup Location: \\buchsrv1\techshare\

Backup Summary:

Items	Included in backup	
🧑 All users	Default Windows folders and lo...	
🖥 System image	Included	

Schedule: Every Sunday at 7:00 PM <u>Change schedule</u>

⚠ A system repair disc might be required to restore a system image. <u>More information</u>
Only one system image per computer can be kept at the backup location. <u>More information</u>

                                              [Save settings and run backup]   [Cancel]

---

8. Click on **Save settings and run backup** when you are ready to complete the configuration.

9. Now you will see that the Windows backup on the client machine is configured and ready to go. You can come back in here and modify settings as needed in the future.

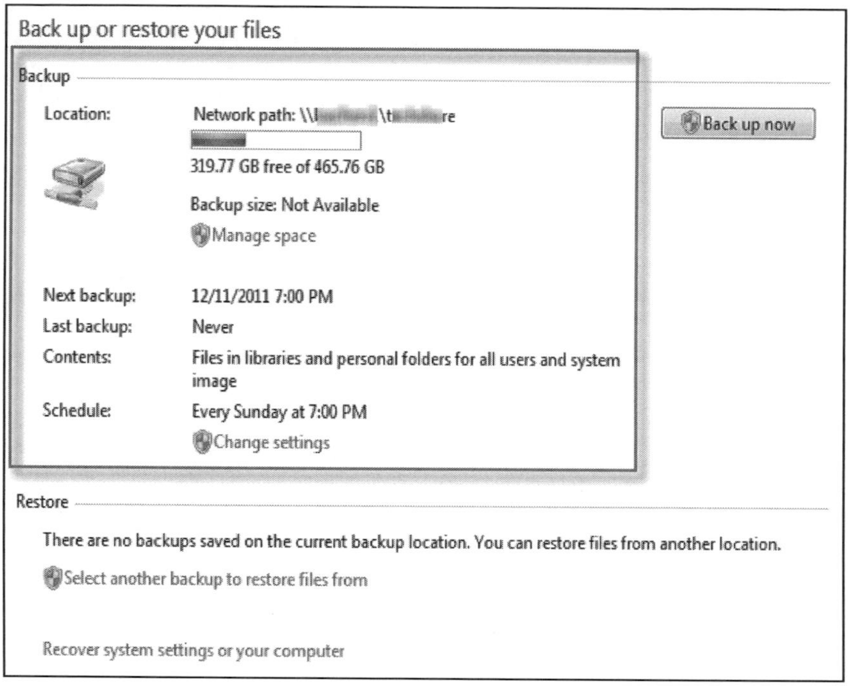

In your share, this is what the backup data will look like. The Complete PC Backup data will be in a `WindowsImageBackup` folder, just like BMR for servers. If you included data in your backup, it will be the computer name and the Windows backup icon, as shown in the following screenshot:

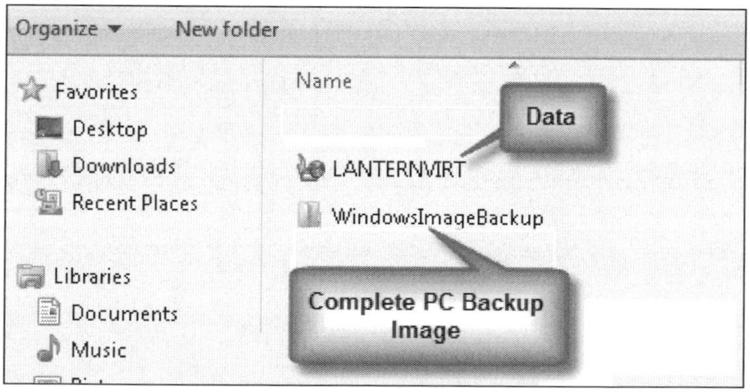

Now go to DPM and configure it to protect the share that you are sending all of these Complete PC Back up images to. It is recommended that you organize this share with some type of naming schema and a folder for each client; for example; your share is called `PC backups` and has folders inside called `client 1`, `client 2`, and `client 3`. Then when you go to setup your right image of `client 1`, you direct it to that share in the `client 1` folder. This will help locate the Complete PC Back up image data for the client you need when you go to restore the Complete PC Back up image of that client from DPM.

Again this is not what administrators really want from a solution because it is not 100 percent centralized. It means you have to initially go to each client and set it up; you also will have to troubleshoot on the clients if the backups start to fail. However, it does get the job done and is a reliable workaround, especially since backing up the complete PC/system state directly from DPM is not possible.

Other resources for DPM client protection

There is more to DPM client protection. There are some topics and tasks around DPM client protection that administrators want to perform, but the "how to" articles on how to do them are hard to find. We have compiled a list of these items here. We will provide a summary and reference links to learn more about the item. If one of the items is something you need to configure in your DPM environment, just visit the link for complete steps.

Setting size restrictions on client protection

This blog post shows how you can set or remove disk quotas for protected client computers that are protected by DPM:

```
http://blogs.technet.com/b/dpm/archive/2011/05/02/a-script-to-set-or-
remove-disk-quotas-for-protected-client-computers-in-system-center-
data-protection-manager.aspx
```

Allow non-admin users to perform end user recovery of DPM protected data

There is a well-known problem with DPM client protection. Non-administrator users on client computers cannot recover data on their own. In DPM 2012 this is still an issue. This link describes the process to fix this issue on the client computer:

```
http://blogs.technet.com/b/dpm/archive/2011/05/10/how-to-configure-
the-dpm-client-to-allow-non-admin-users-to-perform-end-user-recovery-
of-dpm-protected-data.aspx
```

Client Auto Deployment Management pack

This link describes how to automate the deployment and protection of laptop computers by using System Center Operations Manager (SCOM) and System Center Configuration Manager (SCCM):

```
http://technet.microsoft.com/en-us/library/hh758054.aspx
```

Summary

In this chapter, we dove into client protection with DPM. You should have a better idea of how and what to plan for when it comes to backing up end users, planning for off-site protection and the challenges that come along with that, various ways of installing the DPM agent, and client image-level backup. In the next chapter, we are going to learn about protecting computers in workgroups and untrusted domains using DPM.

10
Workgroups and Untrusted Domains

In this day and age of technology, computing resources often cross many boundaries. Organizations tend to have multiple domains and a need for some computers or servers to be in a workgroup. One of the requirements of a DPM server is that it is a member of a domain. With computers expanding beyond the domain, DPM is a member where there is an ever growing need to protect services and it has the ability to protect computers outside of its borders. There is more than one way to accomplish this with DPM.

In this chapter, we will the cover protection of computers in workgroups and untrusted domains using DPM. There are several items to consider when protecting outside of DPM's domain and configuring to set this up. We will review these items in this chapter along with what is supported and not supported. Here are more details of what we cover in this chapter:

- Supported and not supported workgroup/untrusted domain protection
- Using certificate-based authentication with the DPM protection
- Setting up and working with workgroup protection in DPM
- Protection across trusted domains
- How to configure and protect machines in workgroups and untrusted domains
- Protecting domain controllers in untrusted domain
- Protection in DMZ
- Troubleshooting common issues with protection of workgroups and untrusted domains

Supported and not supported workgroup/ untrusted domain protection

There is often discussion in the DPM community about what can and cannot be protected by DPM when in a workgroup or untrusted domain. This list has not changed much since older versions of DPM. To kick off this chapter, we first need to understand what are the limitations.

The following is the list of currently supported protection in workgroups/untrusted domains with DPM 2012 (this list is maintained at `http://technet.microsoft.com/en-us/library/hh757801.aspx`):

Workload	Workgroup	Untrusted domain
Files – Basic – All server and client SKUs	Supported	Not supported
Files – Clustering	Not applicable	Not supported
System State – Windows Server 2003, Windows Server 2008, Windows 2008 R2	Supported	Supported
SQL Server– Basic – SQL Server 2000, SQL Server 2005, SQL Server 2008	Supported	Supported
SQL Server - Mirroring	Not supported	Not supported
SQL Server - Clustering	Not applicable	Not supported
Hyper-V – Basic – Windows Server 2008, Windows 2008 R2	Supported	Supported
Hyper-V – Clustering	Not applicable	Not supported
Hyper-V – Cluster Shared Volume	Not applicable	Not supported
Hyper-V – Clustering	Not applicable	Not supported
Hyper-V – Cluster Shared Volume	Not applicable	Not supported
Exchange – Basic – Exchange Server 2003, Exchange Server 2007, Exchange Server 2010	Not applicable	Supported
Exchange Server – Clustering	Not applicable	Not supported
Exchange Server – CCR	Not applicable	Not supported
Exchange Server – LCR	Not applicable	Supported
Exchange Server – SCR	Not applicable	Not supported
Exchange Server – DAG	Not applicable	Not supported
Microsoft SharePoint Server	Not supported	Not supported
Laptop and desktop computers	Not supported	Not supported

Workload	Workgroup	Untrusted domain
Bare Metal Recovery	Not supported	Not supported
End User Recovery	Not supported	Not supported
Disaster Protection	Supported, if using certificate-based	Supported, if using certificate-based

Using certificate-based authentication with the DPM protection

DPM has the ability to authenticate with computers in workgroups or untrusted domains using certificates; this functionality is new to DPM 2012. Before CBA was introduced, the DPM administrator had to depend on local accounts to protect workgroup servers. CBA is used for organizations that have policies against creating local user accounts. Let's look at some background information of certificate protection in DPM before we cover setting this up.

DPM certificate protection prerequisites are:

- .Net 3.5 SP1 on the protected computer
- Each machine (virtual machines included) must have their own certificate

Certificate requirements are:

- X.509 v3 certificates
- Enhance Key Usage should have client authentication and server authentication
- Key length should be at least 1024 bits
- Key type should be exchange
- System Center 2012 — DPM does not support self-signed certificates

DPM supports protecting the following workloads when using certificates in untrusted domains:

- SQL Server
- File server
- Hyper-V

DPM does not support protecting the following when using certificates in untrusted domains:

- DPM
- Exchange server
- Client computers
- SharePoint server
- Bare Metal Recovery
- System state
- Primary DPM server and secondary DPM protection

The following are the steps for setting up certificate authentication with DPM:

1. You will need an internal Certificate Authority setup to issue the certificates. A guide on setting up a Certificate Authority on Windows Server 2008 R2 can be found at `http://www.buchatech.com/2010/07/setup-configure-a-certificate-authority-on-windows-server-2008/`.

2. Request a certificate from your CA for the DPM server.

3. Install the certificate on the DPM server. This should be imported into the local computer's `Personal` store on the DPM server.

4. You need to get the thumbprint of the certificate. To do this, go to the certificate in the `Local Computer\Personal\certificates` store on the DPM server. Double-click on the certificate and select the **Details** tab and scroll down to the thumbprint. Select the thumbprint and press *Ctrl + C* to copy it. Copy the thumbprint to a safe location.

5. Run `Set-DPMCredentials` on the DPM server to generate the metadata file named `CertificateConfiguration_<DPM SERVER FQDN>.bin`. This file will be used when installing the DPM agent on computers in untrusted domains and workgroups. This metadata file will be placed in `%systemdrive%:\CertMetaData\` on the DPM server by default.

   The syntax for this command is `Set-DPMCredentials -DPMServerName DPMSERVER.DOMAIN.com -Type Certificate -Action Configure -OutputFilePath %systemdrive%\CertMetaData\ —Thumbprint "ch644d9dh1c801ab40d4b31ou0cfcb200a8a1256"`.

6. If you ever lose the metadata file use this syntax to regenerate it. The syntax is `Set-DPMCredentials -DPMServerName DPMSERVER.DOMAIN.com -Type Certificate "-OutputFilePath %systemdrive$\CertMetaData\ -Action Regenerate`.

7. Install the DPM agent on the protected computer.

8. Request a certificate for the protected computer.

9. Install the certificate in the local computer's `Personal\certificate` store.

10. Copy the certificate's thumbprint.

11. Copy the `.bin` file from the DPM server to the protected computer.

12. Open an elevated command prompt and navigate to `C:\Program Files\ Microsoft Data Protection Manager\DPM\bin`.

13. Run `setdpmserver -dpmCredential CertificateConfiguration_ DPM01.contoso.com.bin -OutputFilePath c:\Temp -Thumbprint <ClientThumbprintWithNoSpaces>`. This will create another metadata `.bin` file and this will need to be copied up to the DPM server in the `system32` directory in Windows.

14. On the DPM server open DPM PowerShell.

15. Run `Attach-ProductionServerWithCertificate.ps1`.

16. You will be prompted for information such as `DPMservername` and `PSCredentials`.

 `PSCredentials` contains the name of the client's `.bin` metadata file you copied up to the DPM server in the `system32` directory in Windows.

That's it, now your protected server in the workgroup or untrusted domain should show up in DPM and you can begin protecting it.

Setting up and working with workgroup protection in DPM

To thoroughly explain how to set up and use the protection for workgroup servers it is important to know how this function actually works and what it consists of.

Local accounts or trusts

There are two ways of protecting production servers that are not members of the same domain as the DPM server itself. You can set up a two-way transitive trust between your domain that your DPM server resides on and the domain that the production server that you want to protect with your DPM server resides on.

The best way is to use certificate-based authentication since it provide a higher security but in those cases you do not want to create a two-way transitive trust between your domains; you can use a local account that the DPM Agent will use.

DPM agent

The installation of the DPM agent is the same but the configuration will differ from the normal configuration. When configuring the DPM agent to use a local account for its authentication to the DPM server you must use the -isNonDomainServer switch for the command SetDpmServer.exe. The following is the syntax for the SetDpmServer.exe command:

```
SetDpmServer.exe -dpmServerName <serverName> -isNonDomainServer
[-userName <userName> [-productionServerDnsSuffix <DnsSuffix>]] |
[-updatePassword]
```

When using the -isNonDomainServer switch you must also specify the local account that the DPM agent should authenticate with to the DPM server. Depending on your DNS configuration you may also need to use the -productionServerDnsSuffix switch. It is important that the DPM server and the production server can ping each other using their NetBios names.

Protection across trusted domains

Say your company acquires another company. In such a case, the domains are to be trusted; you can protect the production server that resides in the trusted domain just as you would if they were residing within your domain.

The level of trust between the DPM server domain and the production server domain must be a two-way transitive trust. There are some security considerations that must be thought of before you fully trust another domain.

Configuring and protecting machines in workgroups and untrusted domains

There are many reasons why organizations can have more than one domain without a trust between them. When an organization has these types of domain setup, there is sometimes a need to protect computers across them. In this section, we will cover the steps it takes to configure this. We will go over more than what you see in the TechNet steps such as connection and what to do about DNS. The steps to protecting a computer in a non-trusted domain are entailed in the following sections.

Communication

The communication is initialized and this part will cover what and how the communication is made.

Host files

Both the DPM server and the protected server need to communicate. This can be accomplished by creating entries in the local host file on both the DPM server and the protected server. Once this is done you should be able to ping the DPM server from the protected server and ping the protected server from the DPM server. The host file can be found in the `etc` directory in `%systemdrive%\ Windows\ System32\drivers\`.

DNS

To configure DNS perform the following steps:

1. On the DNS server in the DPM domain, create a new forward lookup zone for the domain of the non-trusted domain computer.

2. Allow unsecure updates to it, so that the protected computer is in the non-trusted domain. This is required because the protected computer is not joined to the domain, such that it will not be able to register itself in the DNS when set to allow only secure updates.

> Allowing insecure updates in a DNS zone is a potential security risk so proceed on this with caution. Be sure that you are ok with computers in the non-trusted domain to update DNS. If this is not ok with policy in your environment, consider the host file entry approach.

3. Once the new DNS forward lookup zone is created in DPM's domain DNS, the protected computer will then be able to register its IP address in DNS. This will allow the IP to change when connecting over VPN and DPM will be able to communicate with it.

Firewall

Now you need to adjust the firewall to allow traffic to and from the DPM server as well as to and from the protected computer as follows:

- On the firewall create a rule for allowing all traffic from DPM to VPN and vice versa
- On the firewall allow TCP port 53 from VPN to the DNS server

The following is a list of firewall ports for DPM communication from a DPM 2012 TechNet article available at `http://technet.microsoft.com/en-us/library/hh757794`.

Protocol	Port	Details
DCOM	135/TCP	The DPM control protocol uses DCOM. DPM issues commands to the protection agent by invoking DCOM calls on the agent. The protection agent responds by invoking DCOM calls on the DPM server.
		TCP port 135 is the DCE endpoint resolution point used by DCOM. By default, DCOM assigns ports dynamically from the TCP port range of 1024 through 65535. However, you can configure this range by using Component services.
		Note that for DPM Agent communication you must open the upper ports from 1024 to 65535. To open the ports, perform the following steps: 1. In IIS 7.0 Manager, in the **Connections** pane, click the server-level node in the tree 2. Double-click the FTP Firewall Support icon in the list of features 3. Enter a range of values for the **Data Channel Port Range** option 4. After you enter the port range for your FTP service, in the **Actions** pane, click on **Apply** to save your configuration settings
TCP	5718/TCP	The DPM data channel is based on TCP. Both DPM and the protected computer initiate connections to enable DPM operations.
DNS	53/UDP	Used between DPM and the domain controller, and also between the protected computer and the domain controller, for host name resolution.
Kerberos	88/UDP	Used between DPM and the domain controller, and also between the protected computer and the domain controller, for authentication.
LDAP	389/TCP	Used between DPM and the domain controller for queries.
NetBIOS	137/UDP	Used between DPM and the protected computer, between DPM and the domain controller, and between the protected computer and the domain.

DPM-Agent communication (DCOM) requires that ports between 1024 and 65535 are open. This range of ports will not work in every environment depending on the firewall team's policy. There is a way to adjust these ports if you need to. You can configure a fixed dynamic port range. You can configure the range to something such as from 62000 to 67050. To adjust this follow these steps:

1. On the DPM server, open the registry using the command `regedt32`.

 Be sure to use `regedt32` not `regedit`.

2. Create the following key under `HKEY_LOCAL_MACHINE\Software\Microsoft\Rpc\Internet\`.

3. Create the datatype for the key as follows:

    `Ports REG_MULTI_SZ (PORT RANGE)`

    `PortsInternetAvailable REG_SZ (REG_SZ:Y/N)`

    `UseInternetPorts REG_SZ (REG_SZ:Y/N)`

4. An example would be:

    `Ports: REG_MULTI_SZ: 62000-67050`

    `PortsInternetAvailable: REG_SZ: Y`

    `UseInternetPorts: REG_SZ: Y`

After completing the previous steps you need to restart your DPM server.

VPN

DPM and the protected computer need to be able to communicate as if they are on the same network. This is accomplished using VPN connections, site-to-site VPN, MPLS, or DirectAccess. As always an "Always on" type VPN connection is recommended, the best options for this are the site-to-site VPN or DirectAccess. Once you have your connection set up you can move on to installing and configuring the DPM agent.

For more information on DirectAccess visit the following URL:

`http://technet.microsoft.com/en-us/library/`
`dd637827%28WS.10%29.aspx`

For more information on site-to-site VPN in Windows visit the following URL:

`http://technet.microsoft.com/en-us/library/`
`ff687658%28v=ws.10%29.aspx`

Installing and configuring the DPM agent

Now you need to install and configure the agent on the protected computer before DPM can protect it. The installation is the same as installing the DPM agent on a protected computer in the same domain as the DPM server but configuring the agent is different. The following are the steps for both of them:

1. To install the DPM Agent on a non-domain computer you need to run or copy the agent installer on the protected server. The agent can be found in this path on your DPM server: `%systemdrive%\Program Files\Microsoft System Center 2012\DPM\DPM\ProtectionAgents\RA\4.0.1908.0`.

    The agent will be named as `DPMAgentInstaller_x64.exe` for 64-bit and `DPMAgentInstaller_x86.exe` for 32-bit. The 32-bit agent is contained in the `i386` folder and the 64-bit is contained in the `amd64` folder.

2. Simply run the `.exe` based on your system 32-bit or 64-bit and this will install the DPM agent.

Once the DPM agent is installed on the protected server it needs to be configured. When configuring the DPM agent on a computer in a workgroup or untrusted domain you need to be logged in as someone with local administrator level access. To configure the agent for a workgroup or untrusted domain computer follow these steps:

1. Open an elevated command prompt, and navigate to `installation drive>\Program Files\Microsoft Data Protection Manager\DPM\bin`.

2. Run `SetDPMServer.exe -DPMServerName <DPMServerName> -IsNonDomainServer -UserName <NewUserName>`.

3. You will be prompted for a password for the user account as shown in the previous syntax. Enter a password and press *Enter*.

The user account you use when configuring the protected agent has to be unique. This means that the user account with the same name cannot be used on another protected server. DPM does not like this and you will run into errors.

There are also some important notes to take regarding when passwords expires.

 If allowed by policy in your environment, it is recommended to set the password of the user account being used by DPM on the protected server to never expire. If the password expires, it will need to be reset on the protected server and DPM. A blog on doing this can be found at `http://www.buchatech.com/2012/07/dpm-failed-to-communicate-with-the-protection-agent/`.

If you look at the membership of the user account that was created, you will notice that it is a member of the following groups. It is required for that user account to be a member of these groups:

Member of:
- Distributed COM Users
- DPMRADCOMTrustedMachines
- DPMRADmTrustedMachines

These groups typically have the DPM server's computer account in them. Because we are in a workgroup or an untrusted domain the DPM server's computer account is replaced with the user account we used when configuring the DPM agent. DPM uses this account and permissions of these groups for managing access to protected servers. The following a further explanation of each of these groups:

- `DPMRADCOMTrustedMachines`: This specifies the group with the DPM server's machine account as the only member

- `DPMRADmTrustedMachines`: This specifies the group with the DPM server's machine account as the only member

- `Distributed COM Users`: This specifies the group containing the DPM server's machine account

Now we need to attach the DPM Agent on the DPM server. To set this up follow these steps:

1. Go to your DPM server and launch the DPM Administrator Console.

2. Click on the **Management** bar.

3. Click on **Agents** and launch the agent install.

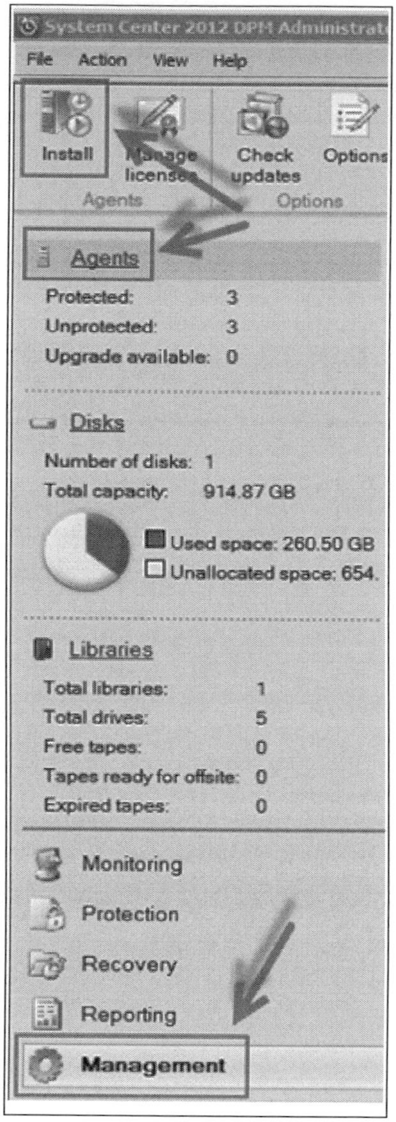

4. Select **Computer in a workgroup or untrusted domain** and click on **Next**.

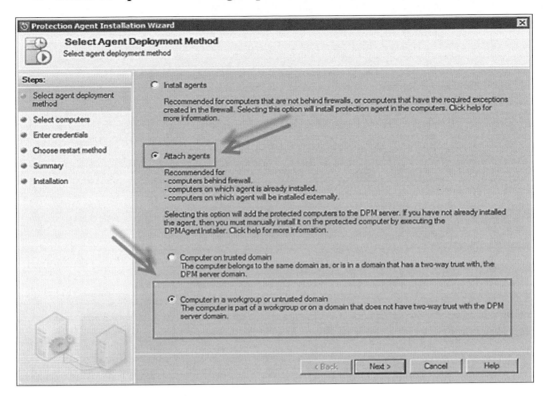

5. Put in the computer name, input the user account, and the password (remember this is the same user account that you provided when configuring the DPM Agent on the protected computer earlier). Click on the **Add** button, and then click on **Next**.

![Protection Agent Installation Wizard - Select Computers dialog. To add a computer not joined to any domain or in a non-trusted domain, type the computer name or the fully qualified domain name and the local user credentials that were specified after DPM agent installation on the computer. Computer name: ProctedServer.otherdomain.com, Username: newuser, Password field filled. Add > and < Remove buttons, Selected computers: Computer. Buttons: < Back, Next >, Cancel, Help.]

6. Review the **Summary** screen, and then click on **Attach**.

7. Once it's finished, click on **Close**.

That's it. Now your DPM should start protecting your computer in the workgroup or untrusted domain.

You can use `Attach-NonDomainServer.ps1` as an alternative method of attaching the DPM agent. The syntax for this would be as follows:
```
Attach-NonDomainServer.ps1 -DPMServername [Name of DPM
server] -PSName [Protected computer] -Username [username]
-Password [Password]]
```

Protecting the domain controller in an untrusted domain

Protecting domain controller is critical regardless of whether this is in the same domain or an untrusted domain. DPM can protect a domain controller in an untrusted domain. However there are some limitations. We will cover these limitations here as well as looking at what is possible.

First of all, as mentioned earlier in this chapter under the *Supported and not supported workgroup/untrusted domain protection* section, Bare Metal Recovery is not supported. The good news is that system state protection is available and this is enough to protect the backing up of your domain controller in an untrusted domain. When backing up the system state of a domain controller with DPM this is what it protects:

- Active Directory domain services (NTDS)
- The boot files
- The COM+ class registration database
- The registry
- The system volume (SYSVOL)
- Certificate services (only if the server is a CA in addition to being a domain controller)

Restoring from the system state will take longer than Bare Metal Recovery to get the server back up and running, but it has been proven to work every time. To set up protection of a domain controller in an untrusted domain, follow the steps under the *Configuring and protecting machines in workgroups and untrusted domains* section in this chapter. For more detail on protecting domain controllers with DPM, refer to *Chapter 5, Workload Protection*.

Protection in DMZ

Microsoft is very clear on one thing regarding the protection of DMZ servers; it is not supported. You probably think that it should work just the same as the workgroup protection and you are right. So why doesn't Microsoft support it? The answer is the firewall configuration for establishing a protection is far too open for Microsoft to say that they can achieve a fully supported secure scenario. It is a good thing that Microsoft is very clear on this point, and within, Microsoft will solve this issue.

To summarize this, you can protect your DMZ servers with DPM 2012 but it is not supported by Microsoft.

Troubleshooting common issues with protection of workgroups and untrusted domains

When you have set up the protection of a workgroup server, the troubleshooting should follow this troubleshooting line:

- Communication between the production server and the DPM server
- Local Windows logs of the production server
- Local DPM agent logs of the production server
- Local DPM server logs

Summary

You made it through the workgroups and untrusted domains chapter. In this chapter, we looked at what is and is not supported in regards to protecting computers in workgroups and untrusted domains. We also covered using CBA with DPM and how to set this up, configuring protection of computers across workgroups and untrusted domains, protection in the DMZ, and troubleshooting common issues when protecting computers in workgroups and untrusted domains.

In the next chapter, we will dive into DPM disaster recovery scenarios. This will look at recovering DPM when a disaster strikes and what you can do to protect your DPM specifically.

11
Disaster Recovery

DPM 2012 is one of the tools needed to recover your organization's data if a disaster strikes. In this chapter, we will cover what you can do to help your organization prepare for an event that most likely never occurs, and this will also be helpful to test and ensure that we are ready if needed.

In this chapter, we will cover the following topics:

- The purpose of a disaster recovery design
- Planning and implementing DPM chaining
- Planning and implementing cyclic protection
- Off site DPM strategies
- Protecting DPM with third-party software
- Backing up network design

The purpose of a disaster recovery design

We need to ensure in our design of the Data Protection Manager (DPM) solution that we are always able to recover the data that the organization needs; a well-designed solution will ensure that no single event will prevent us from recovering data.

With DPM, the following major parts are needed to ensure that recovery of the organization is possible; in this chapter, we will cover what we can do to protect these parts.

The Active Directory domain

DPM requires Active Directory to recover data. If the Active Directory is lost, the first step is to recover it from a tape, and this procedure is covered later in the *Recovering your organization's data when the only thing left is back up tapes* section.

If the Active Directory is lost and no valid backup is available, recovery can still be performed to alternative servers/locations. Also, major applications like Exchange will stop functioning as all users and computer objects need to be recreated; in short, do not lose your Active Directory.

The Data Protection Manager server

The DPM agents connect to a DPM server; if the backup server is lost, recovering it should be one of the first steps. This will ensure that we do not need to change anything on the backup agents before starting recovery.

If the DPM server is lost and no chaining is used, the agents need to be reconfigured to recover data.

Databases

DPM uses a Microsoft SQL database to keep a track of the backups and where they are stored on disk and tape. This means that we always need to have a valid backup of the SQL database to ensure fast recovery.

Short-term storage

In most cases, DPM creates a backup to disk that is accessible directly from the backup server. Any direct disk storage type can be used, but most designs use the direct-attach storage type to keep price and complexity as low as possible.

If the storage used for short-term backup is lost or corrupted, it is not possible to recover from short-term backup to the agents; we can only recover data from long-term storage (tape) or from a chained DPM server.

Long-term storage

DPM uses tapes for long-term storage; there are other options that are covered later in this chapter.

If both short-term and long-term storage is lost it is not possible to recover data from the DPM server, unless the DPM server is protected by a chained server, so it's very important to move media off site if possible, to avoid that a single event like a flood or a fire can prevent a recovery of the organization's data.

If the storage used for long-term storage is lost or corrupted, the ability to recover from tape is also lost.

If this occurs at the same time, the short-term storage is lost. We need to recover from a chained server (if it exists).

Public Key Infrastructure

DPM can use certificates for authentication and encryption of tape storage. If Public Key Infrastructure is lost, DPM is unable to authenticate agents in workgroup or untrusted domain scenarios, which are using certificates for authentication. So, recovering directly from the server to an agent is not possible without issuing new certificates.

If certificates are being used for tape encryption and are lost with the DPM server, it is not possible to recover data from tape.

Windows Azure passphrase

DPM can use Microsoft Azure cloud as a target for backup. This data is encrypted from the server before moving it to the cloud, and the passphrase is needed to decrypt the data. If the passphrase is lost, and if the DPM server has to be rebuilt, it is not possible to recover data from the Azure cloud.

Recovering your organization's data when the only thing left is backup tapes

If your organization is ever in the situation where everything except for off-site tapes is gone, these will be the first steps needed to be performed with DPM to start recovery:

1. First step is to write-protect the tapes; this is not a software feature but the physical lock on the tapes. This is to ensure that no matter what mistakes are made when trying to recover data, losing the tapes is not the end result.

2. After ensuring that the tapes are safe, we need to establish a new domain controller as DPM requires a working domain to be operational.

The steps provided here are for recovering data in a worst case scenario.

Normally, an organization should always have a domain controller on an off-site location that can be used to save time in the recovery procedure. A local backup on the domain controller or to a removable media will also save time and reduce complexity.

From the hardware point of view, we need a tape library or standalone drive that can read the tapes we need to recover from. So if the tapes were created on LTO-4, we can use an LTO-4, LTO-5 or LTO-6 drive.

We will need a server where we can create a domain controller for a temporary domain and one for the restored production domain. We also need a server where we can attach the tape library or standalone drive, and a network connecting the servers.

After hardware and networking have been sorted out, the next steps needed are as follows:

1. Install a new domain controller. In this example the domain controller is `RecoveryDC01` in the domain `recovery.local`. This domain controller is only used until the production domain controller is restored.

2. Install and configure DHCP on the recovery domain controller; this is needed for Bare Metal Recovery of the production domain controller.

3. Install a new DPM server. In this example the DPM server is `RecoveryDPM01` and is joined to the `recovery.local` domain.

4. After installation of DPM, we need to attach the tape library to the server, and before we add the tapes to the library we need to ensure that the tape is write-protected (this is to ensure that an error won't delete the tapes that are needed for recovery).

5. In the DPM Administrator Console, under the **Management** tab, select **Rescan**; this will scan for new libraries and attach them to the DPM server.

6. After the loader is attached to the DPM server, click on **Inventory** and select the detailed inventory. This will load each tape and read the tape label after the inventory has completed. All tapes with backup data will be shown as **(Imported) Tape Label**.

Slot 3	Tape available	Free	BLY...	-
Slot 4	Tape available	(Imported) Domain Controllers-00000006		
Slot 5	Tape available	(Imported) Domain Controllers-00000005		
Slot 6	Tape available	(Imported) Domain Controllers-00000004		
Slot 7	Tape available	(Imported) Domain Controllers-00000003		
Slot 8	Tape available	(Imported) Domain Controllers-00000002		
Slot 9	Tape available	(Imported) Domain Controllers-00000001		
Slot 10	Tape available	(Imported) Data Protection Manager Config DB-00000001		

Context menu:
- Remove tape (I/E port)
- Identify unknown tape
- View tape contents
- Erase tape
- Mark as cleaning tape
- Mark tape as free
- Recatalog imported tap

7. After inventory, we need to re-catalog imported tapes. So right-click on the tapes and click on **Recatalog imported tape**. The catalog procedure reads the data on the tapes and adds it to the inventory on the **Recovery** section of the DPM interface.

8. We then need to recover the system state on a domain controller to get the domain functional again. If there are multiple domain controllers, recover the one with the majority of the roles on it and use ntdsutil to force the FSMO roles to the recovered domain controller.

If the DNS infrastructure is not being hosted by Active Directory, that infrastructure needs to be operational before the domain will be functional.

9. Recovery needs to be copied to a network folder; in the recovery environment the data can be stored to either the recovery domain controller or the DPM server.

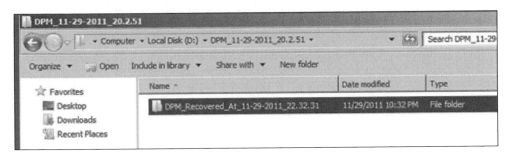

When the recovery is complete, the data will need to be shared.

The data folder, containing the Windows Image Backup files, needs to be shared so that we are able to access them from the Windows 2008 R2 recovery environment.

So, in this example, the `WindowsImageBackup` folder will be in the `DPM_Recovered` folder and that folder needs to be shared.

In this example, the recovered data is restored into `D:\DPM_11-29-2011_20.2.51\` `DPM_Recovered_At_11-29-2011_22.32.31` and that folder contains the `WindowsImageBackup` folder and should be shared. Here, we use `Restored` as a share name.

Bare Metal Recovery is only supported from Windows Server 2008 to Windows Server 2012. There is no support for Windows 2003.

On the server that will be the production domain controller, start up the Windows 2008 R2 DVD and go into the **Repair** option at the installer screen. Note that if 2008 R2 SP1 was installed, ensure that the media used for recovery is slipstreamed with SP1.

Go into **Restore your Computer** from a system image you created earlier and select **Advanced**. This will start the networking and we will get an IP address from the DHCP server on RecoveryDC01.

At the **Re-image Your Computer** prompt, enter the server and path where the share was created, for example, \\recoverydpm01\restore.

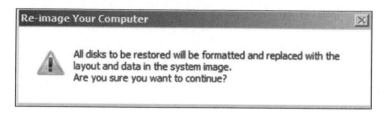

Select the image file you want to recover and start the recovery; after a while the server will restart and we then have a domain controller back up and running.

Getting the domain functional is the first of many steps to get the organization back online. As mentioned at the start of the section, always keep a separate backup of a domain controller to save valuable time for a complete recovery.

Protecting the Data Protection Manager database

Protecting the SQL database is a key feature of DPM. There are a few different scenarios to cover. The first scenario is a single-server installation; we need to add the databases from the locally-installed SQL Server to the protection group.

Adding the database to a protection group will ensure regular backups of the DPM configuration.

We need to ensure that we have both short- and long-term recovery options for the database. This will enable us to recover the database and catalogs in case of short-term storage failure or off-site. If the database is lost we need to catalog long-term storage before a recovery is possible, and backups on short-term storage is not supported for recovery. So always protect the DPM database as it will slow down your recovery time and risk the ability to recover the data from short-term storage. If there is no long-term storage, the database can be recovered using dpmbackup or from a chained DPM server

In this example, we keep the recovery points for **5** days with an hourly backup for the database.

As additional protection, schedule a backup with the dpmbackup.exe tool that is provided by Microsoft. It backs up the DPM database, and creates shadow copies that can be used for backing up replicas.

If you want to create a backup of the local DPM database, use the following command:

```
Dpmbackup.exe -db
```

The previous command creates a backup of the DPM database and places the backup file at `%DPMInstallLocation%\Volumes\ShadowCopy\Database Backups\dpmdb.bak`. This file will be overwritten every time the job runs.

If there is no chained DPM servers or backup to tape, it's recommended to schedule the DPM database, back up daily with Windows Task Scheduler, and after completion, copy the database to another server.

The backup job generates a regular SQL backup file that can be restored from the SQL management tools.

The `Dpmsync.exe` tool can also be used to restore the database, as follows:

```
Dpmsync.exe -restoredb -dbloc C:\dpmdb.bak -instancename dpm01
\msdpm2012eval
```

This will restore the database from the backup file into the local DPM database.

After restoring the database, no matter what method is used, DPM needs to synchronize the database with the replicas.

```
Dpmsync.exe -Sync
```

The `Dpmsync.exe` tool will synchronize the agents and disk replication against the state of the database from the restored database.

Planning and implementing DPM chaining

DPM chaining gives us the ability to let a DPM server protect the data from another DPM server. This can help us move data to a secondary datacenter while still keeping the data locally available for fast recovery. Also, the entire load from the multiple backup is being handled server-to-server, so no additional load is being placed on the servers being protected.

This can also help in protecting agents; if the primary DPM server goes down for a longer period of time then we can switch protection, so that the agents now are being protected from the second DPM server. This will help in limiting the risk of data loss even if we lost one of the DPM servers.

This can also help us get around the recovery point limit of 64 on file-based protection groups.

For the chained DPM server to function, there must be network connectivity from the secondary DPM server to the clients, as this is required if the agents need to fail over. If there is no access, the chaining of DPM servers will not work.

On the primary DPM server, we install the agent on the server(s) we want to protect, we then create a protection group and set up the short and long term recovery goals.

On the secondary DPM server, we then install the backup agent on the first DPM server; we then create a protection group and select the data from the first DPM server we want to protect.

This can continue for as many DPM servers as are necessary; so if we want to have the data located on additional locations, we can add a third DPM server protecting the second, and so on.

This will ensure that data is stored on multiple servers removing the single point of failure but adding a cost of hardware and licensing.

On the primary DPM server, we install the agent on the client we want to protect and set up a protection group; in the following example, we are protecting C: \ and E: \ of a file server:

On the secondary DPM server, we install the agent on the primary DPM server, as we would on any other client.

After installing the agent, it's recommended to set up throttling on the agent; the agent throttling for a DPM server is the same as any other DPM agent. So under **Management | Agents**, right-click on **Computer Name** and check the **Enable network bandwidth usage throttling** checkbox.

In this example, we have limited the DPM-to-DPM communication to 50 Mbps during work hours. This is to ensure that DPM won't put a load on the production network as there isn't a dedicated connection for backup.

On the secondary DPM server, we can then browse the primary DPM server and under **Protected Servers**, we can browse the servers being protected.

On the protection group, set up the protection goals for the secondary DPM server. Protection groups are limited to 64 recovery points for file-based workloads, so if we want to make a recovery point multiple times a day, we limit how long we can keep data in the short-term-based storage pools; when chaining DPM servers we have longer retentions on short-term storage.

Our file server, FS01, is set up to create a recovery point 6 times a day so that we can keep data on the primary DPM server for 10 days without going to tape for recovery.

If we then set up protection from the secondary DPM server for a recovery point once every day, we can get 64 days' history from the secondary DPM server without having to use tape for long-term storage. This will enable us to recover files' recovery points 6 times a day for the first 10 days, and on day 11 to 64 we use a daily recovery point.

If we never want to go to tape, but require recovery options for a whole year, we can set up the primary DPM server with 10 daily recovery points and the secondary with a weekly recovery point kept for 64 weeks. This will enable us to restore files from 6 different recovery points for the last 10 days and once a week for the next 64 weeks.

However, never going to tape with native DPM is something that should be treated with respect. As described earlier, we need our SQL database to keep a track of the recovery points and we need the Active Directory to be able to use DPM.

If we never go to long-term recovery, we can end up in a situation where it will be impossible to recover data if the Active Directory and/or database is lost.

So, back to our items needed to ensure recovery, always keep the DPM database protected and always keep your Active Directory alive; should both fail you need to rely on long-term recovery for rebuilding your organization's data.

One other function of chained DPM servers is the ability to switch protection server. If our file server, FS01, is being protected from DPM01 and all the resources from DPM01 are being protected on DPM02, we can choose to switch protection. So DPM02 will be the DPM server protecting the file server. This is normally used if the primary DPM server goes down for an extended period of time due to hardware errors or other critical events.

Protection Group Member /		Type
⊟ 📄✅ **Protection Group: 2nd** (Total members: 2)		
⊟ 🔵 **Computer: DPM01.internal.systemcenterdemo.dk**		
C:\ on FS01.internal.systemcenterdemo.dk		Volume
E:\ on FS01.internal.systemcenterdemo.dk	📇 Perform consistency check ...	
	📋 Create recovery point...	
	📇 Stop protection of member...	
	📇 Remove inactive protection...	
	📇 Switch disaster protection	
	📇 Modify disk allocation...	
	📇 Resume disk backups...	
	📇 Resume online backups...	
	📇 Resume tape backups...	
	📇 Recovery point status...	

On the secondary DPM server we can select the resources we want to protect directly. Right-click the items and click on **Switch Disaster Protection**.

Protection Group Member /	Type
⊟ 📄⚠ **Protection Group: 2nd** (Total members: 2)	
⊟ 📄 **Computer: FS01.internal.systemcenterdemo.dk(Protection-Switched)**	
C:\	Volume
E:\	Volume

Switching the protection will trigger a consistency check on the resources. This will continue the protection of the resources until the primary DPM server is operational. Remember that the switch protection will use the old recovery objective. So if the secondary DPM server was set to a daily backup for 60 days, it will continue to use that schedule until the objectives for the recovery group are changed.

Moving back to the primary DPM is the same process. Right-click the items in the protection group and click on **Switch Disaster Protection**; this will move the agent protection back to the original DPM server and the secondary server in the chain will continue protecting items from the primary DPM server.

Another use for chained DPM servers is to install the DPM server on smaller remote sites, create local backup, and then add the protected data from the remote site to the DPM server on a larger location.

This will ensure protection of the organization's data and fast recovery as most restores can be handled locally. This will also help reducing the cost of handling tapes, as all tape rotations can be handled centrally, instead of having to rely on non-IT staff to change the tape and store them securely.

A chained DPM server is a cost effective way of ensuring that the organization's data can be spread around multiple locations; so if the main location should suffer a critical failure, we are still able to recover data from a secondary DPM server located on a remote site.

On the chained DPM server it's important to protect the database. This can be done as we would in a single-server DPM solution by creating a protection group and using `sqlcmd`.

Available members		
⊟ 🖧 internal.systemcenterdemo.dk		
⊟ 🖳 DPM02		
⊞ ☐ 🔀 All Shares		
⊟ 🗔 All SQL Servers		
⊞ ☑ (Auto) DPM02\MSDPM2012EVAL		
⊞ ☐ 🖴 All Volumes		
⊞ ☐ 🖳 System Protection		
⊟ 🖳 DPM03		

Selected members	
Selected Members	**Computer**
DPM02\MSDPM2012...	DPM02.internal.syste...
DPM02\MSDPM2012...	DPM02.internal.syste...
DPM02\MSDPM2012...	DPM02.internal.syste...
DPM02\MSDPM2012...	DPM02.internal.syste...
DPM02\MSDPM2012...	DPM02.internal.syste...
DPM02\MSDPM2012...	DPM02.internal.syste...

It is also possible to use the next chained DPM. So on DPM03 we protect the database from DPM02, again we also need a `sqlcmd` backup of the database to ensure that we can always recover the database if needed even if DPM03 is not reachable.

Planning and implementing cyclic protection

DPM cyclic protection uses the same method as the chained DPM server but is limited to the second DPM server, each protecting the other. An example could be:

- FS01 is protected by DPM01 that is then being protected by DPM02
- FS02 is protected by DPM02 that is then being protected by DPM01

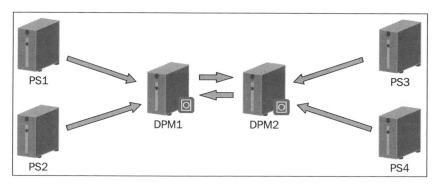

This will distribute the backup load between the two servers and will still enable us to recover the organization's data if one of the DPM servers should fail for any reason.

So on DPM01 we protect the FS01 file server directly, and on DPM02 we protect the FS02 file server directly.

So we now have the servers protecting each other, and again, it's very important that the SQL databases on the DPM server are protected using a protection group and sqlcmd.

Off-site DPM strategies

Off-site DPM servers are often used to remove any single point of failure for your organization's data, so even if a site is lost, it is still possible to recover the data from an off-site location.

The secondary DPM server

Installing a secondary DPM server in a secure remote location that can protect the DPM servers on the primary site is one way of moving data offsite, as all your organization's data will be accessible from this server. It needs to be a site that fulfills your security department's requirements, so a broom closet isn't always the best option.

If there are no secure locations, consider using a substitute location for hosting a provider with a VPN connection between the sites. Again, note that the agents being protected need network connectivity with the secondary DPM server.

If possible, always keep a domain controller on the same site as the off-site DPM server; this will reduce complexity and save time, even if you have to perform a full recovery, as DPM needs a functional domain controller.

In the primary location, we have in our example the file server FS01 that is being protected by the DPM01 DPM server, so the day-to-day backups are handled on the LAN from FS01 to DPM01.

On our off-site location, we have a DPM server OFFSITEDPM01, which is connected to the primary location with a site-to-site VPN connection.

This OFFSITEDPM01 DPM server protects the DPM01 server in the primary location; so if the primary sites fail for some reason, we are still able to recover data from the offsite DPM server.

So the agents on the primary site will use the protecting groups on DPM01 and using the VPN tunnel on the secondary site the OFFSITEDPM01 server will protect DPM01 with DPM chaining.

We can also protect multiple sites / DPM servers with the same OFFSITEDPM01 server but need to pay attention to DPM scale.

If the installation goes beyond DPM scale for one DPM server, we can set up multiple servers on the off-site location.

When all the data is off-site at one location we need to place the tape library there, so that we only need to maintain tape rotation at one location. This can save time and money not having to move the tapes off-site from other locations.

On the primary sites, we can keep the data from 1 to 10 days on the local DPM servers for short-term storage and then protect the data off-site. Then move the data to tape from a central location. This way, should the primary site fail, we still have access to daily backup and long-term storage on tape.

Backing up to the cloud

DPM has always been able to protect data with servers on multiple sites. Moving data to the cloud provides an extra layer of security as the network and storage device is managed by the vendor, so no single event on-site will prevent the ability to recover the data.

For customers who require the data to be moved offsite for security reasons, moving it over a high-speed connection often proves faster and more flexible than having tapes picked up and moved offsite each day.

DPM 2012 SP1 offers an integration with Windows Azure to be used for cloud storage. DPM utilizes the Windows Azure's online backup agent available for Windows Server 2012.

Currently, the Azure Cloud integration supports protection of Hyper-V and file-based workloads, system state, and SQL Server.

Status	Service [Sub-Region]
✓	Windows Azure Online Backup[East US]
✓	Windows Azure Online Backup[North Europe]
✓	Windows Azure Online Backup[Southeast Asia]

When you explore the storage blogs on the Windows Azure portal at http://manage.windowsazure.com, you can see that there are three primary locations for the Online Azure Backup data.

GEO-REPLICATION ON OFF

Secondary Region: europewest

By default the geo-replication of the data is enabled, so we will have our storage data located in two different datacenters.

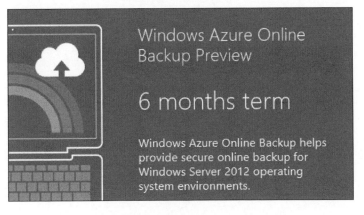

Microsoft provides a 300 GB trial for a period of 6 months to test out the integration with DPM and Windows Server 2012. Pricing is currently unknown, but given the aggressive pricing of other cloud services from Microsoft, we expect a highly competitive pricing model.

To integrate with the Azure Online backup, we need to sign in either with an online trial account or a production account. This username and password is managed through the Azure management portal (`https://manage.windowsazure.com/`).

This integration will enable the option in the console to add cloud as a protection group endpoint.

After connecting the account with the DPM server, a throttle policy can be set. This is to avoid the online backup taking all available bandwidth on the Internet connection. The traffic will be encrypted with SSL on the transport layer.

If DPM needs to recover data from the cloud, there is a requirement for a staging storage. The storage space required needs to be on the DPM server, so if a 50 GB VHD file is being restored from the cloud, we need 50 GB free on the DPM server, thus the storage cannot be shared with the DPM storage.

We can't use the same storage that have been allocated to the DPM short-term storage; so when designing the DPM installation we need to ensure that we have free space outside of the short-term storage pool that can be used for staging when recovering data from the Azure integration.

![Register Server Wizard - Encryption Setting screen]

Register Server Wizard

Encryption Setting
Encryption Setting

Steps:

- Backup Vault
- Proxy Configuration
- Throttling Setting
- Recovery Folder Settings
- Encryption Setting
- Register server for azure backup

Enter a passphrase to encrypt all backups from this server. Note that your existing backups will still be accessible after this change.

- Passphrase must be 16 characters long.
- Use strong password guidelines.
- Do not use recognizable words or phrases.

Enter passphrase (minimum 16 characters)

`•••••••••••••••••••••••••••••••••••••` [Generate passphrase]

Confirm passphrase

`•••••••••••••••••••••••••••••••••••••`

[Copy to clipboard]

⚠ Please make sure to keep a copy of your passphrase in a safe location. If the passphrase is lost or forgotten, customer support will not be able to assist you in recovering access to your backed up data.

Data placed in the Azure cloud is encrypted with a passphrase that is set during installation; this will ensure that your organization's backup stored in the cloud is not accessible for anyone else even if the username/password for the Azure account was used by someone else. If the passphrase is lost it is not possible to recover the data from a rebuild DPM installation, therefore you need to ensure that the passphrase is stored securely in some place safe (or two).

Before the data is encrypted, it is also compressed to save bandwidth and storage costs when moving data to the cloud.

![Create New Protection Group - Select Data Protection Method screen]

Create New Protection Group

Select Data Protection Method
DPM can provide disk and tape based data protection.

Steps:

- Welcome
- Select protection group type
- Select group members
- Select data protection method
- Select short-term goals
- Choose consistency check options
- Summary
- Status

Protection group name: `Cloud Test`

Protection method

Select your protection method.

- ☑ I want short-term protection using: `Disk` ▾
- ☑ I want online protection
- ☐ I want long-term protection using tape

  Protection using tape options are disabled as no tape libraries were detected.

Thanks to the tight integration with the DPM console, we can select our protection group and enable the online protection feature. For online protection to work, the workload should be Hyper-V, SQL, and Windows filesystem. The short-term protection to disk is mandatory, while the long-term protection is optional. Select the drive we want protected in the Azure cloud:

To start the recovery of the data, right-click on the item you want to select and click on **Recover** to start the recovery; the restore will go from Azure cloud to the staging location on the DPM server.

When recovery from the cloud is needed, we select the protected data we want to restore and that will be restored locally to the staging area and to a specified endpoint.

VTL to external drives

DPM does not support external drives / removable medias for long-term storage. For many organizations, handling tape for smaller backup solutions adds an extra layer of cost and complexity.

Cristalink's Firestreamer (`http://www.cristalink.com/fs/`) adds support for using local storage as long-term protection emulating a tape library and storing the data directly in the filesystem.

Using external drives as a target for DPM is a cost effective way of getting data offsite, thus helping small sites protect their data without having to invest in a tape library.

However, I would rather drop a tape from the table than a rotating drive, and there are several vendors that sell rugged external drives that can help negate the oops factor.

If we have five external drives each being used for a weekly backup, we need to format the drives and add them to the Firestreamer.

So in Firestreamer go to **Media**, create, and add a file media. Select **10** media and prefix the barcode with the drive location, and using the external drive as the target, add the size of the drive/media. So if it's a 2 TB drive, create 10 medias at 195,000 MB if the size of the drive formatter is 1.95 TB.

The size of the media is only important if you later move it to removable media and want to ensure that it can be stored on an external USB drive.

Go to **File** and click on **Save as**, and then save the map file on the same drive where the media was created. This will prepare the external drive for the first week's backup.

In DPM we need to lock the library again and perform a full inventory.

⊟ 🗎 **Library: Firestreamer Media Changer (Inventory in progress...)**			
⊞ 🗁 **Drives (In use: 1|Idle: 0)**			
⊟ 🗁 **Slots (Tape available: 9|Empty: 1)**			
Slot 1	Tape available	Free	TCRDQ71R3H1_DISK110000...
Slot 2	Tape available	Free	TCRDQ71R3H1_DISK110000...
Slot 3	Tape available	Free	TCRDQ71R3H1_DISK110000...
Slot 4	Tape available	Free	TCRDQ71R3H1_DISK110000

After the inventory is completed, we can see the tapes available for DPM prefixed with our drive numbe, so that we can find the data again if needed.

Customize Recovery Goal	☒

You can customize the long-term recovery goals for daily, weekly, monthly, or yearly backups. To customize the recovery goals, specify the backup frequency, retention range, number of backup copies, and tape label for each increment of backup to be applied to this protection group.

ⓘ To modify the tape label, click the label text to select it, and then click the label text again to edit it.

Recovery goal 1

☑ Back up every: `1` ⌃⌄ `Weeks` ▾ | Tape Label
Retention range: `4` ⌃⌄ Weeks | External Drives-LT-1Weeks-Copy0
Number of backup copy: `1` ⌃⌄

On our protection group, we create a full copy every week and keep four weeks of history backed up in time. This is an example that will ensure that when we re-use the fifth set of external drives, the retention time is passed and the virtual tapes can be re-used. If you want to keep a longer rotation, retention just needs to be changed to reflect the requirements.

When the weekly protection jobs to tape have completed, we need to prepare the next drive for use with Firestreamer and DPM.

In the DPM Administrator Console, unlock the Firestreamer loader, and then select **Unload All** in **Firestreamer | Actions**. This will remove the media from the virtual loader; if the disk drive is a removable one, use the safely remove hardware and eject media options to prevent disk corruptions when it is being removed from the server.

Repeat the procedure for the next external media.

In Firestreamer go to **Media**, create and add a file media, select `disk + 1` as the barcode prefix and place the files on the external drive. Click on **File | Save as**, to save the media map files.

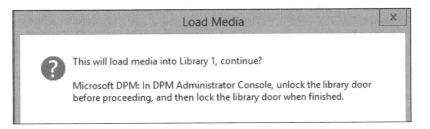

Load the media to end the creation of the media in the Virtual Tape Library. And back in DPM, lock the door and perform a full inventory, and we are ready for the next rotation.

Alternative off-site options

In this chapter, we have covered multiple ways to move the data offsite. There are several hosting companies that provide the offsite DPM server as a service making sure that the hardware and software is operational.

This will make the DPM offsite a service like hosted spam, which is out of the mind and responsibility of the onsite IT staff.

One of these is Microsoft Hosting Partner NVINT (`http://www.nvint.com`) that provides a fully managed hosted DPM solution, helping customers move data offsite into a managed datacenter and helping with recovery test and reporting.

Another option is to use replication to move data from a local VTL box to a remote location, making the replication out of band from the DPM solution. If recovery is needed from a site failure, the DPM server will have to be re-installed and then use the replicated long-term storage as a source for the recovery.

Protecting DPM with third-party software

In the earlier version of DPM, it was a requirement to use third-party software to protect the short-term replica to disk. Since we got to tape integration, we don't have a requirement for using other vendors' software to keep the DPM implantation safe.

However, we can still use agents to protect the configuration database. Another usage is to replicate the short-term storage to a different location, so if an ISCSI target is used and the target supports replication, we can replicate the data in multiple locations without the need for DPM chaining.

It's also important to exclude the `dpmra.exe/csc.exe` process from the antivirus and exclude the `%DPMInstallationFolder%\DPM\XSD` and `TEMP\MTA` directories on the DPM server.

Antivirus products installed on the DPM server must be set to delete and not clean on any files it tries to clean.

 The following article applies to both DPM 2010 and DPM 2012:
`http://technet.microsoft.com/en-us/library/ff399439.aspx`

Backup network design

DPM is able to utilize a dedicated network for backup. This will ensure that the regular production network will not be highly utilized when large protection jobs are running.

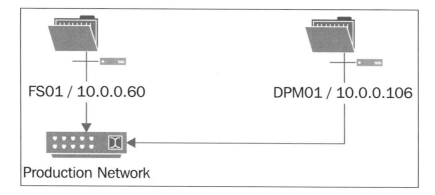

Without a dedicated backup network, user and backup traffic will go through the same network. We can, with DPM throttling, limit how much traffic DPM can utilize to ensure that there is still bandwidth left for users and applications. However, this will slow down the backup and recovery process.

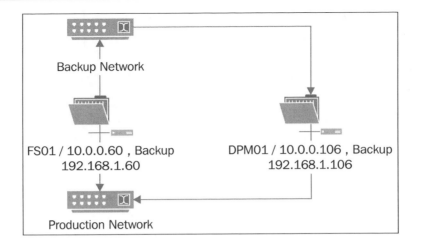

The DPM server will use the dedicated backup network 192.168.1.x to protect the FS01 file server and the users connecting to the server will use the regular production network for accessing the server.

Adding a second network dedicated to backup will ensure that there is always full bandwidth available for users and applications, and if there is a need for larger recoveries, they won't slow down the network. Adding a dedicated network isn't without cost and complexity, so it needs to be carefully considered if it's needed.

To let DPM utilize the backup network, we need to define the network through the PowerShell prompt, using the following command:

```
Add-BackupNetworkAddress -DpmServername DPM01 -Address 192.168.1.0/24
-SequenceNumber 1
```

On the DPM server and the protected server we need to add an IP address of the backup network. If there is no DNS server, host files need to be used to ensure name resolution. This simplifies the implantation as we don't need a dedicated DNS for the backup network.

One other requirement is that the protection agent and DPM server can resolve the hostname on the backup network.

One method for this is to edit the host file on both the protected server and the DPM server so that they will both resolve the IP address on the backup network.

After ensuring that name resolution will use the new backup network's IP address, the DPM recovery agent needs to be stopped to ensure that the new network will be used.

Running `stop-service dpmra` from PowerShell or `Net Stop DPMRA` will stop the service.

60 seconds		0
Send	Adapter name:	Backup
1,4 Mbps	Connection type:	Ethernet
	IPv4 address:	192.168.1.106
Receive	IPv6 address:	fe80::95d4:ff8:a7a6:2a6c%15
436 Mbps		

The backup network requires a dedicated network. Multiple networks can be used and the priority can be controlled with the sequence number where the lowest number has priority.

After setting up the network and name resolution, it's time to kick off the backup job, and through **Performance Monitor** we can see that we are using the backup network NIC instead of the production network.

Using DPM beyond the supported cloud providers

With DPM 2012 SP1, we have support for backup to Azure. There are currently no other supported methods for using public cloud storage.

If your organization can look beyond supportability from Microsoft, there are other methods of moving data to the cloud.

Russian Microsoft MVP, Yegor Startsev, has demonstrated an integration between Dropbox and Cristalink's Firesteamer.

The Dropbox integration ensures that data stored in the Dropbox folder is replicated to the backend stores on Amazon S3, while the Cristalink's Firestreamer is a virtual tape library that emulates a tape library and stores the tapes as files in the filesystem.

Using DPM's certificate-based encryption of the tapes will ensure that a compromise of the Dropbox/Amazon storage account will not put your organization's data at risk. Dropbox adds sync to the solution, so no additional steps are required after backup is complete.

 This solution from Yegor is covered on his site at the following link:
`http://ystartsev.wordpress.com/2011/07/08/dpm-firestreamer-dropbox/`

Another variation of the same solution is to use Amazon Glacier service with Firestreamer and FastGlacier for uploading to Amazon, as the Amazon S3 version relies on server-side tape encryption for security in this integration.

Pricing

Pay only for what you use. There is no minimum fee.

Storage Pricing

Region: EU (Ireland)

* $0.011 per GB / month

Storage pricing is about $12/month for storage online, and there is an additional cost for transferring data in and out of Amazon's storage system.

 The following link has detailed pricing information, as your mileage may differ:
`http://aws.amazon.com/glacier/#pricing`

There is no supported integration between DPM 2012 and Amazon Glacier. This integration demo is shown with Firestreamer software (http://cristalink.com) and **glacier-put** utility (http://fastglacier.com) to upload data to Amazon Glacier.

As we don't have a tight integration between Amazon Glacier and DPM, we utilize the virtual tape library from Cristalink to copy the data from short-term to long-term protection located in the filesystem.

When the long-term backup job is completed, we can see what tapes have been utilized. We then need to unload the tapes from Firestreamer to avoid any other jobs writing to the tapes as we move them to the cloud.

After adding our Amazon Glacier account to the FastGlacier application, we can then copy the data containing the virtual tapes library files to the cloud. There is also a command-line option for this, so scripting can be used to move the data from local storage to the cloud.

If we need to recover data from tape, then we need to copy the data from Glacier to the local storage and then add the file to Firestreamer.

There is cost and time involved every time you need to recover data from Glacier; so a balance on how long to keep the VTL locally before moving it to the cloud for *long-term storage* will need to be found.

Summary

In this chapter we have taken a look at what steps we need to take to ensure that we can always recover our organization's data, even if multiple events occurs at the same time.

The key takeaway is to always have your backup data on more than one location and always keep a fresh backup of your Active Directory and databases for Data Protection Manager. This way, we are in a good position to start recovering data if needed. This is also a process that the backup admin should undertake at least on a yearly basis, to verify that the steps are well documented and valid.

In the next chapter, we will cover the automation aspects of DPM, helping the business at scale, when manual tasks take too much time, and also to ensure consistency.

12
DPM PowerShell, Automation, and Private Cloud

There is a lot you can accomplish in DPM using PowerShell along with some things that can only be done for DPM via PowerShell. Something that is often overlooked when planning or running private cloud is data protection. Using DPM and **System Center Orchestrator** (**SCORCH**) along with the rest of the System Center 2012 suite is a way you can ensure protection of private clouds. In this chapter, we are going to provide you with tips and techniques for working with your DPM using PowerShell and automation of DPM using SCORCH. We will cover the following topics in this chapter:

- Connecting to DPM through remote PowerShell
- Using PowerShell ISE to work with DPM cmdlets
- Automating DPM in your private cloud
- DPM and System Center Configuration Manager

What we will not be covering in this chapter is the basics of PowerShell. We assume if you are reading this book you have a basic understanding of PowerShell. If you need a review around the basics of PowerShell visit the following link:

`http://technet.microsoft.com/en-us/library/bb978526.aspx`

DPM has what is called the DPM Management Shell (DMS). This is a scripting shell that can be used to perform DPM functions. The DMS is built on PowerShell. This can be used on the DPM server, a client computer or from a SCOM server to manage DPM servers. The power in using DPM to manage DPM versus a typical command line is that PowerShell is object oriented. Because PowerShell is object oriented you can do stuff like having objects flow by piping commands together. Examples of using objects with DMS are data sources, protection groups, disks, tape libraries, and more. Once an understanding of DMS is achieved, many management functions can be performed from a command line and even automated for integration into private cloud.

Connecting to DPM through remote PowerShell

With DPM you can use PowerShell remotely to help administer your DPM. There are a few things you need to do to get this working. You need to do the following:

- On the DPM server adjust the execution policy for PowerShell
- On the DPM server you need to set it to receive Windows PowerShell remote commands
- On the DPM server either turn off the local Windows firewall or allow incoming traffic on TCP 49316 and UDP 1433/1434 (SQL Communication)
- On a client computer install DPM Remote Administration for the DPM Management Shell

From the previously listed items, we will cover the execution policy and set the SCDM server to accept remote PowerShell commands. Installing the DPM Remote Administration console was covered in *Chapter 4, Monitoring and Managing the Performance of DPM*. Installing the DPM Remote Administration will also install the DPM Management Shell. With the DPM Management Shell you can run DPM specific cmdlets against your DPM server.

The first thing we need to do is adjust the execution policy for PowerShell on the DPM server. To do this, perform the following steps:

1. Open an elevated PowerShell console.
2. Type this syntax `set-executionpolicy remotesigned` and press *Enter*.
3. When you are prompted to accept, type `Y`.

The `Set-ExecutionPolicy` cmdlet, as explained on TechNet, enables you to determine which Windows PowerShell scripts (if any) will be allowed to run on your computer.

In the `RemoteSigned` execution policy, the downloaded scripts must be signed by a trusted publisher before they can be run.

Now, on the DPM server let's enable it to allow remote PowerShell connections. To do this, perform the following steps:

1. Open an elevated PowerShell console.

2. Enter this syntax `enable-psremoting` and press *Enter*.

 The `Enable-PSRemoting` cmdlet, as explained on TechNet, configures the computer to receive Windows PowerShell remote commands.

On Windows Server 2012, Windows PowerShell remoting is enabled by default. You can use `Enable-PSRemoting` to enable Windows PowerShell remoting on other supported versions of Windows.

That should be it for the PowerShell side of things on the DPM server. Now let's open up the required firewall ports. These ports are: TCP 49316 and UDP 143 (SQL Communication). If you don't know how to open up ports on a Windows firewall, visit this link: `http://technet.microsoft.com/en-us/library/dd353100%28v=ws.10%29.aspx`. If you don't have the firewall enabled on your DPM server then you don't need to worry about opening those ports.

Once you have completed all of those steps you are now ready to connect to DPM remotely and administer it via PowerShell using the DPM Management Shell. Now you should be able to open the DPM Management Shell on your client computer. When the shell is open, type the following syntax to connect to your DPM server:

`Connect-DPMServer YOURDPMSERVERNAME`

DPM has its own set of cmdlets. There have not been many changes to the DPM cmdlets since DPM 2010, so we are going to list them here, but we will not go in depth into each cmdlet in this book. There have been some new cmdlets around online backup to Windows Azure with the release of Service Pack 1. They are as follows:

- `Start-DPMCloudRegistration`
- `Start-DPMCloudUnregistration`
- `Get-DPMCloudSubscription`
- `Get-DPMCloudSubscriptionSetting`

You will see these DPM cloud cmdlets with details in the list. You can find the DPM cmdlets at `http://technet.microsoft.com/en-us/library/hh881679.aspx`.

DPM cmdlet	Summary of the DPM cmdlet
Add-DPMBackupNetworkAddress	Specifies a backup network for the server to use.
Add-DPMChildDatasource	Adds a data source or a child data source to a protection group.
Add-DPMDisk	Adds a new disk to the storage pool.
Add-DPMRecoveryItem	Allows you to identify the recoverable items that members of a DPM role can recover.
Add-DPMRecoveryTarget	Allows you to give the DPM role the permission to recover to a location.
Add-DPMSecurityGroup	Allows you to add security groups to the DPM role.
Add-DPMTape	Adds a tape to a DPM library.
Connect-DPMServer	Opens a connection to a DPM server.
Copy-DPMTapeData	Copies the data from a tape for a given recovery point.
Disable-DPMLibrary	Disables the specified library.
Disable-DPMProductionServer	Disables the DPM protection agent installed on the specified computer.
Disable-DPMTapeDrive	Disables the specified tape drives in the library.
Disconnect-DPMServer	Closes and releases all objects for a DPM connection session.
Edit-DPMDiskAllocation	Modifies disk allocation for the specified protected data source.
Enable-DPMLibrary	Enables the specified library.
Enable-DPMProductionServer	Enables the DPM protection agent installed on the specified computer.
Enable-DPMTapeDrive	Enables the specified tape drives in the library.
Get-DPMAccessLicense	Retrieves the licensing information for the DPM server and protected computers.
Get-DPMAlert	Returns all the alerts on the specified DPM server.
Get-DPMAutoProtectIntent	Retrieves the auto-protection setting for a SQL Server instance.

DPM cmdlet	Summary of the DPM cmdlet
Get-DPMBackupNetworkAddress	Returns a backup network specified for the server.
Get-DPMChildDatasource	Returns the protectable file system objects within a data source.
Get-DPMCloudSubscription	Returns the Windows Azure Online Backup subscription object.
Get-DPMCloudSubscriptionSetting	Returns the Windows Azure Online Backup subscription configuration settings.
Get-DPMDatasetStatus	Returns the dataset state of the archived tape.
Get-DPMDatasource	Retrieves the list of protected and unprotected data in a computer or protection group.
Get-DPMDatasourceProtectionOption	Returns the protection options for all data sources of the specified data source type in a protection group.
Get-DPMDisk	Returns a list of disks found in the previous rescan on a DPM server.
Get-DPMGlobalProperty	Retrieves the global properties for this DPM installation.
Get-DPMHeadlessDataset	Returns any incomplete dataset on the archived tape.
Get-DPMJob	Gets a list of current and past jobs on a DPM server.
Get-DPMLibrary	Returns the list of libraries attached to the DPM server and their status.
Get-DPMMaintenanceJobStartTime	Returns the start time of the maintenance jobs.
Get-DPMModifiableProtectionGroup	Retrieves a protection group in an editable mode.
Get-DPMPGSet	Returns the list of DPM PG sets on the specified DPM server.
Get-DPMPolicyObjective	Returns the protection policy for a protection group.
Get-DPMPolicySchedule	Returns the schedule for various protection jobs such as synchronization, recovery point creation (shadow copy), and tape backups.
Get-DPMProductionCluster	Returns a list of all clusters on which the DPM agent is installed.
Get-DPMProductionServer	Returns the list of servers that have the DPM protection agent installed on them.
Get-DPMProductionVirtualName	Returns the virtual names for a cluster.

DPM cmdlet	Summary of the DPM cmdlet
Get-DPMProtectionGroup	Retrieves the list of protection groups on the DPM server.
Get-DPMProtectionJobStartTime	Returns the start time of a protection job.
Get-DPMRecoverableItem	Returns a list of recoverable items in a recovery point.
Get-DPMRecoveryItem	Allows you to retrieve and display the recovery items attached to a role.
Get-DPMRecoveryPoint	Returns all available recovery points for a data source.
Get-DPMRecoveryPointLocation	Returns the location of a recovery point.
Get-DPMRecoveryTarget	Retrieves the recovery target for the specified role.
Get-DPMReplicaCreationMethod	Retrieves the replica creation method that is specified for a protection group.
Get-DPMRole	Allows you to open a DPM role for editing or to display a DPM role and its properties.
Get-DPMSecurityGroup	Allows you to retrieve and display the security groups for a DPM role.
Get-DPMTape	Returns a list of tapes in the library across drives and slots.
Get-DPMTapeBackupOption	Returns the library, drive, and other backup or archive options for a protection group.
Get-DPMTapeDrive	Returns a list of drives in a library on a DPM server.
Get-DPMTapeSlot	Returns the list of slots in the library.
Get-DPMVolume	Returns a list of volumes on the DPM server.
Lock-DPMLibraryDoor	Locks the door of the specified library.
Lock-DPMLibraryIEPort	Locks and loads the media present in the IE port.
New-DPMPGSet	Creates a new DPM PG set.
New-DPMProtectionGroup	Creates a new protection group on the DPM server.
New-DPMRecoveryNotification	Builds the notification object used for recovery.
New-DPMRecoveryOption	Allows setting of recovery options for various servers.
New-DPMRecoveryPoint	Creates a new recovery point for the data source.

DPM cmdlet	Summary of the DPM cmdlet
New-DPMRecoveryTarget	Allows you to create a new recovery target object.
New-DPMRole	Allows you to define a new DPM role.
New-DPMSearchOption	Builds an object with the search options to search for a particular string within the set of specified recovery points.
New-DPMServerScope	Creates a scope object that is used by the Connect-DPMServer cmdlet to create a scoped DPM connection.
Remove-DPMBackupNetworkAddress	Stops the DPM server from trying to use the specified network.
Remove-DPMChildDatasource	Removes a data source or child data source from a protection group.
Remove-DPMDatasourceReplica	Removes an inactive replica.
Remove-DPMDisk	Removes a disk from the storage pool.
Remove-DPMObject	Removes a DPM object.
Remove-DPMPGSet	Deletes a protection group set.
Remove-DPMRecoveryItem	Allows you to remove a recovery item from the list that a DPM role could recover.
Remove-DPMRecoveryPoint	Removes a recovery point from tape or disk.
Remove-DPMRecoveryTarget	Allows you to revoke permissions to a location for a DPM role.
Remove-DPMRole	Allows you to delete an existing DPM role.
Remove-DPMSecurityGroup	Allows you to remove a security group from a DPM role.
Remove-DPMTape	Removes a tape from a DPM library.
Rename-DPMLibrary	Renames the specified library.
Rename-DPMProtectionGroup	Renames an existing protection group on the DPM server.
Rename-DPMRole	Allows you to rename an existing DPM role and change its description.
Restart-DPMJob	Reruns the specified failed jobs.
Restore-DPMRecoverableItem	Restores a version of the data source to a target location.
Resume-DPMBackup	Attempts to resume all stalled backup jobs.
Set-DPMAutoProtectIntent	Turns the auto-protection setting for a SQL Server instance on or off.

DPM cmdlet	Summary of the DPM cmdlet
Set-DPMCloudSubscriptionSetting	Updates the Windows Azure Online Backup subscription settings.
Set-DPMCredentials	Configures certificate-based authentication.
Set-DPMDatasourceDefaultDiskAllocation	This cmdlet retrieves the amount of disk space that is allocated to the protected data.
Set-DPMDatasourceDiskAllocation	Modifies disk allocation for the protected data.
Set-DPMDatasourceProtectionOption	Sets the protection options for the specified data source.
Set-DPMGlobalProperty	Sets the global properties for this DPM installation.
Set-DPMMaintenanceJobStartTime	Sets or removes the start time of a maintenance job.
Set-DPMPerformanceOptimization	Enables setting or removing of on-wire compression of data.
Set-DPMPolicyObjective	Sets the policy objective for a protection group.
Set-DPMPolicySchedule	Sets the schedule for various protection jobs such as synchronization, recovery point creation (shadow copy), and tape backups.
Set-DPMProtectionGroup	Saves all the actions performed on the protection group on the DPM server.
Set-DPMProtectionJobStartTime	Sets or changes the start time of a protection job.
Set-DPMProtectionType	Allows you to specify the protection type to be used with the protection group.
Set-DPMReplicaCreationMethod	Sets the replica creation method for disk-based protection.
Set-DPMRole	Allows you to save any changes you have made to a DPM role.
Set-DPMTape	Marks the specified tape as Archive, Cleaner, Free, or Not Free.
Set-DPMTapeBackupOption	Sets the tape backup and library options for a protection group.
Start-DPMAutoProtection	Searches for and identifies new SQL Server databases under the instances that are configured for auto-protection, and adds them to the protection group.
Start-DPMCloudRegistration	Registers the DPM server with Windows Azure Online Backup service.

DPM cmdlet	Summary of the DPM cmdlet
`Start-DPMCloudUnregistration`	Unregisters the DPM server with Windows Azure Online Backup service.
`Start-DPMCreateCatalog`	Generates a catalog for the specified data source.
`Start-DPMDatasourceConsistencyCheck`	Performs a consistency check on the specified data source.
`Start-DPMDiskRescan`	Scans for new disks or disks where configuration has changed.
`Start-DPMLibraryInventory`	Starts an inventory of the tape in the specified library.
`Start-DPMLibraryRescan`	Starts a rescan job in the background to identify new libraries or ones that have changed.
`Start-DPMOnlineRecatalog`	Returns a detailed list of data on a tape.
`Start-DPMProductionServerSwitchProtection`	Switches protection of a data source between the primary DPM server and the disaster recovery server.
`Start-DPMSwitchProtection`	Runs on the secondary DPM server to switch protection for a set of data sources.
`Start-DPMTapeDriveCleaning`	Starts a clean tape drive job.
`Start-DPMTapeErase`	Starts a tape erase job.
`Start-DPMTapeRecatalog`	Returns information about the data on a tape.
`Stop-DPMJob`	Stops a running job.
`Test-DPMTapeData`	Verifies the data that is set for a recovery point.
`Unlock-DPMLibraryDoor`	Unlocks the door of the specified library.
`Unlock-DPMLibraryIEPort`	Unlocks the IE port for the specified library.
`Update-DPMPGSet`	Updates and saves the changes made to the specified PG set.
`Update-DPMProductionServer`	Gets updated information about the protected computer.
`Update-DPMProtectionGroup`	Refreshes the protection group configuration to update any changes to protected data sources.

Using PowerShell ISE to work with DPM cmdlets

Let's start this section off with some background on PowerShell ISE. PowerShell ISE stands for **PowerShell Integrated Scripting Environment** and is sometimes just referred to as **ISE**. PowerShell ISE is included by default on Windows Server 2012 and Windows 8. This is Windows PowerShell v3. The Windows Server 2008/2008 R2 and Windows 7 client computers come with PowerShell v2. If you want PowerShell v3 on Windows Server 2008/2008 R2 and Windows 7 it will need to be installed. The install for v3 is located at `http://www.microsoft.com/en-us/download/details.aspx?id=34595`.

ISE is a tool that is intended to make working with PowerShell easier. With ISE, you can create/edit PowerShell scripts using the script pane; test/debug PowerShell scripts by stepping through your code or cmdlets, and it also gives you a graphical interface known as the command pane that can be used to work with cmdlets. To learn more about PowerShell ISE visit `http://technet.microsoft.com/en-us/library/dd759217.aspx`.

When using ISE on a DPM server you are not actually using the DMS at this point. You are simply using the DPM PowerShell module and this contains the DPM PowerShell cmdlets. There are several advantages to using PowerShell ISE with DPM. These are as follows:

- The DPM PowerShell module is pre-loaded for you to work with but also you can quickly switch to other PowerShell modules within ISE
- You can work with the cmdlets in a GUI as well as the parameters
- You can step through your syntax for troubleshooting
- The built-in DPM PowerShell scripts can be loaded into ISE and used from there

The following is a screenshot showing the use of ISE with DPM:

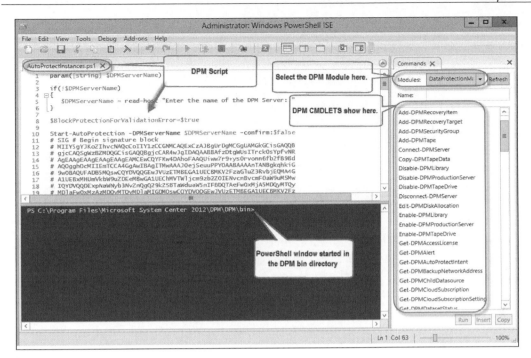

The following screenshot is an example of what it looks like when you select one of the DPM cmdlets in the ISE command window:

Notice in the previous screenshot that when the DPM cmdlet is selected, its parameters are exposed for you to work with. This is a good way to become familiar with the DPM cmdlets. Once you have completed the parameters for the cmdlet you can **Insert** into the PowerShell window or simply **Run** it.

Note that the built-in DPM scripts can be found at the following location:
`<INSTALLDRIVE>\Program Files\Microsoft System Center 2012\DPM\DPM\bin`

Automating DPM in your private cloud

In this section, we are going to look at automation with DPM and DPM's role in the private cloud. The best method for automating DPM is to utilize System Center Orchestrator (SCORCH). SCORCH can hook into many other technologies to automate. SCORCH does this by using integration packs. The integration packs contain activities that can be performed in an area of technology. SCORCH has an integration pack for DPM containing common activities that an administrator would need to perform in DPM. DPM plays an important role in the private cloud and automating DPM is part of the story in bringing DPM into the private cloud. Now let's look into each of these topics in more detail, starting with DPM's role in the private cloud.

DPM and private cloud

Let's get into how DPM fits into the private cloud story. DPM protection of cloud is all about automation and self-service. These are accomplished by combining DPM, System Center Orchestrator (SCORCH), and System Center Service Manager (SCSM).

The private cloud technology is built to be highly resilient and highly automated through the use of readily available technologies. It is cloud still runs in a data center or across multiple data centers and needs protection. They are susceptible to data corruption, administration mistakes such as bad updates or misconfigurations, and applications that go awry. This is where DPM comes in to provide protection against these issues.

With all that being said there are new challenges to protecting the private cloud. Self-service creates a new challenge in not always knowing what is out there or when new workloads are added by end users. Protection needs to automatically be added to newly added workloads as well as self-service recovery for end users. We are going to get into automating DPM with SCORCH but we will not dive into publishing these in SCSM as this is outside of the scope of this book. For a good resource on learning SCSM consider this book at `http://www.amazon.com/ Microsoft-System-Service-Manager-Cookbook/dp/1849686947`. So, the first part of bringing DPM into your private cloud is to build automation workflows in SCORCH and then publish this automation through SCSM's self-service portal giving end users the ability to access data protection on their own.

Next we are going to learn more about DPM and SCORCH, but first we need to take a closer look at how the private cloud's architecture works and where DPM lives within that. The following are the layers of the private cloud:

- Service delivery layer
- Software layer
- Platform layer
- Infrastructure layer
- Service operations layer
- Management layer

In terms of the private cloud layers, DPM sits at the management layer. The purpose of the management layer is to support IaaS, PaaS, and SaaS through service and operations that funnel up the infrastructure, platform, and software layers. DPM is more on the operation side of things, placing it in IaaS. The following screenshot will assist you in understanding where DPM falls in line with the other System Center products in the private cloud model.

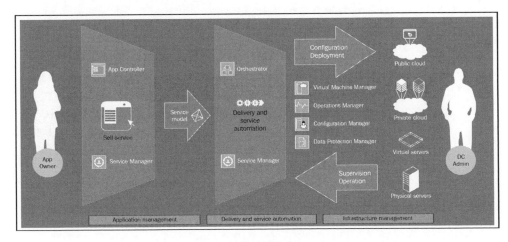

The following is a table from this link `http://social.technet.microsoft.com/wiki/contents/articles/13994.system-center-2012-integration-guide-data-protection-manager.aspx#Role_in_the_Microsoft_Private_Cloud` that directly maps DPM's capabilities to the different layers in the private cloud. This gives further definition of where DPM falls within the private cloud story.

Layer	Description
Service delivery layer	Service providers may provide protection services using DPM to their tenants, which are surfaced in the service delivery through the service catalog or a self-service portal.
Infrastructure layer	DPM can influence the infrastructure layer by requiring such configurations as dedicated recovery networks.
Service operations layer	This layer includes processes for performing a protection service with DPM. This may include automated processes using tools such as Orchestrator Runbooks.
Management layer	DPM provides backup services in the management layer.

To sum this up, DPM sits under operations of the management layer, making it a part of IaaS in the private cloud. In this role, DPM provides the capability to administrators and end users to protect and restore data, service, and infrastructure components.

Automating DPM using Orchestrator

As mentioned earlier, automating DPM through SCORCH is key to bringing it into the private cloud. To accomplish this, you need DPM of course, but you also need to deploy SCORCH. To learn more about deploying SCORCH visit `http://technet.microsoft.com/en-us/library/hh420337.aspx`. Once you have SCORCH deployed, you need to integrate it with DPM. To integrate with DPM we need to download a System Center DPM Integration Pack for SCORCH. SCORCH works with DPM 2010 and DPM 2012. The integration packs can be found at the following links:

- System Center Integration Pack for System Center Data Protection Manager 2010

  `http://technet.microsoft.com/en-us/library/hh531742.aspx`

- System Center Integration Pack for System Center Data Protection Manager 2012

  `http://technet.microsoft.com/en-us/library/hh830726.aspx`

The DPM integration pack for SCORCH enables automating protection for servers regardless of whether they are physical or virtual. DPM and SCORCH can automate protection and recovery of SharePoint, SQL Servers, system state, virtual machines (Hyper-V), and other miscellaneous types of backups.

After downloading the SCORCH integration pack for DPM, we need to register and deploy the integration pack to SCORCH. The very next step is to extract the integration pack files. Run the integration pack file you downloaded. This filename will end with a .exe extension. When you launch the integration pack it will prompt you for a location to place the extracted integration pack. It is going to extract word DOC/X and a .oip file. .oip is the extension of the integration pack that SCORCH needs. Next are the series of steps to register and deploy the DPM integration pack.

Perform the following steps to register an integration pack in SCORCH:

1. On your SCORCH server launch the **Deployment Manager**.
2. In **Deployment Manager**, expand **Orchestrator Management Server**, right-click on **Integration Packs** and select **Register IP with the Orchestrator Management Server**.

3. Click on **Next** in the wizard that opens.
4. On the **Select Integration Packs or Hotfixes** screen, click on **Add**.
5. Browse out to the .oip file of the integration pack you want to import.

6. Click on **Open**. This will bring that integration pack into the wizard. Click on **Next** to continue.

7. On the final screen review the summary and click on **Finish**. When the wizard finishes your integration pack will be imported.

Perform the following steps to deploy an integration pack in SCORCH:

1. In **Deployment Manager**, expand **Orchestrator Management Server**, right-click on **Integration Packs** and select **Deploy IP to Runbook Server or Runbook Designer**.

2. Select the DPM Integration Pack from the list and click on **Next**.

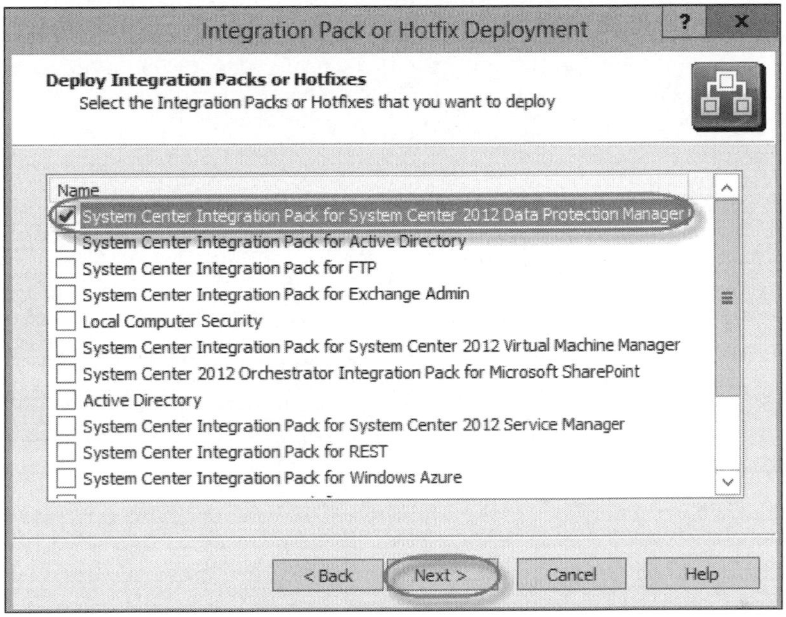

3. On the next screen you need to enter the name of your Runbook server/s or any computer/s with the Runbook designer install. You can also search for computers using the ellipses button. Click on **Add** to include them in the list of servers the DPM integration pack will be deployed to.

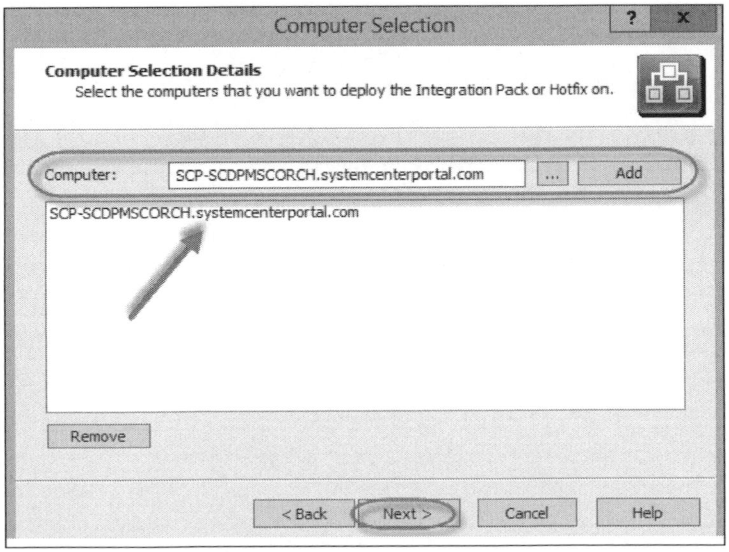

4. Click on **Next**.

5. On the **Installation Configuration** screen you need to make some decisions about the integration pack deployment. Choose to install the DPM integration pack now or schedule it to deploy later. You also need to choose to stop any running Runbook servers or deploy without stopping them. If you choose to stop them, any Runbooks that are in progress will stop. Make your selections and click on **Next**.

6. On the next screen review the summary and click on **Next**.

Now that we have the integration pack for DPM installed in SCORCH, we need to set up a connection to the DPM server. After we make the DPM connection we can look at the activities that are contained in the integration pack.

There is a WinRM service running on SCORCH. The DPM integration pack uses Windows PowerShell remoting to issue commands on the DPM server. This communication is facilitated through the WinRM service. A WinRM listener is used to request and send data. By default the WinRM service is running but the WinRM listener is not configured. Before we can configure the connection to DPM in SCORCH, we need to configure the WinRM listener. To configure the WinRM listener, perform the following on the SCORCH server:

1. Click on **Start** and then on **Run**, then type `gpedit.msc`. This will open **Local Group Policy Editor**.

2. Navigate to **WinRM Client** via **Local Computer Policy | Computer Configuration | Administrative Templates | Windows Components | Windows Remote Management**.

3. Double-click on **Trusted Hosts** and select **Enabled**.

4. In the **Trusted Hosts** list, enter the FQDN or IP address of your DPM server and click on **OK**.

This is it for configuring the WinRM listener on the SCORCH server. Next we can configure the connection to the DPM server. Perform the following steps to configure a DPM connection in SCORCH:

1. Launch Runbook Designer, click on **Options** on the top menu, and select **SC 2012 Data Protection Manager**.

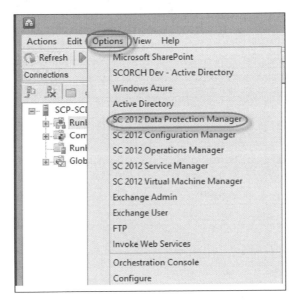

2. After the **SC 2012 Data Protection Manager** screen opens click on the **Add** button. This is where you will set up your connection to DPM.

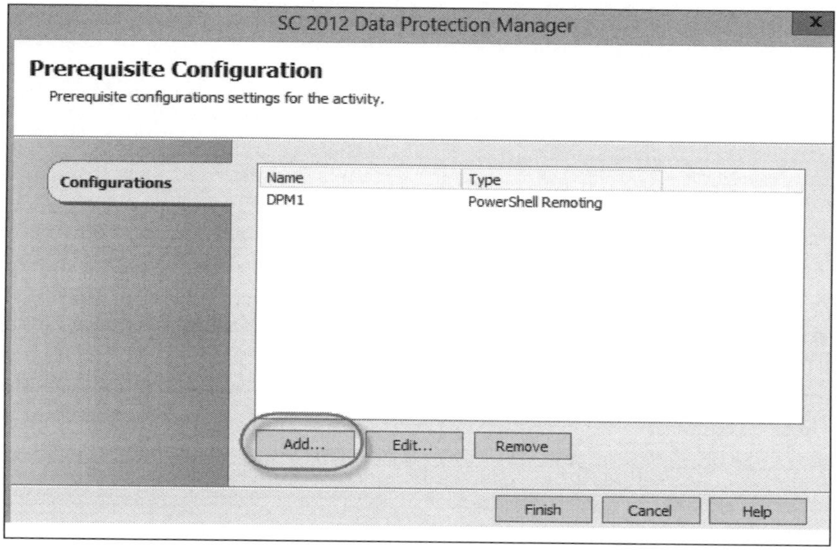

3. Give your connection a name. Click on the ellipsis button and select **PowerShell Remoting**. Click on **OK**.

4. In the **Properties** window, you need to fill out information for the connection to your DPM server. You can see these fields in the following screenshot. Leave the **Authentication Type (Remote only)** field set to Default, **Port (Remote only)** to the default setting, and **SSL (Remote only)** to False unless you know that you are using SSL. Click on **OK** when you are finished.

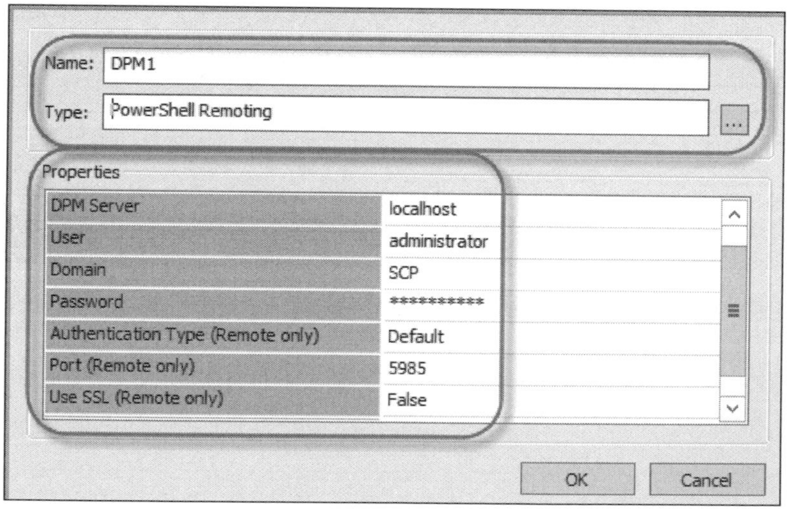

5. The configuration for this connection will now be saved and you will see it listed by the name you gave it. Click on **Finish** to close out.

 Note that you can have connections to multiple DPM servers. You simply need to click on **Add** multiple times and add each connection.

6. The next step before configuring any automation in SCORCH for DPM is to look at the activities that are available for DPM. You will find the newly added DPM category in the **Activities** pane on the right-hand side of the Runbook Designer as shown in the following screenshot:

You can learn more about each of the System Center 2012 Data Protection Manager Activities at `http://technet.microsoft.com/en-us/library/hh420346.aspx`.

Now we have the activities in place, we can go ahead and build some automation. This is done by building a Runbook. A Runbook in SCORCH is a series of activities that make up a workflow for something.

Each item in a Runbook is an activity, meaning they will get data or perform some sort of action. The arrows in between them with the text `Link` are connections between the activities that tie them together and show the path that the Runbook will follow.

If you were to double-click on each of the activities in Runbook you would see the properties and this is where you configure them. The following screenshot depicts what the **Get Data Source Activity** properties look like from one of the Runbook examples we have coming up. You can see here we need to input the location of our data source and the name of it for SCORCH to find it. Also notice that the **Name** field contains the name of our DPM connection that we set up in SCORCH.

Properties
Define the properties used by the activity.

General	Configuration
	Name: SC2012 DPM

Properties	Properties
Filters	Data Source Location — {Data Source Location (e.g. Productio
Run Behavior	Name — {Data Source Name from "Initiate VM

The following are two examples of DPM Runbooks in SCORCH.

The following screenshot shows that Runbook is going to create a recovery point for us. It will also generate alerts for us in DPM based on whether it fails or succeeds. We could use a Runbook like this to schedule recovery points or publish this Runbook to an end user using Service Manager and allow the end user to create a recovery point on demand.

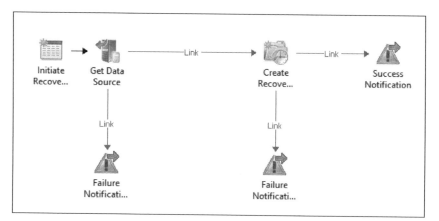

The following second Runbook example is going to initiate a Runbook recovery of a virtual machine. Let's put this in a real-world scenario to show you how this could be used. Let's say a developer is running a virtual machine on a private cloud. That developer has made some bad code changes and needs to restore the virtual machine back to a healthy state. He is working late and IT is not around. This developer could go out to Service Manager self-service portal and request to restore this virtual machine. Service Manager would then kick off a Runbook that restores the virtual machine for the developer without the need for anyone from IT to wake up in the middle of the night and perform this task.

To sum this up, the following Runbook will get the data source, locate the recovery point for that data source, and recover the virtual machine.

That is all we can cover about SCORCH in this book. There will be a new book coming out soon from Packt Publishing dedicated to SCORCH.

DPM and System Center Configuration Manager

System Center Configuration Manager (SCCM) is a systems management tool that can perform the following: software deployment, compliance settings management, and comprehensive asset management of computers and phones including servers, mobile devices (tablets smart phones), laptops, and desktops. In this section, we are going to look at how to utilize SCCM to push out the console and agents for DPM.

Deploying the DPM Remote Administration console via SCCM

In this section, we are going to learn about the process of deploying the DPM Remote Administration console to IT admin computers via System Center Configuration Manager 2012 (SCCM 2012). The following are the steps you will need to perform to make this happen:

1. You will need some place to group your IT admin computers so that you can target the DPM Remote Administration console to them. Create an **IT Admin Computers** device collection in SCCM 2012. This is what we will use to group the IT admin computers.

Icon	Name
	All Desktop and Server Clients
	All Mobile Devices
	All Systems
	All Unknown Computers
	IT Admin Computers

Device Collections 5 items
Search

2. Now we need to copy the contents from the DPM media onto your distribution point share. This will be the CCX86 and DPM folders. Note that in the example for this section we copied these to C:\App Deployments.

As of right now you need to copy all the contents. We don't know the specific files that make up the remote administration console. If you need to save space you can copy one or the other folder and use it. CCX86 is for 32-bit computers and DPM is for 64-bit computers. If you know you will only deploy to 64-bit computers, then get the DPM folder only.

The next step is to go and create a package for the DPM Remote Administration console:

1. In the Config Man console, go to \Software Library\Overview\ Application Management\Packages and create the new package.

2. The create package wizard will come up. Go ahead and complete the highlighted fields as shown in the following screenshot and click on **Next**.

Remember that in the lab for this section we copied the DPM software from the media to `C:\App Deployments`. This is the directory we are setting as the **Source folder** for this package. Your source folder path will be different.

3. Chose standard program and click on **Next**.

   Here is where you need to put in the correct command-line syntax to make sure it installs the DPM Remote Administration console versus the full DPM product. The following is the syntax you will need to put in the **Command line** field. Refer to the following screenshot:

   ```
   setup.exe /i /cc /client
   ```

   Again, CCX86 is for 32-bit computers and DPM is for 64-bit computers. Create your package accordingly with the source folder set to the right path.

4. Fill in the rest of the options as needed for your environment and click on **Next**.

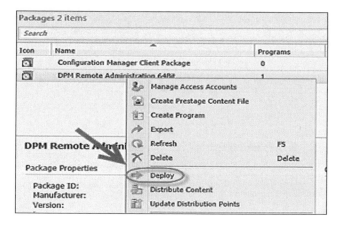

5. Specify the type of operating systems this package can be deployed to and click on **Next**.

6. Confirm your settings and click on **Next** to create the package.

7. Okay! Now we need to deploy the package to the **IT Admin Computer** collection we created earlier. Right-click on the package in the list and select **Deploy**.

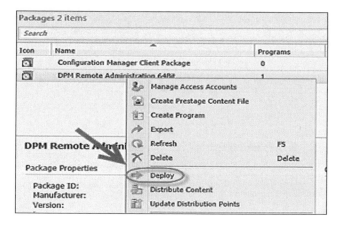

8. Point the package to the correct site collection.

9. Select a distribution point to host the package.

10. Set the package to optional or required. In this section we used required.

11. Schedule the deployment. For this section we set it to run as soon as possible. On the next two following screens in the wizard select the options that make sense in your scenario. The options we show here are for this section and may not work for your specific scenario.

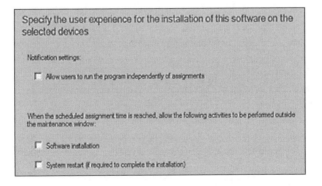

12. In the subsequent screen, you can decide the level of interaction with the end user.

13. Next you have further control over the deployment, as shown in the following:

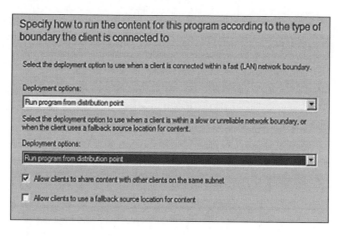

14. Click on **Next** on the **Summary** screen for the package to be deployed to the device collection.

15. Go ahead and click on **Close**.

16. Now if you go to your device collections, select your administrator collection and click on the **Deployments** tab at the bottom. You should see the DPM Remote Administration console listed. This means SCCM will attempt to install it on the computers inside of this device collection.

17. If you chose to deploy as soon as possible, you should see some action once your admin client computers update their policy. To check on the progress of the deployment in the SCCM console navigate to `\Monitoring\Overview\Deployments` and click on **Deployments**.

You will see your package listed. Click on your package and you should see the following:

In this book we are not going to go into how to update the policy at the client end or troubleshooting if issues arise.

To install the DPM agent to computers via SCCM, the steps are essentially the same as those that we used to deploy the DPM Remote Administration console via SCCM. The only difference is that we need the DPM installs instead of the DPM Remote Administration console install. These are:

- For 32-bit computers - `(INSTALL DRIVE):\Program Files\Microsoft System Center 2012\DPM\DPM\ProtectionAgents\RA\4.1.3313.0\i386\DPMAgentInstaller_x86.exe`

- For 64-bit computers - `(INSTALL DRIVE):\Program Files\Microsoft System Center 2012\DPM\DPM\ProtectionAgents\RA\4.1.3313.0\amd64\DpmAgentInstaller_AMD64.exe`

You need to copy these to your SCCM server and create an application or package from it. You can then follow the rest of the steps we used to push out the DPM Remote Administration console.

This should be enough to get you going to deploy the DPM Remote administration console and DPM agents through SCCM. For more information on SCCM 2012, visit `http://technet.microsoft.com/en-us/library/gg682144.aspx`.

Summary

We are now at the end of this chapter and the end of our DPM 2012 journey. Thank you for sticking through this DPM 2012 ride with us. We hope you have gained some new knowledge around DPM 2012 that you can take back to your environment. Let's recap what we learned in this chapter; we covered DPM and PowerShell along with some new cmdlets, using PowerShell ISE with DPM, DPM's role in the private cloud, automating DPM with System Center Orchestrator, and how to deploy the DPM Remote Administration console via SCCM.

Index

VSS requester 17
VSS service 17
VSS writer 17
VTL
about 188
Firestreamer 188

W

Windows applications
about 10
Exchange server 10
SharePoint 11
SQL server 10
system state 11
virtual platforms 11
Windows clients 11
Windows clients 11
Windows Clusters protection, DPM used
about 150
DHCP clusters, protecting 151
file server clusters, protecting 150
workgroup protection
DPM Agent 222
local accounts 221
setting up 221
working with 221
workgroups
communication 223
machines, configuring 222
machines, protecting 222
workgroup/untrusted domain protection
supported 218
unsupported 218

Y

Yegor 261

Thank you for buying

Microsoft System Center Data Protection Manager 2012 SP1

About Packt Publishing

Packt, pronounced 'packed', published its first book "Mastering phpMyAdmin for Effective MySQL Management" in April 2004 and subsequently continued to specialize in publishing highly focused books on specific technologies and solutions.

Our books and publications share the experiences of your fellow IT professionals in adapting and customizing today's systems, applications, and frameworks. Our solution based books give you the knowledge and power to customize the software and technologies you're using to get the job done. Packt books are more specific and less general than the IT books you have seen in the past. Our unique business model allows us to bring you more focused information, giving you more of what you need to know, and less of what you don't.

Packt is a modern, yet unique publishing company, which focuses on producing quality, cutting-edge books for communities of developers, administrators, and newbies alike. For more information, please visit our website: www.packtpub.com.

About Packt Enterprise

In 2010, Packt launched two new brands, Packt Enterprise and Packt Open Source, in order to continue its focus on specialization. This book is part of the Packt Enterprise brand, home to books published on enterprise software – software created by major vendors, including (but not limited to) IBM, Microsoft and Oracle, often for use in other corporations. Its titles will offer information relevant to a range of users of this software, including administrators, developers, architects, and end users.

Writing for Packt

We welcome all inquiries from people who are interested in authoring. Book proposals should be sent to author@packtpub.com. If your book idea is still at an early stage and you would like to discuss it first before writing a formal book proposal, contact us; one of our commissioning editors will get in touch with you.

We're not just looking for published authors; if you have strong technical skills but no writing experience, our experienced editors can help you develop a writing career, or simply get some additional reward for your expertise.

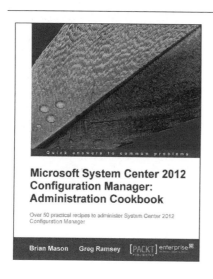

[PACKT] enterprise 🎗
PUBLISHING   professional expertise distilled

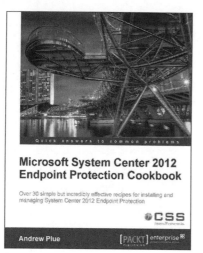

Microsoft System Center 2012 Endpoint Protection Cookbook

ISBN: 978-1-849683-90-6   Paperback: 208 pages

Over 30 simple but incredible effective recepies for installing and managing System Center 2012 Endpoint Protection

1. Master the most crucial tasks you'll need to implement System Center 2012 Endpoint Protection

2. Provision SCEP administrators with just the right level of privileges, build the best possible SCEP policies for your workstations and servers, discover the hidden potential of command line utilities and much more in this practical book and eBook

3. Quick and easy recipes to ease the pain of migrating from a legacy AV solution to SCEP

Microsoft System Center 2012 Configuration Manager: Administration Cookbook

ISBN: 978-1-849684-94-1   Paperback: 224 pages

Over 50 practical recepies to administer System Center 2012 Configuration Manager

1. Administer System Center 2012 Configuration Manager

2. Provides fast answers to questions commonly asked by new administrators

3. Skip the why's and go straight to the how-to's

Please check **www.PacktPub.com** for information on our titles

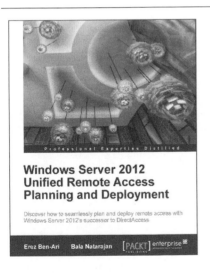

Printed in Great Britain
by Amazon.co.uk, Ltd.,
Marston Gate.